THE MEDIA AND RELIGIOUS AUTHORITY

The
Media
and
Religious
Authority

Edited by Stewart M. Hoover

The Pennsylvania State University Press
University Park, Pennsylvania

Chapter 8 was first published as "I'll Fly Away: Baadasssss Mamas and Third Cinema in Sankofa," in Black Magic Women and Narrative Film: Race, Sex, and Afro-Religiosity by Montré Aza Missouri (New York, NY: Palgrave Macmillan, 2015), pp. 109–139.

Library of Congress Cataloging-in-Publication Data

Names: Hoover, Stewart M., editor.
Title: The media and religious authority / edited by Stewart M. Hoover.
Description: University Park, Pennsylvania : The Pennsylvania State University Press, [2016] | Includes bibliographical references and index.
Summary: "Explores how modern means of communication are changing religion, and how contemporary mediations of religion challenge and refine the aspirations and prospects of religious authority"—Provided by publisher.
Identifiers: LCCN 2016006167 | ISBN 9780271073224 (cloth : alk. paper) | ISBN 9780271073231 (pbk. : alk. paper)
Subjects: LCSH: Mass media—Religious aspects. | Authority—Religious aspects.
Classification: LCC P94 .M3545 2016 | DDC 201/.7—dc23
LC record available at http://lccn.loc.gov/2016006167

The Pennsylvania State University Press is a member of the Association of American University Presses.

It is the policy of The Pennsylvania State University Press to use acid-free paper. Publications on uncoated stock satisfy the minimum requirements of American National Standard for Information Sciences—Permanence of Paper for Printed Library Material, ANSI Z39.48-1992.

CONTENTS

ACKNOWLEDGMENTS

This book has a number of sources, each significant to its final form and contents. At its core is a set of empirical case studies. These originated as the work of participants in a doctoral fellowship program that supported several cohorts of students from a variety of fields and a number of different institutions as they carried out dissertations under the broad umbrella of "media and religion research." As they appear here, these case studies are substantial extensions of those projects. Their authors are now established in their fields, and their work on these projects has benefited from the ebb and flow of scholarly engagement. As these projects developed, it became clear that they pointed to a large, theoretical exploration of the question of authority. That thread of this book was itself launched in a panel at the international conference of the International Society of Media, Religion, and Culture, held in São Paulo in 2008. That discourse has developed and matured, and these two streams now coincide here, with the reflection on the question of media and religious authority now in dialogue with these case studies of various mediations of religion.

I therefore wish to first acknowledge the authors here who have generously engaged in the process of developing this work. They needed to be flexible and patient, and I hope that they feel their investment in this project has paid off. I do.

More thanks are in order, though. First among these is my gratitude to the Lilly Endowment, which generously supported the doctoral fellowship program across several years. In particular, I would like to thank Craig

Dykstra, vice president for religion at Lilly, and Chris Coble, at the time a program staff member at Lilly, for their interest and support. My deepest gratitude also goes to my collaborator on that project, Lynn Schofield Clark, my colleague in research and scholarship across a number of years. The University of Colorado and its School of Journalism and Mass Communication, which hosted our efforts, also deserve mention. That School has now been superseded by a new College of Media, Communication, and Information, and the efforts that Lynn Clark and I initiated in that prior context have now become institutionalized in a Center for Media, Religion, and Culture.

A number of other people have been essential to this project as well. Diane Alters, Scott Webber, and Monica Emerich provided invaluable service as coordinators of the Lilly Fellowship Program, and Doña Olivier, the administrative assistant to our efforts at the time, was critical to that program's success.

In the final stages of the production of this book, Ryan Bartlett has been of exceptional help, providing keen editorial and conceptual insights and efforts to the project. I also thank Kendra Boileau of Penn State University Press for her interest in, and faith in, the project, and Ryan and I thank Hannah Hebert of the Press for her help in seeing this through.

STEWART M. HOOVER
Boulder, Colorado

Introduction

Stewart M. Hoover

The twenty-first century dawned with dramatic changes in relations between long-standing sources of social and cultural power and meaning.
The ongoing processes of globalization, both in its economic and cultural
forms, have reorganized and reoriented relationships between peoples and
nations. These forces of change have served both to reify particular expressions of culture and politics and to place those expressions within larger
contexts of competition, struggle, and—potentially—accommodation and
reorientation.

Within these processes, nothing has exerted itself to more effect (and
in a way, surprise) than religion. For most of the last century, it was convenient—particularly in the West—for intellectual, social, and cultural
authorities to overlook religion as a force in society, culture, and politics—both domestically and internationally. Against this, religion began to
rise in importance in the last decades of the century through such events
as the Islamic Revolution in Iran and the emergence of Evangelical politics
in the United States.

The events of 9/11 of course raised the profile of religion to an entirely
new level. In the years since, lay and scholarly discourses have struggled to
contend with the persistence of religion as a force in domestic and global

politics and society. This renewed attention to the place of religion has led to its discovery all around us, in places and in registers that are both emergent and persistent but previously overlooked. We can see that religion is now both local and global, that its presence is felt in national political contexts as well as in transnational culture and politics. We can also see that there is reason to ask whether evidence of the resurgence of religion is instead evidence of its persistence in new forms, particularly in settings beyond the formal domains of discourse, such as popular and entertainment cultures.

Implicit in all of this are two issues fundamental to understanding religion and its role in politics and society in the new century. The first of these is the important role that the media and the mediation of religion, religious symbols, and religious experience have come to play in the resurgence of religion. The second is the question of religious authority. To the extent that new forms and contexts of religious identity and practice are emerging, the traditional sources of religious symbols, truth claims, and meanings find themselves in competition with these new and emergent ones. But the relationship between emerging mediations of religion and religious authority is not simple or straightforward. It is complex, layered, and nuanced, and the purpose of this volume is to describe it in these terms.

Media are clearly at the center of many of these developments in the world of religion. This is obvious in formal media settings such as journalism, where religion "coverage" is on the rise, though it is still contested and troubled turf. It is also obvious in the production and distribution of specifically "religious" media by religious bodies, which is also growing in volume and significance worldwide. But the media play an important informal role as well. The Iranian Revolution, for example, relied heavily on the "small media" of cassette tapes for the spread of its ideas. Iran's "Green Revolution" following the 2009 elections there and the "Arab Spring" protests of 2011 centered on media as well, though this time the digital "new media." The Evangelical revival in the United States was in great measure a function of its mediation via such forms as televangelism and other kinds of para-institutional, commodified popular culture, including Christian music, religious films, and the religious publishing industry.

Religion has also become more and more a feature of the "secular" entertainment media, from television programs such as *Touched by an Angel*, to *Oprah*, to *Battlestar Galactica*, to *My Name Is Earl*, to theatrical films such as *Ghost*, *Bruce Almighty*, *Avatar*, and the *Twilight* series, to the recording industry. A growing literature considers how such things might have a role to play in constructing contemporary religion.

To the extent that the media are becoming more important in these ways, there are clearly implications for religious authority. Some of these implications are obvious, some less so. It is obvious that the media today directly confront religious authorities' ability to control their own symbols and symbolic resources. Mediations of symbols such as the crucifix (in the case of Madonna's classic "Like a Prayer" music video) delink legitimated and authoritative readings of those signs from the signs themselves. Media also confront authority through the sheer number and range of mediations of religious and quasi-religious imbrications and truth claims that circulate in contemporary media contexts. This potentially serves to dissolve the boundaries of the discursive settings (religious observances, religious instruction, etc.) where religion has been legitimately discussed. Global media further confront authority by relativizing it, bringing a wider range of religious symbols, discourses, and claims to the attention of global publics. Thus in any local context there is today at least the possibility that the local "gods" must be seen alongside gods from a wide range of other contexts, both national and global.

It is a straightforward matter to see these things in institutional or structural terms. The media industries are widely understood today to be important actors on the national and global stage. They confront political authorities as readily as they do religious ones. Global corporate media are even claimed in some circles to constitute an extra-national or meta-state political force. Governments treat media as competitors and threats, often moving to control them when and where they can. Thus it makes some sense to see media in relation to religious authority in similar ways. Religious leaders seek opportunities for "airtime" to promote their views in broadcast media (such as the Tim Tebow pro-life television commercial during the 2011 American football Super Bowl broadcast). Certain films are seen by—and criticized by—certain religious authorities in terms of their direct challenge to official readings of doctrine or history (as in the Vatican's criticisms of *The Da Vinci Code* and *Avatar*). Of course, religious leaders have also sought to create or own "media."

Thinking of these relations in structural terms alone, however, overlooks a much more varied, layered, and complex landscape of interactions between various levels of "lived" religion and "lived" and "consumed" media. In recent decades, media theory has evolved away from an orientation to formal media structures and their productions and toward an appreciation for the way popular reception practice can and does make its own meanings out of media. As a field, culturalist media studies has stressed these "meanings made," and has contemplated media and media contexts beyond the formal realms of journalism and broadcasting. This has meant that the "popular" and entertainment media—across a range of platforms and channels—are seen to be of increasing importance in the construction of cultural and social meanings and effects. The diversification and fracturing of sources and channels in the digital age has made it even more important to think of media in other than purely institutional-structural terms

This is made even more pressing in an era of cultural globalization, where the circulation of meanings and values is ever more widespread, diverse, and interactive. The very grounds on which mediations of religious and quasi-religious imaginaries and claims might be encountered and understood are shifting. New insights, new truth claims, new symbols, and new practices today can come from across the world as readily as from across the street. Moreover, insights into relations between media, religion, and culture can be gained from attention to specific cases and contexts from across the globe.

It should be clear then that we need to think about media, about religion, and about authority in new ways. This rethinking would need to address at least the following issues. First, there is the question of the scale of religious change or transformation that might be underway. I am arguing that religion is today being remade by media. This moves beyond the straightforward notion that all religions are mediated and that modern media introduce new ways that religions are understood and practiced. Instead, there is a growing discourse, such as that in the theoretical domain known as "mediatization theory," that suggests that the outcome of the interaction between religion and media is the creation of something entirely new: a difference in kind, not merely in scale.

Second, this difference is expressed along a number of dimensions, but perhaps none is more important than that contemporary media increasingly make it possible for new religious forms—and in particular new religious voices—to emerge. This has two further implications. First, the particular claims, values, and symbols these new voices articulate become part of the discourse of religion. Second, by virtue of their actions, these new voices can build networks and solidarities and potentially achieve some form of authority on their own.

Third, these processes raise the question of the locus and constitution of authority. Traditional authority continues, of course. But it is now joined by other centers and contexts of authority. And these new centers and contexts are not unproblematic. We might be interested in the first instance in how they provide a challenge to prior centers of power in religion, but they themselves may then become subject to a similar challenge and are certainly deserving of similar critique and analysis.

Fourth, authority in these regards is often linked to debates over authenticity. The received view is that this is a necessary linkage, that authority must maintain its control for the sake of authenticity in relation to symbols, practices, texts, and doctrines. A more nuanced view, and one more cognizant of critical poststructuralist notions, would suggest that this is an issue of power. The power to assign things to the category of "the authentic" is the primary power that religious authorities hold, and their claim of this power is their necessary currency of exchange. Critical reflection on this as a discourse of power is thus a central task.

Fifth, this is all not just a question of structural relations and of power as expressed through structure. It cannot be ignored that new forms of mediation are at their base *aesthetic* processes linking practice and identity with such things as taste and sensation. These aesthetic sensibilities and saliencies are of course important in terms of the reception of various media forms, but it can also be argued that sensation and taste can help constitute identities, communities, and movements. Received approaches and understandings have undervalued the aesthetic and sensational, just as they have the popular and informal. To the extent that religious persistence or resurgence was overlooked prior to the late twentieth or the turn of the twenty-first century, this bias toward formal and structural expressions of religion may have been one of the reasons.

This volume is intended to open up the task of rethinking these matters. It does so in two sections. An initial set of chapters revisits the question of authority in relation to these evolving senses of "the religious." Taking account of received ways of understanding authority and the application of those understandings to the question of religion, they broaden and deepen the grounds on which we might look at the larger implications of new mediations of religion for the sources and centers of legitimation within and beyond religious structures. Classical understandings of authority—rooted in Weber's ideas—are in need of serious and careful reflection as they might be applied to modern religion, to modern media, and to modern mediations of religion and spirituality.

Following this, the book then moves in a second section to a series of grounded case studies across a range of cultural, geographic, and religious contexts. They are in-depth, observational, textual, and ethnographic studies of particular instances of media production and reception in Asia, Africa, Latin America, and North America. Some involve formal representations of religion and spirituality. Some involve informal and emergent, even resistive articulations and voices. Some demonstrate clear demarcations between established authority and contexts of practice, others blur those lines. In some, the sources of textual and other meanings clearly reside within formally constituted religious contexts. In others, the media themselves seem to be the sources of these things. Some revolve around formal mediation by large-scale media such as film and television, others are generated by new, social, interactive, and "small" media such as Twitter. Each demonstrates the value of this sort of grounded study as they provide insights into the ways that the elastic relations between religion and media are being shaped today in a variety of settings. Importantly, together they also provide an international, even global view.

In the first chapter, I assess the moment theoretically, looking at the foundational conception of authority found in the classic work of Max Weber. Weber's ideas of the nature of authority and the types of authority underlie much of what we now think of in relation to religious authority. In fact, religion has seemed to be particularly implied in his category of "traditional authority." Weber's thoughts about the constitution of authority are also influential, and they remain apt and perhaps even more significant today as the traditional grounds and boundaries of authority seem to be shifting. That part of the reason for this shift seems to be attributable to modern media, and the contemporary media sphere frames much of what we consider here.

Weber persuasively argues that most valences of authority rest on structures of plausibility. To be legitimate, authority must be perceived to be plausible, valid, and (to an extent) authentic. Regardless of whether it is legal, traditional, or charismatic authority (Weber's fundamental categories), it must be articulated to belief among its objects in order to retain its power. The significant frame of modern public life makes this plausibility problematic, rather than taken for granted. This frame includes the situation in the developed West, where publics today are increasingly resistant to authority and express declining confidence in the important institutions of public life. Elsewhere, particularly in Africa and the Middle East, confidence in politics is still a work in progress. Fundamental socio-structural issues also come into play. Anthony Giddens (1992), for example, has laid out an articulate argument about modern consciousness, in which he suggests that in contemporary life, individuals increasingly engage with the structures of social life reflexively and with a consciousness of the means and sources of the structural conditions of their lives.

Of course none of this is absolute, but Giddens's argument here is instructive, especially as regards questions of the large role of media in these conditions. A good deal of this reflexive autonomy (the power that individuals today seek to exercise over their own senses of self and identity) is articulated with a mediated public sphere that makes systems of power and the structures of power more obvious, at least notionally. The media contribute to a situation where individuals feel that they have "seen behind the curtain" of the nature and constitution of power and authority, making that authority less tacitly plausible. This condition impinges on state authority, of course, but it also has important implications for religious authority. Within this frame, where the media establish large conditions within which religion (and presumably religious authority) must function, we can see many smaller and more conditional contexts of action. The studies here detail such contexts and phenomena, painting a picture of practices that make religious authority problematic in large and small ways and on a variety of levels.

To look at the implications in more detail, we can think about how each study here relates to the Weberian structure of authority outlined in the first chapter. There, I argue that questions of the mediation of religion impinge on Weber's categories in different ways and to different extents. My argument in that chapter is general, becoming more obvious as we look at specific cases. But, on that general level, it might be argued that of the Weberian categories, *legal* authority might well be least implied by the work we see here. Far more implied is the category of *traditional* authority, which was also more obviously connected to religion even in Weber's thinking. To review, traditional authority receives and maintains its position through its embedment in, and appeals to, shared history and received tradition. This more cultural ground of authority might logically be more implied in the sorts of cultural practices seen in these chapters. These studies and these contexts vary in the constitution of tradition and authority in each, but what ties them together is the way that in each one, tradition is confronted, at least in cultural terms.

Weber's third type of authority, *charismatic authority*, is also implied here, along a number of dimensions. First, there is the broad consensual sense that the media, particularly commercial media, establish their own authority by means very much like Weber's charisma: it is based on their attractiveness to audiences more than it is on traditional or structural means. Charismatic authority is also implied to the extent that the specific practices of mediation that we will see are more symbolic, less material, something that also evokes Weber's charisma. The connection to this type of authority is also obvious in the controversy that might flow from calling the practices we see here "religion." On an important level of received validity, they can appear to be superficial, transitory, and ephemeral, as opposed to the received idea of religion as historical and unchanging. This means that, to the extent that the kinds of things we see here become more commonplace articulations of religion, the whole meaning of religious authority may be shifting, away from structure and toward practice. Such a claim is very much a commonplace in contemporary religious studies.

Thinking in terms of charismatic authority also reframes the debates around some received ideas about the media themselves. What is possible in media and in practices of audiences and communities in relation to media is in part conditioned and framed by our consensual understandings of, and valuation of, media. On a large and public level, certain kinds of media are preferred over others (by authorities!). The received view of media has been articulated by cultural voices such as Daniel Boorstin (1992), who decried "the triumph of the image in America." We take for granted that the media traffic in superficiality; when compared to traditional or legal authority, authority rooted in charisma might easily be thought of as more superficial, less significant, less serious, and necessarily less authentic.

Against these assumptions about charismatic authority in relation to the media, there are contrasting implications from two directions. First, we might suggest that the Weberian notion of plausibility in charismatic authority might well suffer or at least be contested by a linkage through media with markets, market competition, and the presumed superficiality of such things as the "commodification" of religion through its absorption into commercial and commodity markets. A second direction might suggest that this new situation might put the whole question of plausibility in a new light, that the marketing of religious charisma might actually legitimate some sources as authoritative more convincingly because of the functioning of these cultural markets. These are two sides of the same coin, seeing as a problem the diminution of the ostensibly "authentic" on the one hand and seeing that very process as one that establishes legitimacy and authenticity on the other.

This is the sort of larger question that this book hopes to address. It is illustrative that the media age, as it were, "opens up" such questions. In this case, and across the cases we consider here, it is a refiguring of Weber's fundamental categories of traditional and charismatic authority that is at issue. The question of the mediation of religion through these contemporary practices repositions the grounds of Weber's theory. Whereas to Weber the issue of "plausibility" was a prior condition for the functioning of his types of authority, we now know (through the work of Habermas, at least) that in the contemporary public sphere(s) plausibility is actually in play, a dimension whose variation becomes a constitutive condition of authority, a dimension along which negotiations of the status of authority might take place. The question might not be so much whether specific centers of hermetic authority have achieved plausibility as a precondition to their status or influence, but rather how the plausibility of various authorities or authoritative claims or voices, once achieved, constitutes their authority.

The second category in question, "traditional authority" in religion, is also in play in a different way than suggested by Weber. Like Durkheim and Tönnies, Weber worked from a received history of religion that saw religious tradition, and its authority, in structural and essentialized terms. Specific religions, and their systems of authority, were known entities with clearly demarcated and known sources and histories, and their meaning and effect could be measured against those things. Thus a key consideration is whether a given utterance or practice or process is consistent with the legacy of history.

The cases we see here invite us to think of things differently. Instead of thinking of authority inductively, in terms that assume its constitution and efficacy, seeing new conditions in terms of their variation on, or challenge to, that efficacy, we must now think of authority in terms of its constitution. Where does it come from? How is it established? Who is involved? Who or what might be challenging or changing it? In these pages, we will see that the implications for authority fall out along three general lines.

First, it is apparent that the practices and functioning of these "markets" have great potential to *differentiate* religions. They illustrate and illuminate various religious resources, symbols, structures, and claims, placing them in a more-or-less horizontal marketplace of choice (cf. Hoover, 2006). The very fact that these various sources are placed alongside others in this context further demands distinctiveness, and thus even further differentiation. Religions in the modern media marketplace then become at least in part a highly refined and almost iconic version of themselves.

Second, these relativized sources of religion are then relativized by their positioning in the marketplace. As religions are presented within the various public and mediated frames, they appear alongside one another. This almost by definition suggests that none has a necessary precedence over the others. None is more important than the others, except as it achieves increased definition and influence through practice.

Third, these sources, to the extent that some surface above the others, must well do so through some form of Weber's "charisma." They must find their place and their voice through means that are outside the bounds of history and structure. The very fact that we think of this as a "marketplace" almost by definition implies that some version of Weber's charisma must be involved.

This all serves to turn around the traditional and received ideas about authority. Rather than flowing from sources in doctrine and history, and therefore from some essentialized notion of "the religious," I would argue that what we see in these pages suggests that authority instead flows from the "other end" of Weber's chain of causation. It is in what he called "plausibility" that the examples we see here draw their force in relation to authority and therefore achieve new and nuanced authority of their own. These are new and emergent centers and sectors of authority, rooted in their ability to find audiences, to plausibly invigorate or invite practice, and to direct attention. In each case we see these processes, but we often see them in formation and in the early stages of their evolution. These are primarily cases that involve "something new": a new trend, a new context, a new medium, a new social or discursive project. Thus the final significance of what we see here is in what it can tell us about where and how practices and meanings of authority will evolve. We can infer some things from these cases about how things are working now, but we can also begin to see where they might go next.

This new century has invited a large-scale rethinking of "the religious," as I have said. Religion has persisted, in part due to modern mediation and the infusion of religion into contexts of—and its use of—means of contemporary mediation. These chapters help us shape and nuance our view of how these things work. They are not all about formal or institutional or technological mediation. Some are about small, local, and informal things. Some deal with means of mediation far removed from the sophisticated "mass media." Some involve the efforts of purposive actors. Others are more casual and emerge out of broader structures of practice. Each of them, though, tells us that we need to be thinking about the ways that contemporary contexts and practices of mediation make the prospects of religious authority increasingly complex, nuanced, and layered.

This book is only a first step in such a process of thinking and rethinking. It invites further discussion and even debate. More important, it invites more empirical work. The projects reported here are only a few of the possible themes and approaches and methods that might be used. The authors here join me in inviting others to address this work by building on it, contesting it, refining it, and enhancing it through scholarship. We do hope we've started a conversation that will continue for some time to come.

The Media and Religious Authority

REFERENCES

Boorstin, D. (1992). *The image: A guide to pseudo-events in America* (25th anniv. ed.). New York, NY: Vintage.

Giddens, A. (1991). *Modernity and self-identity: Self and society in the late modern age*. Stanford, CA: Stanford University Press.

Hoover, S. M. (2006). *Religion in the media age*. London, UK: Routledge.

PART I

Rethinking Authority in an Era of Media and Religious Change

CHAPTER I

Religious Authority in the Media Age

Stewart M. Hoover

The twenty-first century ushered in many changes in culture, society, politics, and the economy. Anticipated as the dawn of an age, this time things really did change, and rather markedly. A widespread public near-panic about feared "Y2K" calamities focused and articulated an inchoate anxiety about the emergent digital age. It served to raise recognition across U.S. culture about the central place of digital media in our lives. That nothing of the sort happened was not the point. What was the point was that we now all understood that a new age—a digital age—had already dawned. The terrorist attacks of 2001 and 2005 were another opening to the new century. The implications of 9/11 in politics, global security, and international affairs have been obvious. Perhaps less obvious at the time—but now quite clear—were its implications for our understanding of religion.

Prior to 9/11, it was far easier to overlook the role of religion in domestic and international affairs (in the United States and the industrialized West at least). Intellectual and cultural elites in the academy, the media, and international affairs had become comfortable with an implicit notion of secularization, where the progress of the twentieth century was a story of the gradual erosion of the influence of religion. In keeping with the original (academic) definition of secularization, it was thought that increasing levels of education together with economic progress would gradually erode the need for religion (Berger, 1967). One message of 9/11 was that religion had not gone away and would not for quite some time yet. In the U.S. context, 9/11, along with rise of religiously modulated domestic politics (expressed most vividly in the George W. Bush administration), brought home the reality that religion must be accounted for in our calculus of contemporary culture and politics.

In the world of scholarship, this realization has opened the door to a variety of emergent fields, voices, and approaches. The fields of religious studies and religion sociology had long been rethinking and reorienting away from essentialist, functionalist, and structuralist theorizing toward the more subtle and nuanced view that what is important in religion is what is *produced* by practice, not what is *intended* by traditions and institutions. But the new century is also a time increasingly defined by the cultural and social implications of changes in communication, the media, and emergent digital cultures. A scholarship at the intersection of media and religion has emerged as well and has begun to come into its own in the second decade of the century.

This media and religion scholarship began by looking at the more obvious questions of what happens when the media frame or cover religion, as in religion journalism or in stereotypes of religion in entertainment media content. It had also looked at what happens when religion uses media, as in televangelism or the media productions of various religious bodies.

Over time, though, and largely since 2001, it has become clear that a third way of looking at relations between media and religion is now much more appropriate. The media sphere, with its range of commodities, practices, resources, capacities, and affordances, is increasingly coming to *produce* religion, to produce new religious meanings and sensibilities, and can be a context increasingly determinative of what is thought of as religion and thought possible in the way of religions, spiritualities, and the things that might occupy the lived spaces once occupied by religions and spiritualities. It is no longer enough to look only at what religions—as traditionally conceived—think or do in relation to a separate media sphere. Instead, we need now to recognize that that media sphere is itself a place where the once-separate domains of "religion" and "media" now meet and in which new senses, symbols, practices, and meanings of religion and "the religious" are constituted and generated.

There has been a vibrant debate in recent years over ways that this situation might be conceived or theorized. A thorough review of these is beyond the scope of this essay, but some outlines are worth describing. One approach has been to suggest that what is happening is a "mediatization of religion" (Clark, 2007; Hjarvard, 2008; Lundby, 2009). This approach assumes that in important ways media and religion still must be thought of as separate, and that the important implications for religion are in how the industries and institutions of the media sphere change the conditions under which it must now function. The key contribution here is the understanding that the structural conditions of the media industries have changed things for religion in very fundamental ways. This approach runs up against the conceptual challenge of a second view, one that argues that what we must focus on is the fact that all religions are in fundamental ways "mediated," and that we must understand how and in what ways modern and technological means of communication (and their inscription with and ascription of the full meaning of "modernity") express religion today (Horsfield, 2015; Meyer & Moors, 2006). This view holds that the question is in the evolving means and contexts of mediation and circulation of religious meanings. Where religions might once have been mediated through means that were elements of their "mechanical solidarity" (to use Durkheim's term) or were integrated into the warp and woof of *Gemeinschaft* (to quote Tönnies), they are today mediated in different ways and by different means, including means that we think of as "modern." The integration and layering of these various means is the point that must be seen more in terms of its continuities with the past than with its disruptions of the present.

A third view focuses on what is produced in the way of religions and spiritualities, or even of emergent senses of "sacredness" and social practices inflected with greater or higher purpose, including contemporary *secular* rituals of meaning, and how all this changes the terms of what is thought of as important and centrally meaningful (Couldry, 2003; Hepp, 2012; Krotz, 2009; see also Herbert, 2003). This perspective is less concerned with what happens to "religion" than with those meanings and functions and practices that might once have been "religious," but today are more diffused across the culture and expressed in ways and in contexts where qualities of faith and transcendence are less important than are material and social rituals of meaning and value.

A fourth view centers the question on how the media sphere is itself generative of religious meaning, affordance, possibility, and action. One articulation of this has suggested that digital media, in particular, have extended the capacities of the media sphere in such a way that an elastic and generative "third space" or range of "third spaces" of digital religion has resulted (Hoover & Echchaibi, 2012; but see also Campbell, 2012; Clark, 2007; Helland, 2012; Hutchings, 2013; Wagner, 2012). By "third spaces,"

Hoover and Echchaibi have intended to point to an affordance of digital and social media: that these practices hail their practitioners into new subjectivities, implying that the digital affords dimensions of generativity and interactivity that are new and unique on their own terms.

Digital media have in fact introduced something new and different and are increasingly determinative of practice, even among the "legacy media" (Hoover & Echchaibi, 2012). Among the most suggestive and intriguing conceptual turns in relation to the spaces produced by digital media is to think of these spaces anthropologically: in terms of what conceptual and physical geographies they imply and what sorts of cultural meanings and strategies they invoke. This has opened up a wide conceptual turf that refers to important work in gender, ethnicity and national identity, generationally inflected meanings and practices, and postcolonial theory.

The point of this discussion is to suggest that to address any issues in contemporary religion we must account for the media, and that we must understand it is not a simple matter of "media" and "religion" as separate spheres and the work of one on the other, but rather a question of where religion is produced today. There are a variety of ways to think about or theorize this situation, but the media, the media sphere, and media practices of production, consumption, reception, popular remediation, and cultural circulation are at the center of that production.

As we've understood that conditions have changed, and in fact as each of the various paradigms of the study of media and religion has recognized, the implications of all this for *religious authority* are now a central and critical question. Certainly, the issue of religious authority looms large even if we are only addressing the more traditional questions of the framing of religion *by* "the media" or the use of media *by* "religion."

In the former case, the treatment or framing of religion *by* the media, press coverage of the scandals in the Catholic Church is an important example. A changing relationship between the church and the media can be seen there. Many media have traditionally shown deference to religion, and particularly to large, structured religious institutions such as Catholicism. This could be seen was evident in the practices of metropolitan newspapers in U.S. cities with large Catholic populations (Hoover, 1998). An effect of the scandals has been the end of that era to some degree. These events illustrated for the news industries the fact that, as public institutions, religious institutions can be subject to the same scrutiny applied to business, politics, and government. They have also shown that such coverage of religion can sell newspapers, not an insignificant factor in media policy and practice. Catholic leaders and some leading lay voices have been slow to grasp this changing situation. The implication for Catholic Church authority is clear. It is no longer able to define the boundaries and limits of its power and can no longer inscribe a bright line between itself and "the media." Its power has been limited in this way.

Implications for institutional authority can also be seen in the other direction, the use of media *by* religion. The situation here is more subtle, layered, and nuanced, but is nonetheless clear and predictive. It can be seen most clearly in the U.S. context in the rise of the most prodigious "users" of religious media in the twentieth century: the conservative, fundamentalist, and evangelical movements. Their facility and comfort with self-conscious and self-directed mediation is one of the hallmarks of these brands of Protestantism. Against a Protestant establishment defined in many ways by its reluctance to engage with popular media (Hendershot, 2004; Hoover & Kim, 2012; Morgan, 2007; Promey, 1996), the conservative branches of Protestantism engaged media fully and aggressively, moving religion out of the comfortable and tacit private and domestic spheres of action favored by the establishment into the open cultural and political marketplace of public culture. The result has been a large-scale redefinition of the American religious landscape, with the formerly dominant Protestant establishment now at least relativized in relation to other religious traditions, or even seemingly in decline (Hoover & Kim, 2012; Gill, 2012). In the field of popular mediation, some religions simply do better than others do, something that deserves a great deal more attention than I can give it here.

These trends in the relationship between "religion" and "the media" seem to have deepened further in the digital era. While the Catholic Church has moved to find a place in the digital realm, its efforts seem likely to meet with mixed success. The digital revolution seems also to be reorganizing and redefining the equities in religious media, with some groups and movements making the transition to the interactive and social media, and others less likely to do so successfully. The point is that, in both cases, we have to recognize the ways the media sphere has become determinative of the outlines and boundaries of practice and action, and its capacities and affordances are increasingly defining what is possible for traditional religious institutions.

RETHINKING RELIGIOUS AUTHORITY

The classic work on authority, which has been applied to religious authority as well, is Max Weber's *Economy and Society* (1968). At its heart, according to Weber, authority depends on plausibility and acceptance. It must be plausible and accepted to be effective (see also Habermas, 1976). From this basis of legitimacy, the relationship between authority and the party over which that authority is exercised, there are three kinds of authority, according to Weber.

There is, first, *legal authority*, that which flows from established laws and political traditions, defined in relation to bounded memberships or citizenships. Legal authority rests on and works through codes and systems of action and practice. In religions, legal authority is related to discipline, enforced practice, doctrinal systems, and prescribed behaviors. Such systems are impersonal, says Weber, with authority flowing through systems of power. Legal authority is limited, however, to the extent that power flows from the legal system to both the governor and the governed. Specific institutions or authorities are constrained by the system, with those in power subject to the rules and needing to regularly refer to and to be seen complying with them.

Second, there is *traditional authority*. Power here accrues by virtue of the existence of a long-standing and accepted set of shared values and traditions. Authority flows here not through the institutional or structural legitimation of law but through authority's embodiment of a position of some long standing within particular cultural, ethnic, national, or religious traditions. Authority in the traditional sense persists because there has been a structured position of authority that the current incumbents now hold. Those incumbents are limited in the same way legal authority is limited, though, because they must be seen to be acting within the tradition in order to maintain their legitimacy. Their claims to the right to define or redefine the tradition are always open to judgment over their authenticity or consistency with that tradition. Where the roots of legal authority are in a way transparent—its legitimacy ought to be derived from its provenance in specific and legitimate processes—traditional authority's roots are necessarily murkier, and in a way they are more authentic to the extent that they are more obscure or hermetic (Durkheim, 2001; Geertz, 1966; Malinowski, 1978). This is particularly the case with religious authority.

The third kind of authority, to Weber, is *charismatic authority*, or authority rooted in charisma. This type of authority focuses more on the individual or groups of individuals exercising authority and their capacities to influence and convince those at whom their authority is directed. Great revolutionary forces and effective political figures are of course examples of this type of authority. There is no external validation as is the case with legal or traditional authority. Rather, legitimation comes from the capacities and qualities of the authoritative figure or figures. The world of religion is, of course, rife with examples of charismatic authority. Presumably, the founders of all the great religions possessed this type of authority. But charismatic authority is both fluid and transient, says Weber. There are also in religion many cases of individuals and groups that aspire to charismatic authority but fail to establish it with any permanence. There are also many cases of charismatic authority rising to contest traditional or legal authority, and in these cases a crisis of legitimacy comes about as some voices support the qualities of the charismatic leadership while others raise doubts based on traditional or legal grounds.

It is valuable to note that each of these types of authority is largely structural. In each case, the concern is with how structures of tradition or law are cultivated and conveyed through the actions of legitimated individuals and groups within those systems. Similarly, charismatic authority is defined by its ability to create structures of affinity and action out of its abilities to convince followers. Power is, of course, the marker of authority, and in each of Weber's categories the exercise of power by certain forces over the beliefs and behaviors of others is the central issue.

In modern times, a dimension of Weber's theory that he touches on but does not emphasize now deserves more attention: the role of consent in the establishment and maintenance of systems of authority. In the nineteenth century, when Weber was writing, this was an issue, but one that was less significant than it is today (for reasons I'll get to presently). Governing in democratic systems depended on the consent of the governed, as we all know, but Weber stressed the issue of legitimacy (a matter taken up more explicitly by Habermas a century later) because he recognized that the whole point of articulating authoritative offices and individuals to their systems was the problem of the plausibility of their authority, something that was increasingly in play in the industrial era. Educated and increasingly socially autonomous publics could be expected to have a view both of the authoritative offices and of the sources of that authority, and those offices needed to maintain their legitimacy because those publics were becoming more reflexive, autonomous, and potentially skeptical (Habermas, 1989). The point is that even in the largely structural world of authority described by Weber there was a decidedly "poststructuralist" register, that of a context of knowledge and action involved in defining, legitimating, and ensuring the consent necessary for authority to function.

Implicit in Habermas's thoughts on the eighteenth- and nineteenth-century public spheres, and much more explicit in Elizabeth Eisenstein's (1979) work on the earlier development of printing and the publishing industry, is a dimension of the situation particularly significant to the realm of religion and religious authority: the challenge faced by religious institutional authority in the media age is a consequence (again, largely structural) of the establishment of the media as a separate and autonomous sphere of economic, social, and—most significant today—cultural authority. Prior to Gutenberg in the early modern West, the established authorities of the state and the church had things pretty much to themselves. Their scope and legitimacy were rooted in their control of social, economic, and political resources. On that base, they were also able to construct the ideological and discursive resources necessary to pursue their goals and interests. In today's terms, we might say that they controlled the sources of *symbolic* as well as *financial* capital.

Marx helped us understand the importance of this symbolic sphere. The constitution of politics and society is not limited to the capture of material resources. In modernity, control of resources involves control of discourse as well. The function of ideology (central to—but not the limits of—"superstructure" to Marx) was to ensure the legitimacy of the matters that were already and always being settled in the material sphere. Thus there is a conceptual or ideological or symbolic project at the heart of social, cultural, and political projects. Marx showed how meaning works at the center of human relations: for example, in how a surplus of meaning around certain things leads to a fetishization of those things—their investment with deeper and more motivational meanings.

Eisenstein helps us understand how the new media technology of printing led to the development of an entirely new industry—publishing— and a new center of cultural and social authority—the publisher—with the power and autonomy to be able to directly challenge the authority of church and state. And this authority was over precisely that area of social and cultural practice—the circulation of surplus meaning—of what we'd today call "symbolic capital." Publishers didn't have armies of monks writing in *scriptoria*, but they did have an expanding economy of cultural production and they were quickly recognized as potential aspirants to social power and ascendancy. Both the church and the state, of course, moved quickly to harness the power of publishing, and a several-centuries-long struggle over the definition of the role of publishing ensued, which is still working itself out today in such things as the role and definition of press freedom in relation to democracy.

In the context of contemporary Western democracies, where religion is structurally differentiated through sectarianism and denominationalism, those particularized authorities find themselves facing the structural reali- ties of a media sphere (the contemporary legatees of the fifteenth-century publishers) that is itself authoritative. More important, in the twentieth and twenty-first centuries the media sphere has become ever more autonomous as a result of the large-scale globalization and privatization of the media industries. A century ago, the dominant media were national, not international, and as the electronic media emerged, they began as public, not private, entities. This has now changed. The media are today largely global, commercial, and private. This means things for state actors, of course, but my concern here is religion, and it has meant that religious authority today has a forceful competitor, one that is far more portentous for religion than for the state because the media trade in precisely the same things religions do—the practices, commodities, and contexts of meaning making. The media are thus an existential and nearly categorical challenge to religious authority. And that challenge is expressed in a range of contexts and across layers and registers of practice.

Renowned scholar of African and Afro-Brazilian religious history Paulo Farias has articulated a definition of religion that is profound, fitted to the age, and deeply illustrative of the existential challenge religions face from the modern media sphere. Religion is, according to Farias (2008), "that which has the power to confirm the meaning of signs." We can now see that this is, in fact, the most profound aspiration of religious authority as it faces the modern maelstrom of cultural and social change in the twenty-first century. Contemporary culture is defined by symbolic and imagic processes (Baudrillard, 1995; Benjamin, 1969; Boorstin, 1992). The field of images is the field of practice where forms of social, cultural, and religious capital are constructed and exchanged. It can be argued that this is particularly true—indeed that it has always been true—of religion and spirituality and religions and spiritualities (Albanese, 1992; Meyer, 2011; Meyer & Moors, 2006; Morgan, 2007).

A NUANCED, SUBTLE, LAYERED CHALLENGE

Religious authority—in the form of particular academic or ecclesiastical authorities—has from time to time attempted to address the challenges of

the media age. Various recent popes, for example, have spoken on the challenges of the media age. John Paul II issued a major statement on the media
in 1997, titled "Communicating Way, Truth, and Life." The U.S. Protestant
and ecumenical churches have also spoken about media, and particular
Catholic and Protestant theologians and academics have weighed in (Fore,
1990; Mohler, 2006; Myers, 1989; Schultze, 2003; Warren, 1997).

These critiques have two things in common. First, they have continued to assume that the spheres of media and of religion or of religiously
modulated moral action are separate and differentiated, and that the effect
of one on the other is the important question. Second, they have assumed
that there is a certain level of volition at the threshold of media behavior.
They have assumed that people, in their daily lives, live as though they
have choice as to whether they will participate in media. They conceive
of the situation as one where human action and human choice come into
play at the threshold of media practice, that it is a question of one choosing
whether to engage with media. The assumption is that there is a relatively
level field of action involved, where the media are but one among many
sources of insight and meaning or objects of practice. There is thus no particular precedence given to media or to mediated sources or resources. In
fact, consistent with the general tendency of cultural elites in the modern
West, mediated sources are seen to be artificial, simulacric, or secondary.
They may be particularly attractive, but only as entertainments and as less
valuable ways to do the work of identity and meaning making.

Religious authority has thus tended to place itself in conflict with one
of the important realities of contemporary Western life: the inevitability
of media. It simply makes no sense any longer to treat media as though its
practice were entirely volitional. On the most fundamental level, most of
us today simply assume media. We do not see media as one marketplace
among many or one shelf among many in a broad inventory of symbolic
resources. Instead, for both structural reasons and reasons of practice, the
media *are* the context, they *are* the inventory. One of the fundamental explanations for this situation is a broadly cultural and anthropological one.
We simply want to be involved, to be part of broader conversations and
part of a "common culture." Even those individuals who have a religiously
defined motivation to criticize or to avoid media are drawn to this common
conversation (Hoover, 2006). We assume media, and the media assume,
and construct, us, in important ways. The media are thus, in a larger sense,
the kind of "third space" I described above in relation to digital practice.
They are a definitive context with its own logics of practice and action.

This can be seen in a different way with regard to children and youth. Parents know that one of the greatest challenges to their authority is the question of what media, media texts, and media practices their children will be allowed to access. A parent might decide to restrict access to a popular program but find that his child is nonetheless quite familiar with it from viewing at a friend's house or hearing about it on the playground. There is, functionally, no childhood that does not have media (Hoover, Clark, & Alters, 2003). And there is also essentially no domestic sphere without media. The media are so ubiquitous that their presence is felt everywhere.

And, as I've suggested, most people are motivated to participate in media, anyway, in order that they—or their children—are not "left out." Cultural and media theorists back to and including McLuhan (Carey, 1989; Ellul, 1964; Gerbner, 1972; McLuhan, 1964; Ong, 1982; Postman, 2006; Smythe, 2001; and others) have been right to suggest that the media are the contemporary hearth, that they are the contemporary storytellers, that they have assumed the basic cultural functions of Tönnies's *Gemeinschaft.* Why would we, then, avoid them or negotiate with them? They are the places where the central rituals of modern life (tragedies like 9/11 and triumphs like the Olympics) are celebrated, and much more.

The challenge of media is thus layered and nuanced. There are the large and broad contextual levels such as the field of national and international ritual action. There is the fact that through the media, small and regional contexts of practice become large and public. Because of the media, it is no longer possible to have a "private conversation." Everything is open to scrutiny, often beyond the bounds of its original articulation. The media are also a context of the articulation of gendered and generational discourses and meanings. The generational meanings are in many ways the most significant here, as younger generations seem more media-active and media-embedded than were their predecessors.

The generational divide also reveals another nuance or layer to our understanding of the implications of media practice for religious authority. One of the conditions of the contemporary era—and a condition determined in important ways by the media—is the increasing reflexivity of modern life. Anthony Giddens (1991) has shown how self-identity and meaning making today take place in unprecedented conditions of public knowledge and knowledge autonomy. People today know more about— or think they know more about—the workings of things than previous generations did. The existence of modern media has inculcated a sense of autonomy or mastery over the making of modern life and modern culture that leaves individuals feeling on the one hand more in control of their lives, and on the other hand more anxious about those lives.

They, and particularly youth, are reflexive as well about the media and the role of media in defining their own identities and cultural contexts. This reflexivity is articulated through people's use of "public scripts" of media practice that describe that practice in relation to commonly accepted definitions of value. These definitions of value are partly rooted in received elite discourses about media. Thus educational media are "good media," "high art" is better than "popular art," and purposive media are more valuable than entertainment or escapist media. These scripts in relation to media have been called "accounts of media" (Hoover, Clark, & Alters, 2003), important positioning and identity statements that define oneself culturally, generationally, and even in class terms by what kinds of media one consumes, avoids, or admits to or denies enjoying.

Cultural authorities thus face an additional challenge in defining themselves in relation to these scripts. Particularly for young people, the way an institution or authority chooses to define itself in relation to media becomes a significant marker (Bellotti, this volume). Thus the very fact of a given religious institution's objective policies or practices regarding media becomes important and persuasive. This can be seen, in relation to religion, in such things as the way certain megachurches are valued according to their relative level of "media savvy." Media and media practices are thus integrated into cultural life and cultural and moral valuation in ways that are deeply embedded, layered, and nuanced. And these are articulated on a number of different levels.

My argument here should not be read as suggesting that these matters are entirely structural or entirely about questions of media identity and identification. The fact is that media are also largely "about something." There is content, and that content can also serve to differentiate from authority or between authorities. Content important to religious authority could obviously be about politics, culture, economy, generations, secularism, or modernity. It could frame religion or specific religions or spiritualities or the near- or far-from-religion. In all these ways modern media and mediation have the potential to inscribe different nuances of religious authority and inscribe or invoke authority.

One of the important characteristics of modern life and modern consciousness that enforces this situation is the commonplace notion of personal moral autonomy that is so central to modern ideas of human rights and human responsibilities. The world's great religions today conceive of the human subject as culturally and morally autonomous and thus able to make his or her own decisions regarding things as mundane as media consumption. Thus most religions assume that they are arming their adherents with the ability to make their own decisions rather than strictly protecting them from things. This has, in fact, been a sea change in the last fifty years. Before the middle of the last century there was a dynamic debate in the religious community over censorship, with the Catholic Church, in particular, actively defining for its adherents what was and was not to be watched, or even available. Protestant institutions were also involved, though a bit less directly, through their support of such things as film industry "self-regulation."

Today, things are very different. No religion wants to be identified with the censorship of prior times. While there are some organizations devoted to religiously modulated efforts at protecting audiences from bad influences (and there is, indeed, a broad consensus that children should be protected from certain kinds of content), it is much more common for religious leaders to focus on the power and autonomy of individuals to make their own moral choices for themselves. In fact, religious institutions and organizations have learned that to engage directly with specific media content is in fact counterproductive. Catholic and conservative-evangelical condemnation of Martin Scorsese's *The Last Temptation of Christ* in 1988 is thought to have led to a publicity bonanza for the film. Less intense criticism by the Catholic Church of the more recent *Da Vinci Code* also inadvertently supported that film. This lesson was learned by the Mormon Church, which carefully avoided condemning the recent reality-television program *Sister Wives* and the Broadway hit *The Book of Mormon*.

Two nuances are important here. First, the notion of autonomy and the implication that individuals should be free to make their own decisions regarding media content, and second, the implication that religion and religious authority should avoid positioning themselves in such a way that they are in conflict with the common and tacit assumption of media practice. Religions should not, in modern times, find themselves challenging the legitimacy of media or media behaviors. To do so conflicts with the reflexive engagement I discussed above. As Weber pointed out, authority rests on consent. Adherents today, who identify first as media audiences, no longer consent to broad-scale anti-media jeremiads from religious leaders.

ACCOUNTING FOR AUTHORITY

I've tried to suggest that to understand media and religion today we need to accept the notion that the media sphere has become the context of determinative moral and cultural action within which much of what we think of as religious practice must function.[1] "The media" is thus something of an autonomous space that has precedence over other contexts of cultural and social value. It does not really help to continue to think of media and religion as separate and hermetic spheres, competing with each other for moral influence. Instead, the media increasingly set the terms, and religions and specifically religious authorities find themselves working within those terms. I've also tried to argue that the reasons for this are largely cultural and practical. They are not the result of structural or economic factors as much as they stem from the increasing place that the articulation of symbols and values has taken in contemporary culture. The media are the industries that define and control that process, and religion (and indeed other institutions) must somehow adapt.

So, what are the large outlines of this situation as it has implications for religious authority traditionally conceived? It is clear that, along the lines of Weber's classic formulation, his three categories of authority are differentially implicated by the situation I have described. It is clearly more about *charismatic authority* than it is about *legal authority*. As I have discussed, the situation is more about culture than it is about structure, and in fact received legalism in religion is very much rejected today as individuals are active in the cultural sphere, exploring and constructing new senses of "the religious" and "the spiritual." Beyond that, it is legalism, and particularly legalism about moral choices such as media behaviors, that has become widely derogated in modern conceptions of the rejected "prior" bourgeois religious cultural surround. The implication of personal autonomy in moral choice is very much at odds with the legalism in religion.

Traditional authority is another matter. A wide range of studies of media and religion have shown that the contemporary mediation of religion through practices of consumption is very much oriented toward implied and assumed senses of "the authentic." If we conceive of the media as a broad cultural marketplace of potential religious "supply" (Hoover, 2006; Hoover & Emerich, 2011), then those commodities in that inventory will be judged partly based on their authenticity. Many religious "seekers" go to the commodities in the media sphere looking for the pure essences of the various religious traditions they intend to imbricate (Clark, 2007; Einstein, 2008; Roof, 1998). Discussions, even arguments, over authenticity dominate many online and digital spaces (Whitehead, 2012). If authenticity is in question, then traditional authority might indeed be persuasive.

This seems to be the case with the relationship between online Buddhism and the Dalai Lama (Helland, 2012; Piacenza, 2012). His Holiness the Dalai Lama has been quite active in digital spaces (or rather his surrogates have), imbuing the online space with a certain aura or tone of religious authenticity. In contrast, recent efforts by the Vatican to enter digital media have been less salubrious. The lesson clearly is that traditional authority is important, and can be a valuable "brand" in the media marketplace, but that its role is nonetheless a negotiated one that relies on the consent of consuming and remediating audiences and publics. For the Dalai Lama to embrace social media is seen by adherents to be an important crossing of cultural and generational barriers. For the Pope to do so might aspire to the same status but suffers from a history of diffidence and legalism that makes it more suspect, at least to the broad youth audience.

Most of what I have described here has much more in common with Weber's notion of charismatic authority. It is very much about images, connections, values, symbols, and practices that might seem ephemeral and transitory in relation to legal and traditional grounds of authority. But the calculus is very different today, as I have noted. The question is much more "what works?" or "what is produced?" than "how does a given practice or set of practices line up with a religious doctrine or tradition?" Adherents today are much more fluid and elastic in their sensibilities, needs, and practices than has been the case in the past. There is thus a kind of "charisma" in those choices made in the religious media marketplace.

There is also "charisma" in the formal and genre characteristics of media and practices of mediation. Birgit Meyer (2011) has pointed out, in relation to the mediation of religion, that the affordances of "sensational forms" of experience and expression come to the center. The logics of practice in the mediation of religion are to a great extent aesthetic logics. Certain media and media practices have certain saliencies and afford certain kinds of expression, meaning making, and social network building. This implies that in relation to media, we must be thinking of Weber's notion of charismatic authority in a more complex, layered, and nuanced way than has been the case in the past. It is not just the capacities or characteristics of certain leaders and groups that connect authority with communities of shared meaning and action. Today, those communities themselves help constitute authority through the mediation of their participation in certain forms of practice. The notion of charisma thus needs to be expanded to think about the "sensational forms" of religious mediation through modern media.

There is of course a kind of "charisma" in certain religious actors who have become prominent in contemporary media. One can't help but evaluate cases like Amr Khaled, the most successful Muslim "televangelist," as examples of a kind of charismatic authority (Echchaibi, 2011). The important point, though, is that the grounds have shifted and the situation is defined more by audience action than by textual or media power. To say Amr Khaled is influential is not to say that his charisma has determined the practices of audiences, but instead to say that those audiences have created him as a global force. In a way this is nothing new. Weber implied this in his notion of "consent." What is different today is the nuance that, instead of thinking in terms of his power to convince audiences, we must think of his ability to place before potential markets symbolic goods that are attracting large numbers of viewers and remediators.

We might say the same thing about traditional or legal religious authorities. His Holiness the Dalai Lama is an example I mentioned above. His authority in the media frame is both his authenticity in relation to tradition but also his accessibility to certain types of mediation and, through that mediation, his relationship to emergent communities of affinity and reference. His traditional authority is important, of course, but it is not sufficient to explain his fit with the digital and social media sphere.

THE BIG PICTURE

What then are the overall implications for religious authority in all this? I've reviewed a number of specific functions and effects here, but there are some large dimensions that are important as we think about the prospects for religious authority in the media age. First, the nature of the contemporary media sphere and the self-consciousness and reflexivity of audience practice and consciousness mean that religious authority can no longer function in one of the ways that was thought typical of authority by Weber and Marx. Authority can no longer be so easily tacit or taken for granted. The ideological practice of authority in earlier times was to make its interests seem consensual and commonplace as the interests of the whole. A large and determinative religious culture would of course function in precisely this way.

In his classic work on the Protestant establishment, E. Digby Baltzell (1964) described how this worked in relation to the dominant religious culture of the United States. The consent to Protestant power rested on a tacit, obscure, taken-for-granted, and opaque role for Protestantism in the culture. Such obscurity is no longer possible. In today's media sphere—and largely because of it—religious authority is more obvious and exposed.[2] Further, religious leaders face a challenge in positioning their traditions in relation to media. As I've said, audiences today, particularly younger audiences, are suspicious of and resist the imposition of authoritative framings of "their" media.

One of the effects on authority, then, is that it becomes *revealed*. Religions have become increasingly differentiated as they have been represented in a globalized religious sphere. Their various symbols, doctrines, and truth claims have been placed in a more or less horizontal inventory in relation to others. They have also become *relativized*. In the media age, it has become more difficult for any one religion to claim precedence over others. They are now seen as equal pretenders to the attention of publics. This relativism in the cultural marketplace of course has deep roots. American Protestantism has long had such a marketplace at its core, rooted in the experience of the nineteenth-century frontier (Hatch, 1989; Moore, 1994).

This differentiated and relativized religious authority, then, faces the situation I've described in some detail here. The media sphere, its industries and its practices, now defines the context of action within which these authorities must act. They have become the primary context and the primary means by which the symbols that define contemporary religion are constructed, framed, and circulated. Religions face a media sphere that is determinative, but that also has its own interest in defining and framing other cultural and social institutions and practices. They are thus framed and interpreted by the media at the same time that they must use those media to pursue their goals and interests. And those framings and interpretations follow logics determined by media conventions and practices, not by the goals or aspirations of the religions themselves (Silk, 1995). Their symbols, and their institutional image, are both out of their control.

However, as I've also tried to show, the implications for religious authority here are more profound, nuanced, and complex than the rather obvious markers that religious authorities see in the ways their symbols are now recast and the challenges they feel having access to publics. The lesson of much current scholarship on media and religion is that what was once the authority invested in structures and institutions is now something constructed by practice. The media sphere is the sphere of symbols and symbolic action and thus articulates a profound and existential reordering of the prospects of religious authority, which at its base also is about the articulation of "the meanings of signs," as Paulo Farias put it.

What we see in this scholarly record is that today meanings result from interactions between traditions, received symbols, new articulations of those traditions and symbols, and the practical actions of individuals as they act as audiences and as producers and remediators of meanings and symbols and traditions. Above all, the media age has empowered audiences, or at least has invested audience practice with a claim of autonomy and empowerment, and that has radically changed the grounds on which religious and spiritual meanings and symbols are now articulated and circulated. These are practices of construction, not only of reception. Authorities can no longer assume a unitary and instrumental flow of meaning and influence from received doctrine through medium to waiting adherents. Those adherents are now active (or imagine themselves to be active) in the process, and that has changed things substantially.

Authority, then, becomes something that is also *constructed*. While it is no longer the case that received authority has a necessary precedence in the making of religious meanings, it can have some claim through its authenticity—or assumed authenticity—in the cultural marketplace. Therefore, authority is negotiated. Its success in pursuing its goals results from a complex negotiation between ascribed and received sources and practices and new, constructed sources and practices. Authority does rest to an extent in the individuals and groups who are active in imbricating these various sources, as well as in new networks of shared value that emerge from media (and particularly digital) practice. What Weber would think of as religious authority thus exercises its power in a context that it no longer controls, and it must share its power with other actors.

A final implication of all this might seem obvious. Religious authority is now, and will continue to be, fluid and elastic. The terms and boundaries of authority are no longer fixed by law, tradition, or the exceptional characteristics of charismatic leaders or systems. In the motile and fluid marketplace of religious symbols, selections, generativity, and circulation are determined not just by the aspirations and prerogatives of the received but by the affordances and products of practice. This will not always be coherent or logical. It often involves contradictions and incommensurables. Its very fluidity is both a direct challenge to the notion of authority and a new framing of the locus and meaning of authority. Across the longer term, it is hard to say what might evolve as new forms and loci of authority compete for ascendance in this emergent and fluid marketplace. Much of the fluidity of action has emerged with the advent of digital media. It is hard to predict what might result as things settle out.

What we do know is that things have changed a great deal, but they have also remained the same. Religions have always been mediated. They have always depended on systems of communication to confirm and convey belief. They have always depended both on symbols and on processes whereby signs were confirmed and conventionalized as symbols within specific contexts and systems of meaning. Moreover, there has always been change in the means of communication and thus in the media through which religions work. For this reason there have been many eras of "new media" and of "media change." There have always been varieties of "media ages" in relation to new means of communication. The Gutenberg revolution was large and epochal, certainly. So was the emergence of industrialized mass communication (the mass press) in the nineteenth century. The differences have been, perhaps, in the pace and scale of change and in the speed and ubiquity of the emergent media. The changes we have considered here are perhaps changes in scale as much as they are changes in kind.

The specific challenges to authority as the result of communication change that we've considered here are perhaps nothing new, either. The nineteenth century was a period of great fluidity and volatility in religion, largely as the result of new means of communication. Frontier and urban evangelism, both important contributors to the evolution of religion in the United States, were at their base communication revolutions that brought about some of the same kinds of forces we've considered here. They differentiated and relativized authority, establishing the sense that religions could be seen in terms of a competitive marketplace of supply.

It may be that what has changed, then, is the scale and pace and ubiquity more than the fundamental dynamics. But, as we have seen, there is perhaps one rather fundamental difference for the conditions of religious authority today. Modern life, and particularly its media, has increasingly empowered individuals and groups and audiences. Particularly in the emergent digital media, it is the autonomy and actions of audiences and their practices of reception, circulation, and remediation that is at the center. There is good reason to describe things as a combination of increasing speed, pace, ubiquity, and individual action and participation while accepting that the fundamental aspirations and motivations of authority—and of publics—have not changed. However, this does not mean that the pace and scale and ubiquity and participation are not leading to entirely new conditions for institutions, structures, and authority. In fact, it seems that they are, and that these new conditions are leading to large effects in those realms of structure and practice we used to think of as the enduring loci of religious authority.

NOTES

1. I make no claim regarding much of what we think of, traditionally, as religious functions in individual piety. There are clear implications there as well, but my focus here has been on the public face of and articulation of religion.

2. I do not mean to suggest here that this process is absolute or that the ideological project of power in religion has been abolished, only that the conditions have changed in fundamental ways.

REFERENCES

Albanese, C. (1992). *America, religions and religion*. Belmont, CA: Wadsworth.

Baltzell, E. D. (1964). *The Protestant establishment: Aristocracy and caste in America*. New York, NY: Random House.

Baudrillard, J. (1995). *Simulacra and simulation*. (S. F. Glaser, Trans.). Ann Arbor, MI: University of Michigan Press.

Benjamin, W. (1969). *Illuminations: Essays and reflections*. H. Arendt (Ed.). New York, NY: Schocken.

Berger, P. L. (1967). *The sacred canopy: Elements of a sociological theory of religion*. Garden City, NY: Anchor.

Boorstin, D. J. (1992). *The image: A guide to pseudo-events in America* (25th anniv. ed.). New York, NY: Vintage.

Campbell, H. (2012). Understanding the relationship between religion online and offline in a networked society. *Journal of the American Academy of Religion, 80*(1), 64–93.

Carey, J. W. (1989). *Communication as culture: Essays on media and society*. Boston, MA: Unwin Hyman.

Clark, L. S. (2007). Introduction. In L. S. Clark (Ed.), *Religion, media, and the marketplace* (pp. 1–36). New Brunswick, NJ: Rutgers University Press.

Couldry, N. (2003). *Media rituals: A critical approach*. London, UK: Routledge.

Durkheim, E. (2001). *The elementary forms of the religious life*. (C. Cosman, Trans.). New York, NY: Oxford University Press.

Echchaibi, N. (2011). From audio tapes to video blogs: The delocalisation of authority in Islam. *Nations and Nationalism, 17*(1), 25–44.

Einstein, M. (2008). *Brand of faith: Marketing religion in commercial age*. New York, NY: Routledge.

Eisenstein E. L. (1979). *The printing press as an agent of change: Communications and cultural transformations in early modern Europe*. Cambridge, UK: Cambridge University Press.

Ellul, J. (1964). *The technological society*. New York, NY: Knopf.

Farias, P. (2008). Remarks to the Porticus global seminar on media, religion, and culture. Sao Paulo, August 8.

Fore, W. F. (1990). *Mythmakers: Gospel, culture, and the media*. New York, NY: Friendship Press.

Geertz, C. (1966). Religion as a cultural system. In M. Banton (Ed.), *Anthropological approaches to the study of religion* (pp. 1–46). New York, NY: Praeger.

Gerbner, G. (1972). Communication and social environment. *Scientific American, 227*(3), 153–160.

Giddens, A. (1991). *Modernity and self-identity: Self and society in the late modern age*. Stanford, CA: Stanford University Press.

Gill, Jill K. (2012, July 19). Future of liberal religion: A counterculture blooms? *Religion Dispatches*. Retrieved

from http://religiondispatches
.org/future-of-liberal-religion-a
-counterculture-blooms/.

Habermas, J. (1976). *Legitimation
crisis*. London, UK: Heinemann
Educational.

Habermas, J. (1989). *The structural transformation of the public sphere: An
inquiry into a category of bourgeois
society*. (T. Burger & F. Lawrence,
Trans.). Cambridge, MA: MIT Press.

Hatch, N. O. (1989). *The democratization of
American Christianity*. New Haven,
CT: Yale University Press

Helland, C. (2012). *Internet communion
and virtual faith: The new face of religion in the wired West*. New York,
NY: Oxford University Press.

Hendershot, H. (2004). *Shaking the world
for Jesus: Media and conservative
evangelical culture*. Chicago, IL: University of Chicago Press.

Hepp, A. (2012). *Cultures of mediatization*.
Cambridge, UK: Polity.

Herbert, D. (2003). *Religion and civil
society: Rethinking public religion in
the contemporary world*. Burlington,
VT: Ashgate.

Hjarvard, S. M. (2008). The mediatization
of religion: A theory of the media as
agents of religious change. *Northern
Lights, 6*, 9–26.

Hoover, S. M. (1998). *Religion in the news:
Faith and journalism in American
public discourse*. London, UK: Sage.

Hoover, S. M. (2006). *Religion in the media age*. London, UK: Routledge.

Hoover, S. M., Clark, L. S., & Alters, D. F.
(2003). *Media, home, and family*.
New York, NY: Routledge.

Hoover, S. M., & Echchaibi, N. (2012).
The "third space" of digital religion.
Discussion paper. Center for Media,
Religion, and Culture.

Hoover, S. M., & Emerich, M. (2011). *Media, spiritualities and social change*.
London, UK: Continuum.

Hoover, S. M., & Kim, S. S. (2012).
Digital media and the Protestant

establishment: Insights from "The
New Media Project." Discussion
paper. Center for Media, Religion,
and Culture.

Horsfield, P. (2015). *From Jesus to the
Internet: A history of Christi-
anity and media*. Oxford, UK:
Wiley-Blackwell.

Hutchings, T. (2013). *Creating church
online: Ritual, community, and new
media*. London, UK: Routledge.

Krotz, F. (2009). Mediatization: A concept
with which to grasp media and
societal change. In K. Lundby (Ed.),
*Mediatization: Concept, changes,
consequences* (pp. 21–40). New
York, NY: Peter Lang.

Lundby, K. (2009). Introduction: "Mediatization" as key. In K. Lundby (Ed.),
*Mediatization: Concept, changes,
consequences* (pp. 1–20). London,
UK: Peter Lang.

Lynch, G. (2012). *The sacred in the modern
world: A cultural sociological
approach*. New York, NY: Oxford
University Press.

Malinowski, B. (1978). *Argonauts of the
Western Pacific: An account of native
enterprise and adventure in the
archipelagoes of Melanesian New
Guinea*. London, UK: Routledge.

McLuhan, M. (1964). *Understanding
media: The extensions of man*. New
York, NY: McGraw-Hill.

McLuhan, M., & Powers, B. R. (1989).
*The global village: Transformations
in world life and media in the 21st
century*. New York, NY: Oxford
University Press.

Meyer, B. (2011). Mediation and imme-
diacy: Sensational forms, semiotic
ideologies, and the question of the
medium. *Social Anthropology, 19*(1),
23–39.

Meyer, B., & Moors, A. (2006). *Religion, media, and the public sphere*.
Bloomington, IN: Indiana University Press.

Mohler, A. (2006, January 22). Raising teens in the media culture, part 3. *Albert Mohler.* Retrieved from http://www.albertmohler .com/2006/01/22/raising-teens-in-the-media-culture-part-3/.

Moore, R. L. (1994). *Selling God: American religion in the marketplace of culture.* New York, NY: Oxford University Press.

Morgan, D. (2007). *The lure of images: A history of religion and visual media in America.* London, UK: Routledge.

Myers, K. (1989). *All God's children and blue suede shoes: Christians and popular culture.* Westchester, IL: Crossway.

Ong, W. J. (1982). *Orality and literacy: The technologizing of the word.* New York, NY: Routledge.

Piacenza, J. (2012). Third spaces: The Twitter feed of His Holiness the Dalai Lama. Discussion paper. Center for Media, Religion, and Culture.

Postman, N. (2006). *Amusing ourselves to death: Public discourse in the age of show business* (20th anniv. ed.). New York, NY: Penguin.

Promey, S. (1996). Interchangeable art: Warner Sallman and the critics of mass culture. In D. Morgan (Ed.), *Icons of American Protestantism: The art of Warner Sallman* (pp. 148–180). New Haven, CT: Yale University Press.

Roof, W. C. (1998). Spiritual marketplace: Baby boomers and the remaking of American religion. Princeton, NJ: Princeton University Press.

Schultze, Q. J. (2003). *Christianity and the mass media in America: Toward a democratic accommodation.* East Lansing, MI: Michigan State University Press.

Silk, M. (1995). *Unsecular media: Making news of religion in America.* Urbana, IL: University of Illinois Press.

Smythe, D. W. (2001). On the audience commodity and its work. In M. G. Durham & D. M. Kellner (Eds.), *Media and cultural studies: Keyworks* (pp. 230–256). Malden, MA: Blackwell.

Wagner, R. (2012). *Godwired: Religion, ritual and virtual reality.* London, UK: Routledge.

Warren, M. (1997). *Seeing through the media: A religious view of communications and cultural analysis.* Harrisburg, PA: Trinity Press International.

Weber, M. (1968). *Economy and society: An outline of interpretive sociology* (Vol. 1). New York, NY: Bedminster Press.

Whitehead, D. (2012). Faith, doubt, and the search for truth in the mommy blogosphere. Discussion paper. Center for Media, Religion, and Culture.

CHAPTER 2

The Media and Religious Authority from Ancient to Modern

Peter Horsfield

On a weekend afternoon in 2007, the dean of St. Patrick's Cathedral in Melbourne became engaged in an altercation with a small group of young skateboarders who were riding their boards around the empty grounds of the cathedral. As his efforts to remove them developed into a game of chase, he became angry and racially abusive. Unbeknown to him, his tirade was secretly videoed by one of the skateboarders on his mobile phone and several months later posted on YouTube, where it was picked up by the news media and became a headline story nationally and internationally. The dean was eventually forced to resign his position. This seemingly private incident on a weekend afternoon, dramatically made public, exemplifies how new media uses are changing the terms and conditions under which religious authority is ascribed, recognized, and socially supported.

Authority in religion is an important factor in the development and character of religious activities, at an individual level. It is also a crucial element in how religion is organized publicly and integrated into wider social and political structures. For that reason, most political states for centuries have had protocols and procedures for how religious authorities may function in relation to wider political authorities and other social institutions. Chaves argues that the modernist movement of secularization as a political and social strategy needs to be understood as being directed toward religious authority rather than religion in general. "Secularization," he writes, "is best understood not as the decline of religion, but as the declining scope of religious authority" (Chaves, 1994, p. 749).

With the reemergence of religion as a significant political and cultural force over the past few decades, and changes in the relative balance between individual autonomy and institutional authority in religion, the "secular" model for the modern political management of religion is being reworked. The questions of what constitutes religious authority and how it is exercised are ripe for reexamination.

As the social marketplace accommodates this growth in religious interest globally, the question of religious authority has become a much broader issue than simply designated leadership positions within recognized religious institutions. In times of significant social change, uncertainty, or crisis, such as we are facing today, people look for meaning and answers not just from those in formal positions of authority. They respond to anyone who is providing useful meaning and resources in relevant and dynamic ways at sites and through media sources that people access in the course of their daily living.

This is particularly the case in the present globalized situation, as the notion of a nation as a singular unified public sphere changes toward that of a proliferation of publics with specific identities and interests that need to be constantly reconstituted. So also, the notion of religion as a relatively stable network of defined institutions within a bounded society is changing toward that of a religious marketplace comprising not only institutional authorities, but also candidates outside institutional structures whose claim for audience attention and loyalty is based on different appeals and credentials. That religious marketplace now operates largely through the public media.

This new religious marketplace presents political leaders and social policy makers with the need to negotiate a new concept of religious authority that is more individually constructed, defined significantly by media audiences rather than institutions, more consumerist in its approach, and more global in the figures and resources on which it draws. Crucial to the successful integration of religious factions within civil society, therefore, is understanding the relationship of religion and media (Meyer, 2006), and crucial to understanding the relationship of religion and media is understanding the relationship of media and religious authority.

While the place of media in the construction of social realities is being explored across a range of religious phenomena, the connection between media and changes in religious authority has been relatively under-examined. Previously, religious authority has been viewed as a relatively autonomous institutional practice. Religious authorities have been quick to argue that while they may use media, their determinations on religious ideas, doctrines, and practices are made on the basis of revelation and tradition, not utilitarian or instrumental grounds. That perspective is now largely discredited. How religious authorities are constructed, recognized, and exercised is intimately bound up with media factors: the media cultures within which and by which religious authority is constructed, how authority is communicated relative to the audiences it is seeking to influence, and the effectiveness with which religious figures are able to associate and position themselves within the mediated marketplace of political, social, economic, and ideological exchange.

This chapter will explore different aspects of that interrelatedness.

WHAT IS AUTHORITY?

The primary reference point for thinking about authority in general is the work of the sociologist Max Weber. Weber (1968) defines authority as legitimized dominance, a perspective that has two dimensions. One is the element of dominance. Authority carries with it an implication of power: the ability to force, coerce, or compel people to act in a particular way. Weber describes this dominance as "the probability that certain specific commands (or all commands) will be obeyed by given groups of persons" (p. 212).

The second element in Weber's definition is that of legitimization. Authority involves more than just the ability to coerce or compel. Authority involves also an element of compliance or acceptance of the coercion by those being coerced on the basis that they attribute a certain measure of legitimacy to what is being done. The exercise of authority, in distinction from the simple use of force, is characterized by a level of voluntary compliance with the power being exercised on the grounds that participants have an interest in obeying (p. 212). Authority is a situation in which people cede their full autonomy and accept the direction of another, on the grounds that what is being required is accepted as a legitimate expectation, given the circumstances.

Chapman illustrates this difference through an examination of the two Latin terms: *potentas* and *auctoritas*. *Potentas* was associated originally with the role of the magistrate and the magistrate's ability to enforce obedience or punishment through coercion—our English sense of *power*. The *auctor*, on the other hand, from which comes the term *auctoritas* or authority, was a figure who played the important role of guarantor in the process of inheritance. Auctors' influence arose not from their power to compel, but from the benefit to be gained from the role they were performing and the weight of their opinions reinforced by their social position, their learning, or the strength of their personality (Chapman, 2005). Letty Russell (1987) characterizes authority, therefore, as legitimated power: "It accomplishes its ends by evoking the assent of the respondent" (p. 21).

For Arendt, the fact that authority is dependent on a perceived benefit and the trustworthiness of the person guaranteeing it makes authority a relationship that links power to the past. The power an authority exercises is a power ascribed based on an existing relationship or perceived value: "The authority of the living was always derivative, depending upon . . . the authority of the founders, who no longer were among the living. Authority, in contradistinction to power (*potentas*), had its roots in the past" (Arendt, 1977, p. 122). While power may be exercised from within or from outside a community, authority is grounded in a community with a recognized history and identity.

This dimension of legitimization of a use of power is so decisive for Weber that he identifies his three "pure" types of authority, not on the basis of the type of force used, but on the basis of how the force and its compliance is justified or legitimized.

Legal grounds refer to legitimization of certain uses of power on the rational grounds of "a belief in the legality of enacted rules and the right of those elevated to authority under such rules to issue commands" (Weber, 1968, p. 215). Legal authority is an impersonal order or system of rules and laws that has been "established by agreement or by imposition, on grounds of expediency or value-rationality or both, with a claim to obedience at least on the part of the members of the organization" (p. 217). Any legal authority, or any person acting as a legal authority, does so only to the extent that they are operating within the system that has been agreed to by the community and to which they themselves are also accountable.

Traditional grounds refer to legitimization of the use of power on the grounds of "an established belief in the sanctity of immemorial traditions and the legitimacy of those exercising authority under them" (Weber, 1968, p. 215) Traditional authority is domination or the use of power by a person or group of people who have been placed in a position "according to traditional rules" and who are obeyed because of their traditional status, with the discretion to act within "that sphere that tradition leaves open to

[them]" (p. 226). Any person acting in a role of traditional authority does so within certain limits, those understood and recognized by subjects as being defined by the tradition and apply to the person occupying the position.

Charismatic grounds refer to legitimization of the use of power on the grounds that an individual is recognized or revered as being extraordinary and "endowed with supernatural, superhuman, or at least specifically exceptional powers or qualities" (Weber, 1968, p. 241). In contrast to legal and traditional authority, charismatic authority has no external validation apart from the credence given to it by those who recognize it as authentic and act accordingly. For that reason, Weber saw charismatic authority as the more dramatic but also the more transient of the three types. Charismatic authority was "the great revolutionary force," capable of stimulating action to produce "a radical alteration of the central attitudes and directions of action with a completely new orientation of all attitudes towards the different problems of the 'world'" (p. 245). However, lacking external validation, it lasts only as long as it is effective for its followers. After its initial impulse, or as the circumstances that gave rise to it change, it commonly disappears or becomes routinized into either a legal or traditional authority structure: "If proof and success elude the leader for long, if he appears deserted by his god or his magical or heroic powers, above all, if his leadership fails to benefit his followers, it is likely that his charismatic authority will disappear" (p. 242).

Though widely used in social and political theory, Weber's typology has also been subject to a good deal of debate, critique, and modification. One of those points of debate has been whether there are grounds of legitimization that Weber has not identified, a potential deficiency readily acknowledged by Weber himself. A number of people advocate for value-rationality as a separate form of legitimization (e.g., Satow, 1975; Willer, 1967). Value-rationality authority is domination using power legitimated by "faith in the absolute value of a rationalized set of norms." As Satow (1975) proposes, within this form of authority, those exercising power are "legitimized by their relationship to the goals of the ideology" (p. 527), the sort of authority that operates within a professional organization or a Protestant church, for example.

Others question whether Weber has identified and named the legitimizations correctly. Kertcher and Margalit in their work on political authority, for example, replace Weber's charismatic authority with what they call performance-based legitimacy. What is distinctive about charismatic authority, they argue, is not the quality of the person per se, as suggested by Weber, but the fact that the qualities of the charismatic leader enable the person to achieve particular goals and meet particular needs of subjects. The legitimization therefore arises not from the personal qualities themselves, but from what those qualities will enable the person to achieve in furthering the interests of the group. Kertcher and Margalit also replace the terminology of Weber's concept of traditional authority with what they call constructed legitimacy, arguing that what is central to traditional authority is not just the tradition itself, but the perceived importance and moral correctness of the tradition. Traditional authorities acquire their authority through the legitimization of moral rightness (Kertcher & Margalit, 2005, p. 10).

Campbell (2007), in her work on religious authority and the Internet, identifies a different set of loci or layers of authority within religious communities that can be understood as falling within the realm of traditional authority: religious hierarchy (roles or perceptions of recognized religious or community leaders), religious structures (community structures, patterns or practice, or official organization), religious ideology (commonly held beliefs, ideas of faith, or shared identity), and religious texts (recognized teachings or official book).

Another criticism of Weber's typology is that it is too static, reflecting an outmoded view of culture as relatively stable and clearly segmented, overlooking differences and diversity in favor of simple categories and generalized commonalities. Poststructuralist perspectives see culture as a much more complex, dynamic, and contested domain than Weber recognizes. In such a view, how authority is recognized, when and why authority is justified and accepted, or not justified and resisted, is more multilayered, subtle, and nuanced than a three-type typology, or even a eight-type typology, can handle. Nor does a simple three-type typology allow for the fact that any one type may be capable of infinite individual variations, some of which may even be contradictory in different contexts. To think about the interaction of media and religious authority, an analysis of authority is required that better reflects that complexity and dynamism.

AUTHORITY AS FLUID, CONTESTED, AND CONTEXTUAL

If one approaches culture as a more dynamic entity than what Weber presumes, it becomes apparent that in any one situation there are likely to be not just several discrete forms of religious authority at work. One can detect multiple loci, layers, or claims to religious authority actively contesting with one another, building their claim for legitimization not only on religious grounds but on nonreligious grounds as well. All of these combine into a complex contest of religious authorities that need to be seen as a whole—it is impossible to separate out any distinctively religious motive or quality.

As I will explore in more detail below, in the early formative centuries of Christianity, demonstrating that one was continuing the tradition of the apostles was an important factor in a person or group establishing the legitimacy of their actions, beliefs, doctrines, or position. However, there was a wide variety of opinions about what constituted the apostolic tradition, and these different opinions engaged in an extended and at times violent contest to have their opinion legitimized. Different uses of media, control of media, and alignment with different media cultures played an important part in this. Most of the major early conflicts in Christianity arose out of or involved media contests or differences in cultures of mediation, which were themselves significantly reworked in later periods of significant media change.

Seen in this light, Weber's concept of traditional authority needs to be significantly rethought. Rather than representing "established belief in the sanctity of immemorial traditions," traditional authority may need to be seen as something that is being continually constructed in the present to support the position of those seeking to acquire or hold power. That is, rather than simply stepping into the shoes of the tradition, it is necessary for a person or group claiming the mantle of traditional authority to make the tradition in a way that supports their cause and converts their power into authority. The media are an important element in this.

Rather than just three dominant forms of authority, therefore, in any situation there are likely to be a multitude of contenders for authority, vying for legitimization on a variety of grounds. All of these can be seen as operative throughout the history of most religions.

Radiated social position and success (social capital). A person or group is often assigned authority in religious matters on the grounds of their status or success in a related field, such as a senior management position within a corporation, being a successful businessperson or politician, ranking on social scales such as the rich list, technorati (in the blogosphere), or their recognition as a sports, media, or entertainment celebrity. Social capital developed in one area can transfer to the religious domain, particularly when the person's capital is in an area considered deficient in the religion.

Recognized general or specific knowledge. Authority in religious matters can often be ascribed to a person having general or specialist knowledge in another area, unrelated to religion, particularly if the area of their knowledge is important for the life or goals of the religious group.

Recognized experience or wisdom. Religious authority can be ascribed to a person on the basis that he or she is recognized as having a wide breadth of knowledge or experience across a range of fields and that wisdom can be applied to religious matters as well.

This process of "cultural transfer," implicit in each of these areas, is one of the key ways a particular religious tradition becomes enculturated or hybridized (Canclini, 1995). Along with these, there are other likely contenders for commanding authority at any time.

Charisma. Charisma is a fluid quality and may reflect talent in a particular area only, or a more generalized ability that crosses a wide field. It is also more temporary. Part of the contest of authority that takes place may include the behavior of a person who is a player in the field based on charismatic authority ascribed to him or her in the past, but who is struggling to retain that authority as they, the group, or the situation has changed.

Ideological authority. In some religious groups, particular authority is ascribed to ideologies that are seen as representing the distinctive beliefs of the group—theological statements such as "The self-revelation of God in Jesus Christ through the Spirit," or speaking in tongues, or acts of self-sacrifice. Even though such theological statements may have no overt or clear practical applications, authority can flow to those people who link their behaviors or statements with accepted beliefs of the group through a semantic association.

Sacred texts. Authority in religion is commonly ascribed to the artifact of a religion's scriptures and its contents—the Bible, Koran, Torah, Bhagavad Gita, for example. Even though there may be substantial disagreement on what the actual contents say or mean, supporting one's actions or claims by quoting passages from the sacred text can bestow an authority beyond that of the individual alone. In a similar way, establishing a ritual or visual connection between the artifact of the text and an individual can also ascribe authority to the individual.

Religious teaching authority. Bodies or individuals such as the magisterium, theologians or theological faculties, rabbis, rabbinic councils, and so on, can acquire authority not just because of their individual competence, but also because of their association with or endorsement by the revered position. In most religions, the collective of religious leaders is often ascribed greater authority and dependability than the sum of the individuals involved, so that the individual's representative authority is enhanced through his or her identification with the collective, as seen in claims made for Roman Catholic authority: "The totality of the bishops is infallible when they, either assembled in general council or scattered over the earth, propose a teaching of faith or morals as one to be held by all the faithful" (Pivarunas, 1996).

The appointed leader or bureaucratic office. This is authority ascribed on the basis that one has been appointed to a position or office within a group or institution that is necessary for the functioning of the institution. This supra-personal authority is constructed and reinforced by various devices, such as giving precedence, interaction rituals such as standing, bowing, or kissing a ring, and communication protocols such as addressing the person by the name of the office rather than their personal name (e.g., Moderator, Your Grace, Rabbi).

Rituals. In a number of religions, key rituals have developed significant authority, frequently protected by superstitions that give them an abstract existence and power separate from those who perform them. Being associated with their conduct or interpretations can ascribe authority above that of the individual.

Martyrs and saints. In many religions, past figures who have lived exemplary lives or died exemplary deaths are preserved in memory through stories, relics, festivals, images, and shrines and hover in the background as authority figures whose perspectives must be taken into account.

Proverbial wisdom. Particularly in strongly oral communities, past experience preserved in adages and proverbs holds an authority that contends with other influences in group thinking and decision making. Tex Sample (1994) describes a debate in a rural community in the United States in which argument proceeded by disagreeing participants citing different adages or proverbs to support their positions, with a view to presenting the most authoritative proverb for the situation.

Visual memory. Individual or group memory of things seen or meanings visualized in some form can become an important force that contends for people's loyalty. Augustine recounts an incident in which a largely illiterate congregation almost removed their bishop for using Jerome's new Latin translation, in which the bush under which Job slept was an ivy rather than a gourd vine, an image that contradicted paintings with which they were familiar. Writing to Jerome, Augustine comments, "The man was compelled to correct your version in that passage as if it had been falsely translated, as he desired not to be left without a congregation—a calamity which he narrowly escaped" (Epis 71.3). In his work, Morgan (1998, 2005) illustrates similarly how visual images of Jesus, for example, may be more authoritative in people's religious understanding than biblical or other written texts.

In any specific religious situation, you are likely to find a range of these different sources of authority coming into play and actively or passively contending with one another for influence and people's loyalty. Given that dynamic situation, religious authority has to be seen as being continually negotiated, established, and reestablished.

The process of authority, therefore, is neither simple nor one-directional. Part of the complexity of religious authority is that people tend to negotiate their own "packages" of recognition and compliance, placing greater value or legitimacy on a particular authority or combination than others. While people may comply with a particular authority, they may do so in a negotiated way—complying in some ways but not in others. Part of that process of negotiation may also involve a person in a position of authority accommodating him- or herself to people's demands in order to retain that authority[1] While authority may be recognized and obeyed, it may not be in terms that the authority would like or believes is appropriate. This complexity means that authority needs to be understood as territorial or quite specifically contextual in scope, applying to particular groups of people within particular regions. In thinking about the character of religious authority, therefore, specific questions need to be asked as to what context, time, or space religious authority is being applied.

LEGITIMIZATION AND COMPLIANCE

As noted above, the strength of religious authority lies not just in the power exercised, but also in the voluntary compliance with that power by those who are subject to it. While one can achieve political order through imposed power, political order based on the power of coercion alone will be unstable and will be subject to (more) frequent acts of resistance and subversion unless it can be legitimized legally or ideologically (Kertcher & Margalit, 2005, p. 8). Chapman (2005) illustrates this in relation to the authority of the legal system: "This sense of authority is reflected in the 'authorities' of the English legal tradition: judges, whose decisions carry legal and coercive power, are nevertheless wise to base their opinion on the 'authorities' of the legal tradition, even though there is no absolute requirement to do so. This might be referred to as 'enabling' authority rather than coercive power. To be effective, coercive power should be based on accepted authority" (p. 105)

Similarly, a religious person or body may take action based on an assumption that they have the authority to do so, but unless what they claim is recognized and accepted as legitimate by those they are seeking to command, there is no authority—only attempted power. This process replicates the media perspective of reception theory, which specifies that textual meaning is not created in its production or in the preferred meaning of the producer, but in an interaction between the text, the context, and the audience. The audience is a crucial player and retains significant power in determining whether any action, including domineering power and coercion, is authoritative.

The audience, therefore, has significant power in determining what is authoritative or not—power can be taken, but authority needs to be given. This perspective turns attention then to the question of the dynamics or methods by which those in power, or who are seeking to be in power, work to secure the compliance of the dominated, as a means of enhancing their power. Within this framework, the question of "In what ways do media become an element or the means by which compliance is secured?" becomes pertinent. In thinking about that question, I want to explore two major grounds on which the exercise of power within religion is transformed into religious authority: legitimization through performance and legitimization through symbolic construction.

LEGITIMIZATION THROUGH PERFORMANCE

Legitimization through performance addresses the fact that the right to exert power is given to people and groups who can demonstrate or have demonstrated that they are able to achieve goals, to make things happen, or to create the conditions that make life safe, enjoyable, and meaningful for those being governed. There are some grounds for arguing that attributing authority to someone on the grounds of performance has become a more important factor in the modern age than it was previously. Arguably, performance has always been a factor, but the time frame and tolerance threshold for judging mis-performance have both shortened, and changes in the political framework have made it easier for the dominated to shift their allegiance on the basis of those perceptions. The case that Kertcher and Margalit (2005) make in relation to political authority may equally apply to religious authority: "Since the French Revolution, the modern nation-state emphasizes performance. Under this political order, rulers bargain with their citizens for collective citizen's rights guaranteed by the state in exchange for duties. In return for regularly paying taxes and participation in wars, the provisions of security, education, and welfare are assured" (p. 12).

There are a number of reasons for this: the rise in Western affluence, the multiplication of goods and services available to individuals, and the increase in social and cultural options mediated through the logic of consumerism and the choice of the marketplace. These combined have shifted the balance of legitimization away from Weber's traditional and legal grounds more toward the grounds of performance. Rather than attribute authority to the traditional on the grounds of the sanctity of immemorial traditions, as may have been the case in the past, today we are more inclined to attribute authority to the traditional only to the extent that we perceive doing so will bring us benefits. We respect and support those in positions of traditional authority and accept the power they exercise on our behalf or even over us, so long as they continue to demonstrate that they are able to produce the conditions that keep life safe, enjoyable, and meaningful for us.

To exist within this cultural context, religion is required to demonstrate its competence against the same criterion of performance, and comparably against its competitors. There are a number of areas where religion has traditionally been competitive: in the practical area, as a community of support, a social meeting place, a provider of health care, education, and welfare; in the moral area, as a generator of moral vision and ethical frameworks, an impetus for moral development, a philosophical support for sacrifice and generosity; in the traditional area, as a preserver of the resources of the past, a site for nostalgia, an orienting perspective on time, a site for cultural participation and aesthetics; in the intellectual area, as a provider of information and perspectives by which people are able to make sense of events and build meaning; and in the spiritual area, as a resource for the pursuit and inducement of harmony, peace of mind, hope, reconciliation, oneness, and integration.

In a global media environment where there are a number of options, the extent to which a religion continues to be seen as authoritative by individuals or communities depends on its capacity to continue to produce benefits in these areas. That is, people will continue to cede practical, intellectual, symbolic, or legal power to religion, providing religion continues to produce benefits for them in the practical, intellectual, symbolic, or legal areas of life.

Underperforming religious authority may be able to be sustained in relatively closed social situations or where competitors can be either silenced or suppressed so that people have few alternatives. These situations still exist in some nations today, and limiting alternatives or eliminating competitors have been strategies utilized extensively by religions in the past to protect their power.

In the West in particular, however, almost all of these performance functions are now competitive, and services once provided exclusively by religion are now available from a variety of alternative sources, including NGOs, the nation-state, social action groups, commercial businesses, or other religions. This growth in competition has been proposed as one of the reasons for the progress of secularization and the decline in religion through the modern period. Chaves (1994) identifies the process of secularization as one of declining religious authority, which he links to the growth of institutional differentiation—that is, alternative providers of performance-based benefits: "This broad shift in perspective appropriately highlights the political, conflictual, and contingent nature of relations among societal institutions in general and between religion and other spheres in particular. Here, society is understood as 'an interinstitutional system' rather than as a moral community. In such an interinstitutional system religion is understood primarily as another mundane institutional sphere or organizational sector; it can no longer claim any necessary functional primacy" (p. 751).

It is apparent that to evaluate media's influence in this by considering just one individual medium or individual media situations is inadequate. The multiplication of goods and services and the increase in social and cultural options that has shifted the center of power from institutions to consumers within the marketplace are inconceivable apart from a whole environment of media-based structure and practice. This media-cultural environment includes the creation of desire through advertising; the spread of awareness of alternatives through the global advertising, marketing, news, social commentary, and person-to-person media network; the construction of difference and imagined product diversity through marketing; the attempted stabilization of the market through branding; and the globally mediated mechanisms of product research, development, production, search, purchase, delivery, and cultivated consumption that are the nuts and bolts of the capitalist system.

The fragmentation of the present global marketplace means that authority is more likely to be ascribed in more circumscribed areas, on a more conditional basis, and for shorter periods of time. Authority is also more likely to be ascribed as part of a wider, eclectic package of authorities managed by the individual rather than the individual relegating that power to a single external body. In his study of new media in the Muslim world, Anderson (2003) notes how the steady adaptation of new media within and across Islamic communities is challenging existing forms of Islamic authority, bypassing traditional practices once considered authoritative, and establishing new networks in which authority is more pragmatic, participative, eclectic, and transient:

Islam is represented on-line in a mélange of wire-service news copy, transcribed sermons, scanned texts of the Qur'an and hadith collections, advice and self-help information ranging from where to find halal butchers and mosques to matrimonial and cheap travel to prayer-times and Islamic educational materials. . . . *This is a social-communicative sphere more comparable to the "creoles" that Benedict Anderson* . . . identified with the civic publics that arose, without prior design, with the earlier spread of print capitalism and particularly with early modern newspapers. That is, the Internet and its surroundings that enthusiasts call "cyberspace" or envision as a new "information age" do not facilitate the spokesperson-activists of established institutions, but draw instead on a broader range of new interpreters or newly visible interpreters of Islam. (p. 48)

While consumer-based choice has been criticized for its excesses, in reality there is no other way for individuals to function within a globally mediated marketplace of excessive information and unlimited options except by making their own judgments about value and benefit and charting their own course accordingly. In order to be considered as an option in that choice-making process, any religion, religious individual, or religious institution must establish their authority through a number of actions: organizing to be present in the people's marketplace; distinguishing themselves from other competitors in order to be noticed; promising practical, moral, traditional, intellectual, aesthetic, or spiritual benefits in line with the needs or aspirations of those in the marketplace; and retaining loyalty by performing, or creating the appearance of performing, in line with those promised benefits.

LEGITIMIZATION THROUGH SYMBOLIC CONSTRUCTION

The second way the use of religious power may be legitimized and effective in generating compliance is through symbolic construction—that is, effectively discerning values that the subjects consider important and constructing the position of authority or use of power as representing or furthering those values.

Even if those in positions of authority are largely ineffectual in their performance or in producing benefits, their authority may be maintained if they are able to align their position and use of power with key values of the subjects. Following this line of argument, Kertcher and Margalit (2005) argue that Weber's concept of traditional authority being justified on the grounds of tradition is slightly off target. They propose that traditional authority is legitimized on the grounds that people see it as morally right.

There are a variety of methods by which people exercising power may symbolically construct their use of power as morally right or authoritative in order to enlist people's loyalty and compliance. One is through the use of unifying myths and vision. Authority is enhanced when those exercising power are able to position themselves and associate their use of power within the symbols and narratives that frame people's world, thereby associating what is being done positively with the group's collective past, history, or tradition. Such an association may be overtly or covertly constructed, specifically integrating themselves into events or values from the collective past, or covertly associating themselves through visual imagery or performed actions that evoke memories of past narratives. Another is to construct themselves as acting in a representative capacity on behalf of God, the tradition, or the collective, thereby camouflaging the personal nature of their use of power behind a screen of representativeness. Another is through the creation of exclusive association with other people or objects of power and authority to enhance the impression of wider recognition and influence, or ascribed social capital. Staged and displayed photographs of religious leaders with national and international politicians, businesspeople, pop culture idols, and celebrities are part of this enhancement of authority through association with other powerful figures (a practice which has been part of the history of most religions). The restricted access or use of objects seen as powerful within the religion is also part of this symbolic construction of authority.

Authority is constructed and sustained symbolically in the construction of the universe, the fundamental sense of moral rightness, within which one's authority is justified, within which actions take place, and by which actions are conjured as normal or natural, unnatural or inappropriate. Bourdieu (1977) has been instrumental in identifying the ways in which the fundamental medium of language and language games structure relationships in particular ways to benefit those in power and disadvantage their competitors by setting the conditions under which a speaker may "command a listener," and the conditions under which a speaker may not only be understood but also "believed, obeyed, respected, distinguished"—fundamental components of authority. Among the elements of such discourses, he identifies "laws which determine who (*de facto* and *de jure*) may speak, to whom, and how. . . . Among the most radical, surest, and best hidden censorships are those which exclude certain individuals from communication (e.g., by not inviting them to places where people speak with authority, or by putting them in places without speech)" (pp. 649–650).

The constructions put in place by such discursive practices are not durable, but need to be constantly renewed through hegemonic practices, described by McQuail (1994) as "a loosely interrelated set of ruling ideas permeating a society, but in such a way as to make the established order of power and values appear natural, taken-for-granted, and common-sensical. A ruling ideology is not imposed but appears to exist by virtue of an unquestioned consensus. Hegemony tends to define what is unacceptable to the status quo as dissident and deviant" (p. 99).

The construction of religious authority, therefore, is an ongoing process, operating constantly not only to meet its obligations or deliver on its promises, but also to continually construct the world that legitimizes its power: "A whole aspect of the language of authority has no other function than to underline this authority and to dispose the audience to accord the belief that is required. . . . *The language of authority owes a large proportion of its properties to the fact that it has to contribute to its own credibility—e.g.,* the stylistic elaborations of literary writers, the references and apparatus of scholars, the statistics of sociologists, etc." (Bourdieu, 1977, p. 649). One could add to Bourdieu's list the convoluted abstractions of theological discourse and the mumbo jumbo of ritual language that have frequently legitimized religious authority.

MEDIA CHANGE AND CHANGES IN RELIGIOUS AUTHORITY

One of the valuable metaphors by which to understand the relationship between media and religious authority is to see all media as the web on which religion at any particular time takes shape. Thinking of media as the web of religious culture[2] brings into our thinking about religion the fundamental and essential role that communication plays in all social and cultural activity. Though they have different names, communication and culture are symbiotic and inseparable. Communication is a social and cultural activity; culture is basically a conglomeration of activities that communicate. You cannot have a cultural event of any kind, including a religious event, that doesn't require communication or that isn't built on a communication practice. In the same way, you cannot communicate without participating in practices that are made available within the culture, that carry with them cultural expectations, values, prejudices, and patterns.

While Weber saw this web of culture as relatively stable—"a relatively closed context of meaning-making for a relatively integrated social group" (Lewis, 2005, p. 9)—more recent cultural thinking sees culture and its communication as much more diverse, fluid, and dynamic, carrying within itself not only forces that move it toward stability but also forces that challenge that stability and move it toward destabilization and change. Institutions over time seek to manage these differences and change by acting in ways to stabilize social order, structures, language, symbolization, and meaning. Such efforts to create stability and a common opinion, however, provoke parallel processes of decentering imagination and resistance that challenge that stability.

The communication or media web of culture, therefore, is dynamic, with complex pathways and networks continually being formed and re-formed. Dominant patterns of communication practice exist beside and are continually being challenged and subverted by alternative pathways, interconnections, relations, and patterns. As recent ethnographic studies of media reception and use are showing, the variety of media webs within any culture is infinite, as individuals put together their own packages of media practice. The interaction of these differences also contributes to the dynamism of culture.

Seeing the web of communication as both fundamental and dynamic allows us to affirm the distinctive place of media and media change in the construction and change of cultures, without reverting to a technological determinism that says that changes in media have a direct and inescapable effect on cultures in a unilateral and unavoidable way. Certainly, new media can cause significant changes in people's ways of communicating, with consequent changes in social patterns, structures, and values. At times these changes can be rapid and dramatic, at others a less dramatic but no less influential ripple effect spreading through the whole pattern of communication practices.

Elizabeth Eisenstein advocates this intermediate view in her major study of the influence of printing in early modern Europe. She questions the view that gives equal value to a range of social factors considered to contribute to the extensive social changes that occurred at that time. While acknowledging that other variables were also involved, she argues that printing as a single medium change warrants special attention because its effect was a multiplying one, acting not just as an additional new way of communicating, but also by altering fundamental methods of data collection, storage and retrieval systems, and communication networks that set the conditions and provided the means by which other changes could take place (Eisenstein, 1979, pp. xv–xvi).

The relationship of religion as one social phenomenon to the wider web of communication of the society is an interactive one and varies from place to place and period to period. New media do not normally impose themselves or intrude without resistance from other major social institutions, such as religion. New media commonly arise from, or are helped in their introduction into a society by, a range of supporting factors or potentialities already present within the society. In the case of Christianity and media, for instance, at times media practices that have been rooted in or developed largely within Christian institutions or by Christian individuals have been taken up by the wider society. At other times and in other places, Christian institutions or individuals have adopted new media or new communication practices available or being used in the wider society and adapted them to their purposes.

Significant changes in media can instigate religious change in a variety of ways. They can add options to established ways of communicating, generating new ways of doing things without totally ousting old practices. New media may create a dramatic shakeout or shift in existing institutional practices, though those shifts may be slow or rapid. New media technologies and practices can be taken up in restricted sectors of a religion first and not be given high ratings in other sectors, until the conditions are right for the wider institution to see the new media practice as natural to the religion. As media changes become domesticated, what was once seen as external to the religion may become the legitimized means of significant transformation of religious culture, knowledge, practice, thinking, and perceptions of space and time, authority, political and economic relations, and organizational structure and social behavior.

The relationship between media and religion, therefore, is nuanced and interactive. Particular media configurations, even those that appear at first as foreign, can become domesticated within a religion and produce changes that in time become an indistinguishable part of the religion's social and cultural life and traditions.

This perspective provides a valuable perspective for thinking about the relationship between media, media change, and the construction of religious authority. Media, because of their central role in establishing and maintaining relationships and the mustering of resources within a community, are a key site of social power. Changes to the communication web on which any religion is built invariably create struggles by individuals or groups, old and new, to maintain or establish their authority by repositioning or realigning themselves strategically on the new web. Those practitioners whose ideas, practices, or identities are more easily adapted to the characteristics of the new web will find it much easier to establish themselves in key positions of authority than those whose religious formulations and practices are tightly linked to the old.

The impact of changes in the media web on which any religion is constructed and relationships of power and authority in the religion, therefore, can be explored through a number of questions:

Who has access to and who is excluded from the religious web, at what level, and with what authorization?

Who has the right to participate in particular gatherings, forums, or institutions where information is communicated, discussions take place, and decisions are made?

Who has the power, literacy, and resources to produce information and the power to receive it and be in "the loop" in relation to key media of religious communication?

What factors enable or restrict that access, such as speaking the language, knowing how to read or write, knowing the jargon (be that theological or technical), belonging to the appropriate class, gender, or race, being perceived as trustworthy, having the resources required to access the web (e.g., a telephone, television set, or computer to access the Internet), having the resources and knowledge to put one's perspectives into the flow of communication, or having superior military or coercive power to impose one's possession?

The impact of media change, therefore, needs to be understood within the context that religious authority is neither fixed nor rigid. Authority needs to continually establish itself through language and communication within a marketplace of competing claims and interests. When the needs of the market change, or when a new contender emerges, the symbolic power of the established position needs to be argued and reaffirmed, not just according to the innate value of their way of communicating, but also its economic relevance, or value, to the new market and its dominant symbolism. This struggle occurs in a range of ways, from attempting to censor or censure the new, through hegemonic efforts to portray the established ways as natural or orthodox, to competing within the marketplace.

These struggles can be seen and need to be considered on a range of levels of analysis: at the level of individual thought and practice, as a person's values, beliefs, perspectives, and practices change; at a subcultural level, as authority patterns within groups change under the impact of new people, new cultural influences, new information, or material conditions; at an intercultural level, as particular forms of Christianity (conservative vs. liberal, Western Christianity vs. southern Christianity) gain dominance over others and acquire greater symbolic capital; and at a macro-social level, as national material conditions and communication patterns change, raising the symbolic and practical value of particular expressions of Christianity over others.

This particularity is important. For while the technological characteristics of new media are important factors in social and religious construction and change, they are just one factor. How the media are used and appropriated also need to be considered. The particular technological characteristics of a new medium do not become culturally significant until they are implemented in particular ways in different contexts. In practice, social arrangements and change are rarely the result simply of new technologies in a deterministic fashion, but a complex product of political negotiation and maneuver, economic pressures, opportunities for implementation, social competition, individual persuasiveness, and sometimes sheer accident or coincidence. There is no inevitable law or cause-effect predictability about how any new medium will develop or the consequences it will have. As Ruth Finnegan (1988) has noted, "The medium itself cannot give rise to social consequences—it must be used by people and developed through social institutions. The mere technical existence of writing cannot affect social change. What counts is its use, who uses it, who controls it, what it is used for, how it fits into the power structure, how widely it is distributed—it is these social and political factors that shape the consequences" (pp. 41–42).

MEDIA AND THE EARLY RECONSTRUCTION OF CHRISTIAN AUTHORITY

Much is made in the New Testament Gospels that when Jesus began his mission, he had no structural authority on which to draw. His authority was a personally embodied one, strongly in keeping with Weber's concept of charismatic authority—someone who came to be recognized by many as being endowed with apparently supernatural or superhuman powers and qualities. The four Gospels develop the meaning of Jesus's authority by drawing on three models of religious leadership embedded in Judaism: that of the oral prophet, the rabbi or sage, and the martyr. Since these are later reflections and constructions of the Jesus story, and only four "authorized" versions out of a much larger number of Gospels written at the time, it is difficult to know the extent to which these models of religious leadership were influential in Jesus's developing self-understanding.

Following the death of Jesus, the earliest Christian movement was diverse, as the ambiguous meanings inherent in the untimely death of Jesus and his proclaimed resuscitation were developed and interpreted to different contexts. Conflicts are evident in the earliest Christian writings between different groups and opinions that are significantly media-related: Jewish and Gentile interpretations; the interpretations of the dramatic and itinerant Christian prophets and evangelists, whose constructions and performances were strongly oral in character; the influential minority of followers who were literate and favored the establishment of a written tradition interpreted orally by authorized teachers; and the martyrs and the symbolic influence of their martyred death.

By the end of the second century, a number of recognizable streams of interpretation had developed: the Jewish Christian stream, which maintained its links with Judaism, saw Jesus as the Messiah but not the Son of God, and favored the authority of disciples within the structure of rabbinic Judaism; the Gnostic stream, which interpreted the Jesus tradition through the lens of the wider philosophical and cultural movement of Greek Gnosticism; Marcionite Christianity, which interpreted Jesus separate from his Jewish roots; Montanist Christianity, which retained a strong emphasis on charismatic practices and structures of authority; and Catholic or Logos Christianity, which adapted Jesus's original message to the Logos philosophy of neo-Hellenism. In keeping with the practice of Jesus, a number of those streams involved significant leadership by women.

Yet pretty much by the end of the third century, that diverse movement of Christianity had been narrowed to one dominant stream, the Catholic or Logos version, whose adherents had succeeded in establishing themselves not only as the dominant interpretation but as the only true interpretation of who Jesus was and what Jesus meant. This dominance was established despite the fact that the Catholic party implemented a particular model of authority and leadership that was restricted to males (despite the fact that Jesus involved women in his mission and affirmed the importance of women in leadership), was strongly literate in its leadership structures (despite the fact that the vast majority of Christians and possibly Jesus himself were illiterate and oral in their communication and cultural practice), and was strongly hierarchical in nature (despite Jesus's teaching that his followers were to eschew hierarchy and the exercise of power in favor of relationships of mutual service).

It is frequently represented in histories and theologies of Christianity that this one particular stream dominated because it was the true embodiment of Christianity. This view needs to be challenged in the light of the struggle for power that took place and the dynamics of that struggle by which the Catholic position established its hegemony. Hatch (1957) advocates the need for reviewing this dominant view:

> If we were to trust the histories that are commonly current, we should believe that there was from the first a body of doctrine of which certain writers were the recognised exponents; and that outside this body of doctrine there was only the play of more or less insignificant opinions, like a fitful guerrilla warfare on the flanks of a great army. Whereas what we find on examining the evidence is, that out of a mass of opinions which for a long time fought as equals upon equal ground, there was formed a vast alliance which was strong enough to shake off the extremes at once of conservatism and of speculation. (pp. 10–11)

There were many reasons for this hegemony that go beyond the scope of this study, but it is valuable to note the particular ways in which strategic uses of media were key elements in this early narrowing of Christianity, an imposed hegemony on the movement of Christianity that continued for more than a millennium. A number of media factors can be identified.

CONSTRUCTION OF THE CATHOLIC BRAND

One of those strategies was a branding one, similar to what we would associate with a media-based corporate branding campaign today. The term "catholic" comes from the Greek adjective *katholikos*, meaning "universal." One of the first uses of the term was by Ignatius around the year 106 in a letter to the Christians in Smyrna. In that letter, though Jesus is identified as definitive of Christianity, Ignatius links the brand "universal" with a particular type of authority structure, one governed by bishops. "Wherever the bishop shall appear, there let the multitude [of the people] also be; even as, wherever Jesus Christ is, there is the Catholic Church. It is not lawful without the bishop either to baptize or to celebrate a love-feast; but whatsoever he shall approve of, that is also pleasing to God, so that everything that is done may be secure and valid" (Ignatius, 106, chapter VIII). The term is used again in the account of the martyrdom of Polycarp in 155. The Muratorian fragment, one of the earliest lists of the books of the New Testament from around 170, also uses it. In both cases it is used in the context of ecclesiastical discipline.

Though the term "catholic" literally refers to all Christian communities (i.e., universal), through its hegemonic use the concept of *universality* has become identified with a *particular* stream of Christian opinion, and increasingly that being defined by the powerful bishop of Rome. By the end of the second century this hegemony had become entrenched. In the year 380 Emperor Theodosius I enforced the exclusivity of the brand politically and in Roman law with a decree, the *Codex Theodosianus*, that the term "catholic Christians" would be reserved only for the version of Christianity he endorsed:

> We desire that all the people under the rule of our clemency should live by that religion which divine Peter the apostle is said to have given to the Romans, and which it is evident that Pope Damasus and Peter, bishop of Alexandria, a man of apostolic sanctity, followed; that is that we should believe in the one deity of Father, Son, and Holy Spirit with equal majesty and in the Holy Trinity according to the apostolic teaching and the authority of the gospel. ... *As for the others, since in our* judgement they are foolish madmen, we decree that they shall be branded with the ignominious name of heretics, and shall not presume to give their conventicles the name of churches. (Thatcher, 1907, pp. 69–71)

The political will of the emperor was embedded in Christian doctrine the following year in the definitive Nicene Creed with the inclusion of the statement "I believe in one holy catholic and apostolic church."

MEDIA AND CONSOLIDATION OF POWER IN A HIERARCHICAL ORGANIZATION

Another major contributor to the overall supremacy of the Catholic Party was the effort put into the creation and normalization of a centrally managed, hierarchical organizational structure that located power and authority in the male leadership position of bishop.

The Catholic Party's hierarchical structure of bishop-presbyter-deacon was not native to early Christianity. Jesus rejected the exercise of power by any one person over another and, reflecting his emphasis on mutual love, promoted a collegial relationship characterized by mutual service. This was enacted in the earliest years of the movement in a communal form of leadership, with particular authority ascribed to those who were part of Jesus's original inner circle and those seen as gifted. This included resourceful women who found in Christian communities opportunities to exercise leadership and gifts in a way that was denied them in the wider society. Therefore, the development and implementation of the Catholic male episcopal structure included a significant effort to subordinate the leadership of women and charisma-based leadership within the male-led hierarchical structure. In line with Innis's (1950) arguments about the importance of writing in the construction of empires, the male bishops' superior ability to access and effectively utilize the resources of writing was a crucial factor in this dominance.

One of the earliest to promote the view that the bishop was the defining authority in the church, with other offices such as presbyter, deacon, and widow subordinate to the bishop, was Ignatius, who died around 117. Ignatius was a bishop of Antioch and could be seen as arguing to justify a system that supported his own power. His ascription of the terms "catholic" or "universal" to this hierarchical view of the church was influential in linking religious authority in Christianity with a particular hierarchical organizational structure. The opinions of Ignatius were contained mainly in seven letters he wrote while under armed escort on the road from Antioch to Rome, where he was to be executed. His writings acquired greater authority because of his impending martyrdom and the drama generated along the way as he passed through. The letters were also widely copied and circulated.

Reinforcing this view was another bishop, Irenaeus of Lyons, who in his major work, *Against Heresies*, written in 180, promoted the position of bishop as a bulwark against the theological threat he saw being posed by Gnostic expressions of Christianity. Irenaeus set bishops apart as the bearers of true Christianity on the basis that they were the ones to whom the original apostles who knew Jesus personally passed on the true tradition. He justifies this idea with a rather mechanical concept of apostolic succession—that is, that the tradition of the apostles is preserved by a sequence or succession of bishops who hand it on to one another. He supports his argument with a constructed sequence of bishops going back to the apostles, though there is significant debate about the accuracy of his list. What we see from this, though, is a transformation of the more charismatic view of religious authority into an institutional one that is more defined and controlled. Irenaeus's dubious demonstration of direct succession also illustrates the point made above, that the exercise of religious authority within Christianity has involved not just acting in a way that implements the authority, but also an active process of constructing a particular worldview, theology, and organizational structure to legitimize the power being taken.

At the time, most bishops would have overseen small Christian communities or groups of communities. Throughout the second and third centuries there was an increase in the number of church councils held locally or regionally in which all bishops participated, though many were poorly educated, barely literate, and therefore scarcely able to participate in the heavy literate theological debates that were taking place at the time. As a result, greater power accrued to those who were bishops in the small number of major cities of the empire because of the greater wealth in their churches, the greater number of clergy under their command, the civil importance of their cities in the imperial order, and their access to the facilities and resources for writing. With the exception of Irenaeus, almost all the major Christian writers of the period of the second and third centuries were bishops or connected with the five major imperial cities: Alexandria, Antioch, Carthage, Athens, and Rome.

Writing was a powerful weapon used extensively by bishops to normalize the structure that supported their power, to organize opinion, to link with other bishops in their common cause, to quote from one another as apparently distant and impersonal sources in support of their own local authority, and to exploit as a common group the concept of one church and the church universal. As Fox (1994) notes, "Literacy also allowed bishops to outmaneuver opponents, display a common front of opinion, abjure or cure mistaken Christians, or 'sign up' lists of names for creeds and disciplinary rulings, texts which allowed yet more power to be mobilized" (p. 134).

The resources that the bishops were able to muster for the production and distribution of written texts (a number came from wealthy families and brought these resources with them) allowed for the production and circulation of manuals of practice that implemented the particular organizational structures being promoted by the Catholic Party. *The Apostolic Tradition,* for example, attributed to the Roman Christian presbyter Hippolytus, was an influential and widely circulated document of seven thousand words or so from the early third century that provided detailed directions on the choice and ordination of bishops, presbyters, and deacons, the preparation of people for baptism and the conduct of baptism, the conduct of the Eucharist, and guidelines for personal religious practices. A clearly hierarchical organization is promoted through directions on who is to be ordained and set apart (bishops, elders, and deacons—"ordination is for the clergy because of liturgical duty"), and who is not to be ordained (widows, readers, female virgins, subdeacons, and those who have received a gift of healing by revelation—"for the matter is obvious"). These particular interpretations of Christianity are universalized within the document by identifying them as the essence of the tradition. The hegemonic nature of this document is apparent in its unquestioned affirmation that this is what Christianity has always been: "Now, driven by love towards all the saints, we have arrived at the essence of the tradition which is proper for the Churches. This is so that those who are well informed may keep the tradition which has lasted until now, according to the explanation we give of it, and so that others by taking note of it, may be strengthened (against the fall or error which has recently occurred because of ignorance and ignorant people)" (Hippolytus, ca. 215, Para 1.2).

Part of the consolidation of the bishop's power and their view of Christianity included keeping tight control of the production and circulation of alternative Christian opinions. Alternative Christian views, such as Gnostic Christianity, Arianism, and Montanism, were declared "heretical," their writings were destroyed, and severe penalties were imposed for anyone found possessing them. Alternative centers of spiritual power and authority, such as that of women and the oral prophets, which had been major forces in the communication and interpretation of Christianity's meaning from its beginning, were brought under the bishop's control. Christian women were forbidden to write, and the role of prophecy, in a clear example of Weber's understanding of the routinization of charisma, was declared a function of the bishop, regardless of whether the bishop possessed charismatic gifts.

The important role played by writing in this episcopal takeover of religious authority is well illustrated in the work of Cyprian, the bishop of Carthage during the mid-third century. Cyprian was an educated, wealthy, aristocratic Carthaginian property owner, possibly of senatorial rank. Trained within the Greco-Roman education system as a rhetorician, he was a skilled debater, likely with experience in politics, the law, and civil administration. He was elected as a bishop two years after his conversion to Christianity—a singular example of religious authority being ascribed based on a person's position in the secular world. As a bishop, and reflecting his Roman imperial experience and interests, Cyprian actively promoted a singular concept of church as the one visible orthodox community of Christians, with a universal unity of monarchial bishops as the sole authority in Christianity: "There is one God, and Christ is one, and there is one church, and one chair (episcopate) founded upon the rock by the word of God" (Letter 43, in Clarke, 1984a).

Cyprian's work and ideas circulated in his writings contributed to the further transformation of Latin (Western) Christianity into the Catholic model, as an imperial structure with clear parallels between church government and civil government. The consolidation of a clergy class separate from lay Christians paralleled the secular separation of the curial class (property owners) from the plebs. This structure of authority in Christianity, parallel to that of the empire, allowed a ready accommodation of Christianity to the empire's political power. With the wealth of the church in Rome, its claims of direct connection with the apostles Peter and Paul and hosting of their burial sites, and the importance of Rome as the center of the empire, it was not long before Rome acquired the position of senior bishop of catholic Christianity.

Cyprian's influence was extended beyond his local North African diocese through the skills and experience he had in building political networks through personal contact and constant writing. Between the years 250 and 258 Cyprian wrote around a dozen treatises, some of them several volumes in length. Eighty-two of his letters from this period are preserved, while others are referred to for which copies no longer exist. Many of his letters were produced in multiple copies with multiple attachments.

The letters of Cyprian that have been preserved indicate that most were not just private correspondence but public documents, intended to be freely copied and widely distributed. His correspondence is broad in its scope, with evidence of communication with Christian communities in Spain, Gaul, Cappadocia, Rome, and elsewhere in Italy. In one of his letters Cyprian includes a list of all the African bishops and their sees, apparently to keep the central records and mailing lists held in Rome up to date. He wrote frequently to other bishops and leaders in other churches, encouraging them, telling him his opinion of things they were doing, or urging them to desist from behavior he considered divisive or damaging.

Many of Cyprian's letters are addressed to multiple recipients—one is addressed to eighteen different people, relaying to them decisions of councils or common action. A good example is Letter 73, written to an unidentified "Iubaianus, my brother," in response to an inquiry about Cyprian's thinking on the question of baptism of heretics. The letter runs to 6,500 words and includes as an attachment a copy of another long treatise, *On the Virtue of Patience*, which Cyprian notes, "We are sending to you as a token of our mutual affection." On another occasion, when questions were being raised about his actions, Cyprian wrote to the presbyters and deacons in Rome to correct misperceptions. This particular letter includes copies of thirteen of his former letters as well. Letter 74, written to refute the opinions of a fellow bishop, included not only a copy of the original letter, but also a further 2,500 words of his critique of the letter.

Cyprian's Letter 49 provides another insight into the central place of writing in the maintenance of the Catholic organizational structure. It is a letter written immediately after the close of a local council to report its findings to the bishop of Rome: "To you, my dearly beloved brother, we are sending over news of these events written down the very same hour, the very same minute that they have occurred; and we are sending over at once to you the acolyte Niceforus who is rushing off down to the port to embark straight from the meeting" (Letter 49, in Clarke, 1984a).

This distribution process indicates the existence of an uninterrupted ease of communication around the Mediterranean region and a constant circulation of Christian letters and other writings around this communication network. Cyprian claims of an open letter written by the Roman clergy that "it has been circulated through the entire world and reached the knowledge of every church and every brethren" (Epis 55.5.2, in Clarke, 1984b). He is able to cross-reference previous letters of his on the assumption that they have been widely circulated and their contents are part of the shared knowledge.

Fox (1994) refers to this as the use of Christian writing for "the organization of opinion" and demonstrates the advantages that writing gave to those Christian leaders who had the resources to utilize it. Haines-Eitzen (2000) argues that this flurry of output reflected "circles of readers and scribes who transmitted Christian literature individually and privately" (p. 84).

A central bishop such as Cyprian could not maintain such a volume of output and copying without scribal support and the organizational or personal resources to sustain it, giving distinct advantages to those who were able to access those resources. On a wider scale, a major center like Rome, with its greater resources, was able to place itself as a clearinghouse for distribution, with extensive secretarial, duplication, archival, and distribution systems in place enabling quick communication through the empire's extensive communication networks.

These few examples illustrate that authority within Christianity is not an inherent quality. It is a construction developed through active contest between different centers of power, in which media—the ability to produce, reproduce, distribute, shape, and control information—are crucial components not just in positioning someone as a person of authority, but in constructing and maintaining the hegemonic worldview in which that authority makes sense. The Catholic Party of Christianity was able to subdue alternative embodiments of the Christian faith through its ability to co-opt and utilize the literate culture and resources of the Roman empire and position itself culturally and politically within the power structures of that empire. With the collapse of the political empire in the fifth century, the Roman Catholic Church had the organizational structures in place to become the dominant imperial political structure in the West. This social and political dominance continued for more than a millennium until the birth of the printing press changed the media-cultural dynamics of some key European nations and regions to facilitate the rise of the new authority structures of the Reformation and the modern world. Those media-cultural dynamics, and the authority structures they have sustained in the West, are changing again under the impact of digital media technologies. The way in which religious authority is being changed and reascribed on this new media playing field is open to new analysis.

NOTES

1. There is an amusing anecdote told of an inner-city pastor whose congregation voted to move from their troubled location to a more comfortable suburban one, contrary to the pastor's wishes. When asked what he would do, the pastor replied, "I must go with them, I am their leader."

2. I first became aware of the concept of media as the web of culture through Hoover (1993). It also builds on Weber's concept of culture as the web of meaning.

REFERENCES

Anderson, J. W. (2003). The Internet and Islam's new interpreters. In D. F. Eickelman & J. W. Anderson (Eds.), New media in the Muslim world: The emerging public sphere (2nd ed., pp. 43–60). Bloomington, IN: Indiana University Press.

Arendt, H. (1977). What is authority? In Between past and future: Eight exercises in political thought (pp. 91–141). New York, NY: Penguin.

Bourdieu, P. (1977). The economics of linguistic exchanges. Social Science Information, 16(6), 645–668.

Campbell, H. (2007). Who's got the power? Religious authority and the Internet. Journal of Computer-Mediated Communication, 12(3), 1043–1062.

Canclini, N. G. (1995). Hybrid cultures: Strategies for entering and leaving modernity. (C. Ciaparri & S. L. López, Trans.). Minneapolis, MN: University of Minnesota Press.

Chapman, M. (2005). Authority. In J. Bowden (Ed.), Christianity: The complete guide (pp. 105–110). London, UK: Continuum.

Chaves, M. (1994). Secularization as declining religious authority. Social Forces, 72(3), 749–774.

Clarke, G. W. (1984a). The letters of St. Cyprian of Carthage, vol. 2, Letters 28–54. New York, NY: Newman Press.

Clarke, G. W. (1984b). The letters of St. Cyprian of Carthage, vol. 3, Letters 55–66. New York, NY: Newman Press.

Eisenstein, E. (1979). The printing press as an agent of change: Communications and cultural transformations in early *modern Europe*. Cambridge, UK: Cambridge University Press.

Finnegan, R. H. (1988). *Literacy and orality: Studies in the technology of communication*. New York, NY: Blackwell.

Fox, R. L. (1994). Literacy and power in early Christianity. In A. K. Bowman & G. Woolf (Eds.), *Literacy and power in the ancient world* (pp. 126–148). Cambridge, UK: Cambridge University Press.

Haines-Eitzen, K. (2000). *Guardians of letters: Literacy, power, and the transmission of early Christian literature*. Oxford, UK: Oxford University Press.

Hatch, E. (1957). *The influence of Greek ideas on Christianity* (1st Harper Torchbook ed.). New York, NY: Harper and Brothers.

Hippolytus. (ca. 215). *The apostolic tradition of Hippolytus of Rome*. Retrieved from http://www.bombaxo.com/hippolytus.html.

Hoover, S. (1993). What do we do about the media? *Conrad Grebel Review* (Spring), 97–107.

Ignatius. (106). *The epistle of Ignatius to the Smyrnæans*. Retrieved from http://www.ccel.org/ccel/schaff/anf01.v.vii.html.

Innis, H. A. (1950). *Empire and communications*. Toronto, ON: University of Toronto Press.

Kertcher, Z., & Margalit, A. (2005). Challenges to authority, burdens of legitimization: The printing press and the Internet. *Yale Journal of Law and Technology, 8*(1), 1–30.

Lewis, J. (2005). *Language wars: The role of media and culture in global and political violence*. London, UK: Pluto Press.

McQuail, D. (1994). *Mass communication theory: An introduction* (3rd ed.). London, UK: Sage.

Meyer, B. (2006). *Religious sensations: Why media, aesthetics and power matter in the study of contemporary religion*. Amsterdam, NE: Vrije Universiteit.

Morgan, D. (1998). *Visual piety: A history and theory of popular religious images*. Berkeley, CA: University of California Press.

Morgan, D. (2005). *The sacred gaze: Religious visual culture in theory and practice*. Berkeley, CA: University of California Press.

Pivarunas, M. (1996). The infallibility of the Catholic Church. *Religious Congregation of Mary Immaculate Queen*. Retrieved from http://www.cmri.org/96prog5.htm.

Russell, L. (1987). *Household of freedom: Authority in feminist theology*. Philadelphia, PA: Westminster Press.

Sample, T. (1994). *Ministry in an oral culture: Living with Will Rogers, Uncle Remus, and Minnie Pearl*. Louisville, KY: Westminster / John Knox Press.

Satow, R. L. (1975). Value-rationality authority and professional organizations: Weber's missing type. *Administrative Science Quarterly, 20*(4), 526–531.

Thatcher, Oliver J. (Ed.) (1907). *The library of original sources*, vol. 4, *The early medieval world*. Milwaukee: University Research Extension Co.

Weber, M. (1968). *Economy and society: An outline of interpretive sociology* (Vol. 1). New York, NY: Bedminster Press.

Willer, D. (1967). Max Weber's missing authority type. *Sociological Inquiry, 37*(2), 231–239.

CHAPTER 3

Media and (Vicarious) Religion

Two Levels of Religious Authority

Alf Linderman

It has been argued that religion has been a blind spot within media studies. It has for the most part not been considered a meaningful category in the general study of the media. The same goes for religion scholars when it comes to the media. Popular culture and the mass media have not been a major concern for religion scholars in general, nor for scholars in the sociology of religion. The focus within religion scholarship has predominantly been on traditional institutional religion and on religious practices and attitudes. Observations of the need for more attention to the nexus between media, religion, and culture have been around for some time. One very concrete case in point reflecting the increased attention devoted to the interplay between media, religion, and culture is the international series of conferences under the rubric of "media, religion, and culture" that started in Uppsala, Sweden, in 1993. There are also a number of edited volumes related to these conferences (Hoover & Lundby, 1997; Hoover & Clark, 2002; Mitchell & Marriage, 2003; Sumiala-Seppänen, Lundby, & Salokangas, 2006; Lynch, Mitchell, & Strahn, 2011; Hjarvard & Lövheim, 2012).

Still, however, there is need for further dialogue around how the combination of religion and media scholarship can contribute to the understanding of how religion comes into play in present (late) modern societies.

In light of all the attention recently devoted to the resurgence of religion, this need is even more emphasized. I would like to argue that the dialogue regarding how the combination of religion and media scholarship could be mutually beneficial should be specific and should take into account examples of theorizing where it is apparent, or at least possible, that one line of scholarship could benefit from input by the other. As an example, I will here discuss the British sociologist of religion Grace Davie and her thought-provoking theorizing around what she refers to as *vicarious religion*. I will especially focus on her statements on how difficult, or even downright impossible, she considers it to actually measure the phenomenon of vicarious religion. My argument is that two specific studies conducted in Sweden in 1999 and 2007, on attitudes toward religious television among the general Swedish population, can be interpreted as implying information relating also to the issue of vicarious religion. Furthermore, after having argued that these empirical studies relate to Davie's concept of vicarious religion, I will move on to the discussion of religious authority. Drawing on my discussion of these two empirical studies in relation to vicarious religion, I propose a notion of two levels of religious authority. On the first level, other scholars have convincingly demonstrated how people seem to show less interest in institutional religion, and consequently also in institutional religious authorities. In other words, people increasingly seem to assume authority over their own relation to religion and their religious identity. On a second level, however, given my discussion of vicarious religion, people seem to like the idea that a small minority maintains religious traditions and practices. In doing this, they are also granting this minority some sort of limited but also specific religious authority. Thus this argument becomes the foundation for my notion of two levels of religious authority. There is a subjective turn in that people show less interest in religious authorities in their lives in general. But given the perspective of vicarious religion, people at the same time seem to appreciate that some people take on the task of maintaining traditional religion and religious rituals. People seem to like that some folks know the proper way to perform religious funerals and other services when such functions for some reason become needed. This, in turn, means they are granted some sort of authority by those who occasionally might need these services.

WHAT IS VICARIOUS RELIGION?

Grace Davie (2006) defines vicarious religion in the following way: "By vicarious, I mean the notion of religion performed by an active minority but on behalf of a much larger number, who (implicitly at least) not only understand, but, quite clearly, approve of what the minority is doing" (p. 24). Davie's conception of vicarious religion stems from her previous work as a sociologist of religion, trying to understand the religious development in Britain and Europe. Among religion scholars, there has been a long-standing discussion around the concept of secularization. One of the central issues in this discussion is the difference found between Europe and the United States when it comes to religious attitudes and practices. In the light of these differences, any simple relationship between the process of modernization and secularization has to be questioned. It seems that increased modernization does not necessarily lead to a reduction in religious beliefs and practices.

Based on Davie's initial reflection on the religious situation in Britain, in 1994 she published *Religion in Britain since 1945: Believing without Belonging*. This book became an important point of reference for scholars in the sociology of religion. Among other things, Davie in this book made it clear that religion and religious life had to be seen as a complex phenomenon including many interrelated dimensions. However, Davie (2007) herself has over time become increasingly dissatisfied "with a way of thinking that almost by definition pulls apart the ideas of believing and belonging" (p. 22). Using the concept of vicarious religion as a tool, she has tried to explore the more complex relationships between different dimensions of religious life.

Davie (2007) gives four examples of how religion can operate vicariously:

- Churches and church leaders perform ritual on behalf of others;
- Church leaders and churchgoers believe on behalf of others;
- Church leaders and churchgoers embody moral codes on behalf of others;
- Churches can offer space for the vicarious debate of unresolved issues in modern societies. (p. 23)

She points to religious rituals at important stages of our lives, such as birth, marriage, and especially death, as obvious examples of when churches and church leaders are performing rituals on behalf of others. For example, when a member of the clergy performs a funeral, this is perceived as a meaningful act by those who mourn the person who passed away. The clergyperson performs this act on behalf of those who mourn.

But there is another side to this vicarious function of religion. Churches and church leaders take on the responsibility to maintain religion and religious rituals for the purpose of being able to offer such services to those who might need them: "Churches maintain vicariously the rituals from which a larger population can draw when the occasion demands it, and while that population expects a certain freedom in ritual expression, it also expects the institutional structure to be kept firmly in place" (Davie, 2007, p. 23).

Davie uses Princess Diana's funeral as an illustration. People who normally would have no contact with the church had a great interest in getting some sort of experience from the ritual performed at the princess's funeral. Churches also became gathering points for many in the time following Diana's death. A precondition for this, of course, is that the institutional structure is kept firmly in place, as Grace Davie states. If churches and the rituals performed in these churches should have the potential to become relevant to people in a given situation, the prerequisite is that there be churches where the competence to perform rituals in a proper way is maintained. This tendency to turn to churches and religious authorities in given situations is the observation from which Davie draws the conclusion that a large number of people, at least implicitly, approve of that which on a regular basis is performed in churches by a small minority of the population in European countries.

Sweden is often described as one of the most secularized countries in the world. But even there we can find examples of a similar kind of phenomenon to the one to which Davie refers. In 1994 the Swedish ferry *Estonia* sank during its journey between Estonia and Sweden. Some nine hundred lives were lost in the accident, mostly from Sweden. This was a shock to Swedish society. Many people could relate to the victims, knowing someone, or knowing someone who knew someone, aboard the ship, and some communities were particularly hurt by the accident since many died in groups traveling together. This accident caused many people to go to churches in Sweden. They went to the many memorial services held after the accident, but also to churches just to experience a quiet sacred room filled with religious symbols (Pettersson, 2013). Since people need the churches, their rituals, and everything that churches, church leaders, and religion represent at these occasions, it is necessary that some people take on the responsibility of maintaining religion and religious traditions and rituals. This, in short, is what Davie refers to when she talks about vicarious religion.

Steve Bruce and David Voas (2010) have dismissed the concept of vicarious religion. According to them, the example of Diana's funeral does not have anything to do with religion. All that is needed is something that adds to the experience of mourning and saying farewell to someone who tragically died: "The church offered a convenient venue and trained personnel, but no one would have much cared if the person officiating at Diana's funeral was a lord rather than a bishop: what mattered was the pomp and circumstance" (p. 246).

The same would consequently also be true in the Swedish case of the ferry that sank. What Bruce and Voas present, however, is only an assumption, for which they present no empirical support. To my knowledge no poll has been conducted regarding how people would feel about the church compared to any other kind of solemn context, with the assumed amount of pomp and circumstance, as the venue for a funeral like that of Diana. It also appears far-fetched to imagine that the constitutive component in Swedes' turn to churches after the loss of the ferry *Estonia* only related to their need for what Bruce and Voas refer to as "pomp and circumstance." The Swedish anthropologist Mikael Kurkiala (2010) points to his own behavior after the deaths of so many when the *Estonia* sank as an example of how humans relate to religion during such events. He went to a cathedral to light a candle. Drawing on this example, he points to the nature of religion as a dimension of life that cannot be reduced to any other. It is very unlikely that Kurkiala would pay a visit to the city hall to light a candle in a similar situation, regardless of how solemn this place might be. I think that Bruce and Voas too quickly conclude that such behavior has nothing to do with religion. Thus I find the concept of vicarious religion worthy of further reflection and, if possible, empirical investigation. This concept holds the potential to explain why churches and religious rituals seem to refuse extinction even in societies considered very secular, like Sweden.

I would briefly like to point to another example. Even in communities where very few people take part in local church services, it is not rare for people in Sweden to have strong feelings about very tangible representations of religion, such as church buildings, and to defend such buildings if they are threatened. Also in this case, Bruce and Voas (2010) dismiss this circumstance as support for the notion of vicarious religion: "Appreciating the churches' contributions to cultural heritage and contemporary welfare enough to wish to preserve them does not make one (vicariously) religious, any more than hoping that the local stately home is not turned into a carpet warehouse makes one a closet supporter of the aristocracy" (p. 254).

Again, Bruce and Voas take for granted that religion is no different from any other social phenomenon. Any social institution that has a certain degree of solemnity and that can produce a certain level of pomp and circumstance can be paralleled with religion. There is, obviously, a risk of circularity in the discussion about vicarious religion. If we define religion as only a matter of solemnity, we conclude that any other institution with a similar degree of solemnity can take on the function that religion had in previous times. And vice versa, if we consider religion to be a distinct category of human behavior, we are more inclined to look for specific roles that cannot as easily be transferred, or reduced, to other dimensions of life. What we need to do, then, is to use various models and concepts to try to understand various religious phenomena. The explanatory capacity, and empirical validity, could then be evaluated. The concept of vicarious religion can be used as one way to explore further the role of religion in modern Europe, and as such I find it stimulating and thought provoking.

In their critical discussion of vicarious religion, Bruce and Voas (2010) talk about two principles on which vicarious religion rests: "The idea of vicarious religion rests on two principles: that a minority of people are religious on behalf of a silent majority and that those in the majority appreciate their efforts. Both must be true for the description to apply" (p. 245).

Do those who are supposed to do something on behalf of others need to have this awareness themselves? It is not clear to me if Davie means that this has to be the case. For Bruce and Voas, it seems natural to expect that those who act on behalf of someone else also have to have the corresponding self-perception. In some situations the notion of such awareness seems more natural than in other situations. There are examples of when a person consciously is doing something on behalf of someone else. Bruce and Voas (2010) offer a few such examples of what they refer to the classic model of vicariousness: "It is not hard to find modern examples of vicarious religion in the classic sense. In southern Europe, men may like their wives to represent the family in church; in traditional Muslim or Jewish societies, women are not obliged to appear at services, because men do" (p. 245).

But in most cases, Bruce and Voas do not see this kind of obvious vicarious action in the area of religion. It would be interesting to study empirically to what degree religious officials and the active religious minority in any sense of the word would feel that they act on behalf of others when they take part in various religious rituals. However interesting that would be, I do not think such obvious awareness is needed for vicarious religion to be present in the sense in which Davie presents it. A religious community could be doing their religious business, continuously hoping that more people would care, without having the awareness that they do this on behalf of those who do not appear to be interested. The very fact that they perform the way they do, and thus maintain the religious tradition and the religious rituals, and in various implicit and explicit ways are supported by large parts of the surrounding community, is sufficient for talking about vicarious religion in the way Davie does.

VICARIOUS RELIGION AND THE MEDIA

Grace Davie considers the media in her discussion of vicarious religion in at least two ways. First, the mass media supply many of the religious rituals that people need in times of death and disaster. The funeral service of Princess Diana was broadcast on television and/or radio not only in Britain, but also in many countries throughout the world. In the case of the Swedish ferry lost at sea, specific religious rituals and memorials were broadcast after the disaster, and church officials of various kinds were brought onto the talk shows when the media dealt with the disaster.

The second way Davie refers to the media is by pointing to the great interest the media have in certain church events and church controversies. While maintaining the idea that religion is a marginal phenomenon in today's western European societies, the media did, for example, express great interest in the death of Pope John Paul II. Davie (2007) considers the funeral of the pope to be "possibly (given the scale of the broadcast) the largest communal ritual event in the world's history" (p. 30). She interprets this ambivalence to religion among media institutions—viewing religion as marginal while giving it massive attention in certain situations—as another possible sign of the vicarious role of religion. The potential of religion to become very important in specific situations makes it interesting to cover certain religious events.

There is, according to Davie, another side to the media's attention to certain religious controversies. Drawing on the examples of media attention to the moral codes of religious officials and the issue of homosexuality, Davie proposes this to be a sign of the way churches can offer space for the vicarious debate over unresolved issues in modern societies. Thus the mass media attend to such issues not for the purpose of reporting on what is going on within churches and religious institutions per se, but in respect to the general interest in issues that are controversial and difficult to discuss in society at large (Davie, 2006; see also Christensen, 2012).

It is not very surprising that Bruce and Voas (2010) do not buy into Davie's examples of how the mass media can play a role in vicarious religion. They note that the media are always interested when, for example, a person representing something acts or says something that seems to be in conflict with that which she or he represents (p. 248). There is definitely some merit to this argument. But Davie's basic assumption, that the media are a venue that makes major rituals available to many people, and thus play a role for vicarious religion, is hard to dismiss (unless, like Bruce and Voas, you dismiss the theoretical concept altogether).

MEDIA STUDIES AS A RESOURCE

As stated above, Davie includes the media as an important component in her reasoning about how religion can operate in vicarious ways. But she does not reflect on the general role of the media. Nor does she consider media studies and media theory. The media are essential to her argument in that it is through the media that the audience can experience religious rituals on occasions like those mentioned above, but she does not discuss the media as such. I would like to argue that a dialogue between media studies and Davie's theorizing on the concept of vicarious religion could enrich our understanding of this concept. Much knowledge is being gathered in the context of media studies about the way we relate to the media in our everyday lives. Perhaps this knowledge could shed light on the way people in modern societies, through the media, can have experiences of vicarious dimensions, not only regarding religion but also in other areas of life. What about how we relate to sports and to politics? An important issue to explore would be how the media can supply a connection to those who maintain something on behalf of the media audience in various dimensions of life beyond religion.

Having made this very general argument as to the value of considering media studies when discussing vicarious religion, I would like to turn to a more specific statement made by Grace Davie to explore how a study of attitudes to religion in the media could contribute to our understanding of vicarious religion. In her article about vicarious religion as a methodological challenge, Davie (2007) writes; "One thing is certain: you cannot *count* vicarious religion. Hence its relative invisibility to those who use primarily quantitative methodologies" (p. 27). She continues to discuss the methodological challenge as she responds to Bruce and Voas's (2010) criticism of her concept of vicarious religion. Davie (2010) writes the following about research methods for the empirical study of vicarious religion: "It involves not only individuals, but institutions, traditions, assumptions, emotions, dispositions—including unconscious ones; it requires therefore an historically informed, highly sophisticated research design to test it adequately" (p. 265).

I would argue that at least in Sweden, you actually *can* measure attitudes that relate to vicarious religion, and you can even do it drawing on quantitative methods. Below, I will show how I think it can be done through the analysis of attitudes toward religion in the media. This is most certainly not what Davie is thinking of when she writes about "highly sophisticated research design." Such a design is perhaps needed if Davie imagines that we could measure vicarious religion in a more direct sense. Until such methodological approaches have been developed, I would like to direct our attention to aspects that actually can be measured and discussed in conjunction with Davie's notion of vicarious religion.

In 1999 and 2007, SIFO Research and Consulting (Svenska institutet för opinionsundersökningar) conducted telephone surveys in Sweden on my behalf. The questions concerned various aspects of people's opinions about religion in the media in general, and in particular with reference to the Swedish public service company the Swedish Broadcasting Corporation (Sveriges Television). This state-owned organization has been broadcasting religion in various ways since its start, and there have been weekly church services on the television schedule since 1987. These religious services do not draw very large audiences if you look at any one particular broadcast. But if you ask about the general frequency of watching religious services on television, one out of ten say that they watch such services once a month or more. If you include those who say that they watch religious services on television at least once a year or more, one-third of the Swedish population report that they watch religious services on television.

The interesting thing in the present context, however, is not how frequently people watch these services, but their attitude to having church services broadcast every Sunday. In the survey conducted in 1999, two-thirds of the Swedish population said that they wanted the Swedish Broadcasting Corporation to broadcast religious services on television every Sunday. In the survey conducted in 2007, the number was lower, but the majority, 53 percent, still wanted religious services on the air every Sunday. Since people do not seem to watch these services on a regular basis, it is obvious that many more want services to be on the air than actually watch them. Why do they want these services broadcast if they do not want to watch them?

A plausible answer is that this item in the survey actually relates to the phenomenon Grace Davie calls vicarious religion. I would argue that people want these services on the air exactly for the same reasons that, according to Davie, are related to the vicarious role of religion. Having religion on the programming schedule of the Swedish public service broadcaster is a way to make certain that religion is "out there" if you ever end up in a situation when you need it. It will ensure that religion will be available through the media, but also that religion will continue to be an inherent and important dimension of modern society. Thus religious buildings, rituals, and traditions will be maintained in society by a few on behalf of those who do not want it right now, but who want to have the opportunity to consume religion in one way or another if needed in the future. As mentioned above, Grace Davie states that vicarious religion cannot be measured in any quantitative sense. She is perhaps right in that it is impossible to measure vicarious religion directly. But the same can be said about many human perspectives and attitudes. When dealing with vague concepts referring to various human perspectives and attitudes, we need to find operationalizations—not only to understand a specific concept in terms of empirical observations and to make the concept measurable, but also to develop the way we understand the concept as such.

I would like to argue that the attitude toward religious services being broadcast on television among the Swedish population is in fact one indicator of the presence and strength of vicarious religion. In doing this, I obviously consider the empirical study of attitudes toward religious services on television to be an operationalization of at least one aspect of Davie's theory on vicarious religion. To empirically measure attitudes that we can relate to the notion of vicarious religion, then, also adds to our understanding of the concept itself. But perhaps even more important, this makes it possible to critically discuss the concept in new ways. If the media are a significant venue for taking part in religion and religious rituals when needed, and people in Sweden seem to value the fact that religion is on the schedule of the nation's public service broadcaster, one could start to ask questions. Studies related to the media can help to ask critical questions about vicarious religion and what we think this concept represents. As stated above, Bruce and Voas criticize the concept of vicarious religion. They offer alternative, and to them more convincing, explanations of Davie's vicarious religion examples. With a specific empirical study as our starting point, we can enter the process of critical evaluation in a different way. We can be more specific, and go beyond the substitution of one assumption for another. Given what we know about people's use of, and attitudes toward, the media, we can ask questions about what kind of religion vicarious religion actually is. Does the word "religion" mean the same thing when we talk about those who are engaged in religious practices, compared to when we talk about those who only want religion to be around in society and who want it to be on television but don't want to look at it themselves? Thus the reference to media studies allows us to ask questions about what vicarious religion really is in other, more specific ways. What kind of religious experience are we talking about with vicarious religion? What is the relation between the experiences of people who belong to a religious community and take part in religious rituals on a regular basis, and the experiences of those who want to have only a little taste of religion from time to time? Are we really talking about religion in the same sense in these two different settings? The operationalization of vicarious religion, and the empirical investigation that this operationalization allows for, are a good starting point for the critical evaluation and discussion of this concept.

TWO LEVELS OF RELIGIOUS AUTHORITY

The purpose of this essay, however, is not to discuss further the concept of vicarious religion itself. My present interest is to draw on the discussion of vicarious religion for the purpose of some reflections regarding religious authority. As stated above, there has been what we could call a subjective turn in the area of religion. Drawing on Charles Taylor's (1992) work on the ethics of authenticity, Paul Heelas and Linda Woodhead (2005) describe the subjective turn as a shift from believing in religious authorities to individual autonomy and subjectivity in the area of religion. They identify a general pattern of this subjective turn. The fact that they can talk about patterns of increased subjectivity, of course, raises questions as to what this subjective turn really is all about. In Sweden, you frequently hear people saying that they are religious, or at least spiritual, in their own way. They want to express that no external authority has the right to define religion or spirituality for them. This is an example of what Heelas and Woodhead call the subjective turn. But if most people, or at least many, seem to respond in similar ways to questions about religion and spirituality, one can start to wonder how "subjective" such answers are. It seems to be the social norm that you should say you are religious in your own way (Willander, 2014). If so, this would no longer be an individualistic standpoint, but rather just the result of people's adherence to the predominant way of thinking about religion in contemporary society

Thus the notion of the subjective turn is not necessarily as straightforward as it may seem. But one thing remains true: individuals in Sweden today more often than not have the self-perception of being free in relation to external religious authorities. On the level of self-perception, there is obviously a general turn from believing in religious authorities to individual autonomy and subjectivity. There are of course many exceptions to the rule. In recent years, we have seen a number of fundamentalist groups in Europe fro whom strong religious authorities still play an important role. This includes groups related to many different religious traditions and communities. One could perhaps interpret such groups, at least in part, as a conscious response to the present lack of authority for religious institutions in contemporary society. Common to these examples of religious groups where authority plays an important role is that individuals typically choose to adhere to a certain community and a certain authority figure. Such authority structures are not dictated by any mainstream social institution. Overall, I would agree with Heelas and Woodhead, and many others, that there has been a general subjective turn in western Europe—not least in Sweden. Thus the primary level of religious authority has been taken over by the individual herself.

At this point, it is interesting to take Davie's notion of vicarious religion into consideration. She struggles to understand why so many people remain members of the national Swedish Lutheran Church, which until the year 2000 was the state religious institution. One of the conceptual tools she uses to shed light on this condition is vicarious religion. She makes the following statement with reference to the Nordic countries:

> The clearest illustrations of all can, of course, be found in those parts of Europe (the Nordic countries and Germany) where some form of church tax is still in place—in other words, where the population as a whole, rather than the actively faithful, contribute to the maintenance of the churches and to the people who work in them. The most striking aspect about the Nordic countries is the relatively small number of people who decide to "contract out" of this system. Some do, but most continue tangibly to support their churches (the financial contribution is not negligible), despite the markedly low levels of both churchgoing and orthodox religious belief in this part of the world. Why do they do this? One assumes that they hope these institutions will continue in existence for a wide variety of reasons. (Davie, 2010, p. 266)

One of these reasons is, as has been elaborated on previously, that the church should continue to have the capacity to celebrate certain rituals when needed beyond the minority of religiously active people (e.g., funerals). When doing my study on attitudes toward religion on television in Sweden, I had a question similar to the one Grace Davie was asking. Why do people want television services broadcast every week when they obviously do not watch them—at least not on a regular basis? Interpreting this study in the context of Davie's notion of vicarious religion allowed me to make sense of this seemingly peculiar condition. They want religion to be maintained in its traditional form for a variety of reasons, and one such reason is that religion and religious rituals should be available when needed.

This, then, also implies a dimension of religious authority. Given Davie's suggestion that the inclination to remain members of the Church of Sweden and thus also to support it financially, and my suggestion that people's positive attitude toward religious services on television is motivated by the latent need for religious competence, there is a dimension of religious authority in this support of the church and of religion on television. However, this dimension of religious authority is secondary to the primary level of authority. The individual has taken over the primary level of religious authority and has full integrity as to whether, and in what way, to express religious and/or spiritual interests. The individual is also in charge of the decision as to when and where to seek religious competence. But when such competence is asked for from the church, given Davie's perspective on vicarious religion, there is a dimension of authority involved, since the individual then would like to know that the church officials know what they are doing. Church officials have vicariously maintained the tradition of how to conduct a funeral the proper way, and thus vicariously have some authority regarding this.

In conclusion, what I propose is to make the conception of religious authority a bit more complex in the specific perspective of Davie's concept of vicarious religion, an idea that became helpful in trying to interpret my own empirical findings. There are (at least) two levels of religious authority, the first being that of the individual, and the second being that of those officials representing the institutions that, implicitly, are supported by the bulk of the general Swedish population.

With this simple example, I want to show that there are good reasons to look a bit more closely at how media scholarship can be fruitful to theories of religion and religious change. I have indicated that the study of attitudes toward the media can help us to explore a recent and important theory within the sociology of religion put forth by a prominent scholar in the field. It allows for specific questions, but also for continued theoretical reflection. Thus I have tried to demonstrate the fruitfulness of taking the interplay between studies of media and religion as the point of departure for reflection on religious authority in late modern Sweden.

80

REFERENCES

Bruce, S., & Voas, D. (2010). Vicarious religion: An examination and critique. *Journal of Contemporary Religion*, 25(2), 243–259.

Christensen, H. R. (2012). Mediatization, deprivatization, and vicarious religion: Coverage of religion and homosexuality in the Scandinavian mainstream press. In S. Hjarvard & M. Lövheim (Eds.), *Mediatization and religion: Nordic perspectives* (pp. 63–78). Gothenburg, SE: Nordicom.

Davie, G. (2006). Is Europe an exceptional case? In After secularization, [Special issue]. *Hedgehog Review*, 8(1–2), 23–34.

Davie, G. (2007). Vicarious religion: A methodological challenge. In N. T. Ammerman (Ed.), *Everyday religion: Observing modern religious lives* (pp. 21–36). Oxford, UK: Oxford University Press.

Davie, G. (2010). Vicarious religion: A response. *Journal of Contemporary Religion*, 25(2), 261–266.

Heelas, P., & Woodhead, L. (2005). *The spiritual revolution: Why religion is giving way to spirituality*. Malden, MA: Blackwell.

Hjarvard, S., & Lövheim, M. (Eds.) (2012). *Mediatization and religion: Nordic perspectives*. Gothenburg, SE: Nordicom.

Hoover, S. M., & Clark, L. S. (Eds.) (2002). *Practicing religion in the age of the media: Explorations in media, religion, and culture*. New York, NY: Columbia University Press.

Hoover, S. M., & Lundby, K. (Eds.) (1997). *Rethinking media, religion, and culture*. Thousand Oaks, CA: Sage.

Kurkiala, M. (2010). Vi bär på en vilja som inte är vår egen [We carry a will that is not our own]. In H. Liljenström & A. Linderman (Eds.), *Bortom tro och vetande: Tankar från en dialog* [Beyond faith and science: Thoughts from a dialogue] (pp. 42–54). Stockholm, SE: Carlsson.

Lynch, G., Mitchell, J., & Strhan, A. (Eds.) (2011). *Religion, media, and culture: A reader*. London, UK: Routledge.

Mitchell, J., & Marriage, S. (Eds.) (2003). *Mediating religion: Conversations in media, religion, and culture*. London, UK: T&T Clark.

Pettersson, P. (2013). *Utmaningar för Svenska kyrkans identitet* (Challenges to the identity of the Swedish Church). Karlstad, SE: Karlstad stift.

Sumiala-Seppänen, J., Lundby, K., & Salokangas, R. (Eds.) (2006). *Implications of the sacred in (post)modern media*. Gothenburg, SE: Nordicom.

Taylor, C. (1992). *The ethics of authenticity*. Cambridge, MA: Harvard University Press.

Willander, E. (2014). *What counts as religion in sociology? The problem of religiosity in sociological methodology* (Doctoral dissertation). Uppsala, SE: Uppsala University.

CHAPTER 4

Religious Authority and Social Media Branding in a Culture of Religious Celebrification

Pauline Hope Cheong

"Follow me on Twitter!" is an expression favored by digitally connected contemporaries. In fact, "Connect with us" and "Follow me on . . ." are increasingly common appeals made on digital media. And yet, as social media marketing develops, how are clergy as spiritual role models and leaders of local congregations responding to such calls to develop an online following as they work and live in digitally mediated environments?

Over the years, American religious organizations have sought to increase their followings by reaching out to external audiences and competing internally among their own faith traditions as members more frequently change spiritual affiliations (Wuthrow, 1994). Like their "secular" counterparts, religious organizations are subject to market forces and must access and manage their resources from the external environment to survive in the "religious marketplace" (Finke & Stark, 1988). Without a state-sponsored religion, rivalry among churches can be intense given the largely unregulated religious sphere characterized by competing secularization, globalizations, pluralism, and privatization trends (Kale, 2004). As Twitchell (2004) observed in *Branded Nation*, "If you want to succeed in the American market, you'd better make church compelling" (p. 56). Today, in light of social media and personal branding, Twitchell's observation could be more fittingly updated to read, If churches want to succeed, they'd better make church *leaders* appealing.

Yet, despite the burgeoning interest in social media and transformative buzzwords like "read-write," "user-generated content," and "participatory information sharing," little research has examined how spiritual leaders are engaging social media to build credibility, community, and ontological security to ensure consistency in practices that give meaning to people's everyday lives, where stable views of the world are constantly under siege (Giddens, 1991). Moreover, recent observations in computer-mediated-communication research, including the "mediatization" of society, are associated with the pluralization of lifeworlds and loss of control over traditional beliefs and practices that affect the ability of institutional religion to define social realities (Hjarvard, 2008). Mediatization has been conceived as a meta-process that shapes contemporary society, along with individualism, globalization, and commercialization (Lundby, 2009). However, this perspective largely negates the agency of spiritual leaders to gain significance in the public sphere through the provision of moral guidance and symbolic content to maintain an active and secure presence in civil society (Lövheim, 2011). As I have noted elsewhere, few scholars have developed conceptual frameworks for studying mediated religious authority, let alone empirically investigated the accomplishment of their authority on digital and social media platforms (Cheong, 2011).

This essay discusses the discursive nature of religious authority and examines how pastors of megachurches construct their authority on Twitter, as part of their multimodal communication strategy to create a personal brand identity. Recently the rise of such "megachurches" has shone the spotlight on a market-savvy class of leaders called "pastor-preneurs" (Twitchell, 2007) who lead large Protestant religious organizations of more than two thousand people in their worship services weekly (Thumma, Travis, & Bird, 2005). These religious organizations have ascended in numbers and influence in the last decade, with currently more than 1,300 megachurches in the United States alone. Their distinctive size and burgeoning growth have stoked debate about the role of the "seeker-sensitive," "distributed" church in general and the commodified, corporatized "McChurch" in particular (White & Yeats, 2009).

Pastors of megachurches have gained so much media publicity that they have been labeled as celebrities (Cooke, 2008) and holy mavericks (Lee & Sinitiere, 2009). Under these circumstances, their leadership practices are an interesting window into the ways voluntary organizations face mounting entrepreneurial pressures to market themselves and reorganize their work by authoring and disseminating content across multiple print and electronic media.

To understand the ways that pastors are discursively branded as celebrities, this essay first draws on a multidisciplinary body of recent literature in marketing, organizational communication, and new media studies to highlight the pivotal role of communication in the construction of religious authority. To comprehend further the operations of these social media pastor-preneurs, this article presents examples of multiple ways these leaders engage in strategic communication via microblogging in order to establish their authority. Here, the empirical focus is on Twitter, one of the most popular microblogging tools, whereby users compose brief multimedia updates and send them via cross-platform mobile messaging and web-based applications like text messaging, instant messaging, and e-mail, or on the web.

As the construction of a carefully crafted and necessarily condensed version of their brand identity is not without ambivalence and paradoxes, this essay will conclude by critically examining the tensions that are operant in strategic arbitration. These tensions include the dialectical interplay between autonomy-community, confession-constrain, and differences-similarities for priests working in mediated spheres.

Given developments in the "corporate colonialization" of everyday life (Deetz, 1992), this essay has significant implications for faith organizations and other civic institutions with regard to their internal organizational set-up and external promotion, particularly as the unprecedented numbers of religious resources online compete for the psyche and pocketbooks of seekers and believers (Serazio, 2009). Examining the microblogging practices of prominent religious leaders offers insights into new online cross-media publishing cultures and the cocreation of faith communities, in addition to illuminating how religious authority is built and maintained. Beyond spiritual organizations, this essay also has implications for authorities in other voluntary and corporate settings, at a time when people's spiritual needs are becoming more prominent than ever (Fogel, 2000), prompting leadership to communicate via motivational storytelling of vision and a higher purpose (Driscoll & McKee, 2007) to instill a sense of spiritual calling, membership, and loyalty (Fry, 2003).

THE COMMUNICATIVE CONSTITUTION OF RELIGIOUS AUTHORITY

As I have reviewed elsewhere, the relationship between the Internet and religious authority may be characterized by the logics of disjuncture and displacement, and the logics of continuity and complementarity (Cheong, 2012a). The first is rooted in the earlier emphasis on the Internet as a decentralized and free space. A dominant conceptualization is that forms of religious authority are altered by digital technologies, which are perceived to disrupt and displace traditional faith doctrines and domains, often embedded in forms of hierarchical communication. More recent research studies have sought to situate religious authority among older media and faith infrastructures. The Internet may have, to some extent, facilitated changes in the personal and organizational structures by which religious leaders operate. But accommodative and mediated practices by some clergy may enable them to regain the legitimacy and trust necessary to operate in the religious sphere.

Specifically, I have proposed that key to understanding contemporary religious authority is the recognition of its discursive, relational, and emergent nature (Cheong, Huang, & Poon, 2011b). As Bruce Lincoln (1994) notes, religious authority is actualized by the "perceived or institutionally ascribed asymmetry between speaker and audience that permits certain speakers to command not just the attention but the confidence, respect, and trust of their audience, or—an important proviso—to make audiences act as if this were so" (p. 4). In the same vein, communication scholars have argued that authority is cocreated and maintained in dynamic interactions between leaders and followers that acknowledge and conversationally manifest the authority (Cheong, Huang, & Poon, 2011a; Taylor & Van Every, 2011). Accordingly, religious authority is approached as an order and quality of communication and, as such, can be analyzed as discursive exchanges embedded in everyday interactions.

In light of changing information architecture, religious authority today involves expansion of communicative competency or "strategic arbitration," which includes skills of managing and reconstructing knowledge norms from competing sources online. Digital and social media use may have, to a certain degree, facilitated changes in the personal and organizational basis by which religious leaders operate, but many priests are appropriating new patterns of interactions, including computer-mediated communication, to relegitimize and construct new practices and patterns of authority. As I and my colleagues Huang and Poon (2011b) have noted:

> Despite their changing roles, many pastors are pragmatic and view communication technologies as a means to relegitimize authority. By acting as strategic arbiters of fragmented expertise, the epistemic authority of leaders is reinforced through the social

production and reproduction of religious realities for their members. Moreover, while access to media resources may contract leaders' capacity to speak, they also valorize the character of authority as leaders secure their autonomy by revising their social identity to reflect more inclusive forms of authority relationships. This does not imply epistemic dilution but rather the reassertion of trust among members, and thereby epistemic standards through arbitration. Furthermore, to counter deprofessionalism, some leaders have been able to grow their media representation and influence through practices online (e.g., sermon publication and webcast productions) that function as authority markers. In addition, because effective exercise of authority depends on clergy's management of a social division of communication relations, acquisition of new epistemic functions through strategic arbitration in social media strengthens normative regulation of power by aligning epistemic knowledge to members' understanding of religious norms. (p. 954)

Prior multi-year, multi-method research studies suggest that rather than force a debate over who is an authority in an informational age, Christian pastors' and Buddhist priests' response has been to act in authority through the construction of norms of credibility in navigating online resources, blogs, or social networking sites. Leaders and laity are encouraged to enter into agreements characterized not solely by dogmatic pronouncements but also by clergy's competencies to connect interactively and encourage their members to adopt a more reflexive approach to learning (Cheong, Huang, & Poon, 2011a).

Other scholars have similarly recognized religious authority as being jointly performed by organizational leaders' and members' situated interactions in rites and rituals in material and digital spaces perceived to be sacred. Lee (2009), for instance, illustrated how Won Buddhist priests have created blogs on the South Korean social networking site Cyworld for self-cultivation, empowerment, and the development of leader-member relationships. These blogs were used to demystify the ideal image of a pure and pious priest, depict the priests' accommodation and loyalty amid gendered organizational norms, and "indirectly deliver" sermons.

Furthermore, as we have pointed out in our anthology *Digital Religion, Social Media and Culture*, several studies appear to highlight multiple changes in the modes of authorial performances as spiritual leaders renegotiate the authority they now seek on social media and offline networks, including new institutional practices (Cheong & Ess, 2012). Notably in our volume, Lomborg and Ess (2012) observed in their case study how the presence of a Danish church on Facebook was praised by its members in terms of the "brand value" for being "progressive," and Musa and Ibrahim (2012) called for deeper understanding of church "brandversations" and the interactions that shape the identity and perception of religious organizations as distinctive, cultural brand communities.

These studies, taken together, illustrate the importance of understanding the communicative constitution of religious authority, where authority is expressed through discourse that not merely describes or reports but impels and establishes "precedence" or hierarchy, what Taylor (2011) calls a "performative" rather than "constative" view of communication where roles and status distinctions are contested and sustained in ongoing negotiations. Accordingly, the analytic focus shifts to the continuous process of *authoring* of persons and members of an organization, which enables organizational purpose and identity to be coherently composed. This conceptualization also implies that authority may be distributed or "spectral" in the sense that sources of authority need not be physically present in the same locale in order for authority to be established, since persuasive conversations work to enact their presence in their absence (Brummans, Hwang, & Cheong, 2013; Fairhurst & Cooren, 2009). In turn, within a mediated society, clergy have to manage new spaces of persuasion arising from multiple sources of issuances of authority online. Understanding the communicative constitution of religious authority thus prompts further research into the ways social media communication facilitates the branding of religious clergy.

PASTOR.COM: BRANDING IN THE RELIGIOUS MARKETPLACE

Competition and rivalry have historically existed in religious spheres or the marketplace, whose economy comprises current and potential followers (demand) and organizations (suppliers) seeking to serve it (Finke & Stark, 1988) with supernaturally based compensators generally bundled with temporal rewards (Stark & Bainbridge, 1987). The strategic management perspective to the study of religious organizations, for example, highlights the importance of optimum product offerings and target market segments to achieve competitive advantages relative to other organizations (Miller, 2002). Yet the corporate-inspired discourse of branding religious leaders for organizational growth, particularly in social media spaces, remains under-examined.

According to James Twitchell (2004), branding is at heart a communication process that involves strategic narratives. In particular, the marketing of megachurches involves a process of storytelling whereby successful churches self-consciously use commercial narrative techniques to make their ideological points and distribute their services to generate cultural capital (Twitchell, 2007).

One form of cultural capital is the social construction of leaders' very identities. Organizational communication scholars argue that an increasingly important product of organizing is a particular self. Organizational discourses work to create, regulate, and control identities through communicative practices, including defining the person directly, providing a vocabulary of motives, explicating moral values, and articulating group categorization and affiliation (Alvesson & Willmott, 2002). The process of "making" these selves occurs through everyday, face-to-face, and mediated organizational cultural practices. The sharing of organizational stories, the celebrating of heroes and heroines, the performance of rituals, and the production and consumption of organizational symbols all work in concert to articulate a preferred organizational self (Tracy & Trethewey, 2005), a "personal brand" (Lair, Sullivan, & Cheney, 2005). This is true for corporations and, increasingly, for the leaders of religious organizations.

Strikingly, strong and persuasive discourse that is religiously tinted has recently surfaced to endorse the adoption of interactive social media for church marketing and the advancement of its outreach and missions, as evinced in expressively titled publications like *The Reason Your Church Must Twitter*, *The Blogging Church*, and *The Wired Church 2.0*. In particular, much impetus is given to Christian pastors to use social media to enact and extend their authority, which brings about attendant responsibilities to perform a crafted and condensed version of themselves online.

According to the prominent faith and nonprofit organization consultant Phil Cooke (2008), religious branding involves the expression of multiple "tenets of brand faith," including the creation story of the church, its creed, icons, and rituals with the usage of sacred words via multiple media forms (pp. 71–81). Specifically, key to successful (read large and growing) ministries is the "personal branding" of the pastor for prominent media outreach. He writes, "In many cases, we choose to focus our branding on the pastor or ministry leader, not just the church or ministry itself. . . . Especially when it comes to preaching and teaching ministries, in most cases we've discovered that people tune in to hear that pastor's teaching; so in branding a national media ministry, we usually focus on the personality that leads that ministry. There's no question that we live in a culture of Christian celebrity" (p. 92).

It is pertinent to note in the above extract how ministry success is directly attributed to the pastor, or more specifically to the pastor's projected "personality" in a mediated culture of the "Christian celebrity." The construction of the branded pastor-preneur is perceived to be essential for the development of "fundraising, partnership or resource relationships," given the public pressures that are deemed to place considerable demands on the spiritual head, who must, in turn, maintain a charismatic and appealing persona. Cooke (2008) also stresses that, "in the media, people ultimately want a relationship with a person, not a program, a building or a ministry" (p. 95). So it follows that irrespective of product attributes, church brandversations should elicit an audience response to and promote consumer identification with a persona and lifestyle that differentiates a pastor's products from a competitor's offerings.

In this discourse, the responsibility of a contemporary religious leader is, therefore, to engage vigorously in self-branding. This form of branding is presented as the creation of a new, innovative, and memorable identity because "in a media-driven culture, bring different is everything" (Cooke, 2008, p. 101). As Cooke states, "God gave you unique DNA, so your job is to discover how your unique gifts and talents can differentiate your ministry from everyone else's" (p. 102). In other words, successful product differentiation in the case of religious leaders is proposed to encompass a significant cross-media identity marketing campaign, showcasing "an overarching theme in their life and ministry" (p. 17).

In short, the brand for religious leaders is their strategic narrative, "the story that surrounds who you are—a story that creates focus for your ministry" (Cooke, 2008, p. 19). Furthermore, prominent ministry leaders are listed as brand examples and model representatives of what it means to lead a booming, life-changing organization; for instance, "Billy Graham is the *salvation* guy. Robert Schuller is the *motivation* guy. . . . James Dobson is the *family* guy. . . . Joel Osteen is the *inspiration* guy" (p. 18). In this way, as explicated below, for megachurches seeking to expand their missionary charge, the building of a distinctive pastor-preneur bio is positioned to be crucial for the strengthening of loyalty and devotion to the church.

Similarly, the branding of religious clergy is promoted in Anthony Coppedge's (2009) e-book *The Reason Your Church Must Twitter: Making Your Ministry Contagious*. In the chapter "Twitter for Pastors," clergy are exhorted to regularly microblog to "help people to better to [sic] relate to them as a person. . . . Simply post a Tweet and, in the process, give people a view into your life and your world."

Here, regular social media updates by pastors are encouraged to facilitate the "humanizing" of their leadership, a component which is seen to be the "missing element in the connection between church leadership and its congregants." Although Coppedge writes that the adoption of microblogging is "far from creating a pop-culture personality," a number of recurring statements in his book, which has been endorsed by prominent megachurch pastors, advocate brand leadership as the strategic management of media, attuned to our image-conscious times. The purported effect of the microblogging, electronically savvy pastor is to build his or her authority via an enhanced public image, as "the connection people want to feel with their pastor and pastoral staff cannot be overstated."

For example, lunch invitation tweets to staff by a senior pastor are recommended to "reinforce *the public perception* that [a pastor] *really does pour* into the team of leaders at the church" (emphasis added). Hence, microblogging works to help clergy achieve a preferred organizational self whereby they communicate their identities to fit prevailing laity and market expectations and demands. As such, as we shall see below, clergy branding entails continuous updates and self-monitoring, even adherence to a strict regime of authoring updates and posts of multimedia materials, accomplished on Twitter by deadlines indicated by a planned "content calendar," a tool recommended on churchmarketingsucks.com.

In sum, organizational communication research and church media marketing discourse have recently focused on occupational self-branding, accomplished in part via strategic narratives on social media. For faith brands involving the creation and performance of leaders' identity, this raises the question of how these clergy perform their authority on Twitter.

@GODVERTISER: MICROBLOGGING CLERGY PRACTICES

Research for this essay is drawn from an examination of branding practices on Twitter by looking at the profiles of top twittering clergy, and an analysis of tweets from clergy of the largest megachurches in the United States.[1] In what follows, I will discuss how microblogging clergy practices encompass at least five of the following forms of communication as strategic arbitration by pastors to shape informational and interpersonal outcomes such that they sustain personal legitimacy and/or organizational practices and hierarchy.

The first practice concerns the naming of Twitter accounts and the creation of personal bios. When opening a Twitter account, all users are

asked to pick a handle username and accompanying URL (http://twitter
.com/*username*) as well as compose a bio (a short personal descriptor of
160 characters or fewer to define who they are on Twitter). Among the
twittering clergy from the top fifty megachurches, their handles and bios
appear to reinforce their brand identity across media, and/or to rouse interest as part of creating a memorable identity.

For instance, several of these accounts have usernames that are a shorthand for the actual names of their creators, who are prominent authors,
broadcasters, speakers, and performers; for instance, @MarcosWitt (the
four-time Latin Grammy award–winning Christian singer and pastor), @
MarkBatterson (author of multiple books and well-known blogger), and
@robertfurrow (Christian television and radio host). It demonstrates how
these pastors are acutely cognizant of multimedia platforms to build distinctive brands, which in turn strengthens their reputation and authority
by allowing them to tell a consistent story. In this way, microblogging
handles serve to raise the profile of these pastors and consolidate their
brand identity.

Another popular form of Twitter handle for top clergy is portman-
teaus, which are catchy words formed from combining two (or more)
words (typically combining sounds and meanings) into one new word.
These neologisms include @godvertiser (a handle for Kenny Jahng, the
media and innovation pastor of Liquid Church, which combines the words
"God" and "advertiser") and @Leadershipfreak (the username for pastor
Dan Rockwell, a linguistic play on the term "Jesus freak"), which serve as
attention-grabbing, unusual hooks to contribute to the creation of a unique
identity.

Moreover, an examination of the Twitter bios accompanying the handles reveals how many of these are constituted to be deliberately engaging,
thought-provoking, and memorable. Table 4.1 illustrates some of these
arresting bios (emphasis added). It is interesting to note how some of these
condensed descriptors are composed to seem amusing or facetious, even
to the point of self-deprecation.

In many of these leadership bios, clergy label themselves as persons of
no importance, influence, or power (e.g., a "nobody," "pilgrim," "Sinner," and
"gardener") and/or playing ordinary relational roles like "loving husband,"
"Father of 5," and "happily married." Several of these bios also include peculiar and whimsical information, like "I dont wear socks," "Massive Consumer
of Breakfast Cereal," and even include information of a belittling nature
("uber-horrible golfer"). Given the national, even international renown of
some of these pastors, it is not difficult to note the irony of these abbreviated

TABLE 4.1 EXEMPLARS OF PASTOR TWITTER USERNAMES AND BIOS

Username	Clergy	Bio
@RickWarren	Rick Warren	*I dont wear socks.* I mentor young leaders & lead the PEACE Plan serving the poor & sick globally. I love Saddleback, serve pastors & write DAILY HOPE. *I like you.*
@PastorMark	Mark Driscoll	*A nobody trying to tell everybody about Somebody.*
@ScottWilliams	Scott Williams	Husband, Father, Pastor, Speaker, Author, CEO of @_NxtLevel. *Al Gore invented the internet & I invented the #FistBump on Twitter!* || #OKC
@Leadershipfreak	Dan Rockwell	*My dream is when people see me they think that guy made my life better.* Blogger, *learner*, MBA, *happily married.*
@aheartforgod	Mike	*A pilgrim journeying to the Celestial City. Won't you join me?* Pastor Mike is making the most of web technologies to encourage disciples. (Matt 28:19)
@kurtwvs	Kurt von Schleicher	Speaker | Vertical Motivator | Connector | *Been called an UBER-HORRIBLE GOLFER, a 1 on 1 people-fishin-coach of sorts, HEY U!* www.gplus.to/BeReal
@chuckbalsamo	Chuck Balsamo	DAILY blogger, *runner, gardener*, loving husband, father, *friend, encourager*, innovative pastor, conference speaker, & best selling author TO BE!
@scottythom	Scott Thomas	Pastor of Ministry Development, The Journey Church. Founder of Gospel Coach. Husband. Father. Friend. Author. Teacher. *Disciple. Redeemed Sinner.*
@chaseathompson	Chase A. Thompson	Husband, Father of 5, Pastor, Adjunct Professor, Broadcaster, *Massive Consumer of Breakfast Cereal.* Check out our show Faith Today below or visit us at Agape!

self-descriptors, which try to portray them as the proverbial "little guy." In fact, humor is achieved by way of contrast, as most of these bios do not contain the traditional occupational titles of "preacher," "senior pastor," or "spiritual director." In this sense, a connection to the ordinary helps to "humanize" these leading authorities and render them more accessible and appealing online, despite their large, often impersonal, globetrotting, multimedia ministry.

In a related manner, another way that clergy are branded on Twitter is through strategic promotions, whereby microblogging is used to help advertise or inadvertently disclose specifics about their products and face-to-face appearances. Consider, for example, the following tweets:

> Keith Butler (@KeithaButler) on 3 Jun 2010 at 4:10 PM: Start your day w/Fresh Water Daily Devotional. Prepare to reign as a champion everyday w/the Word. Order your copy now!

> Jud Wilhite (@JudWilhite) on 5 Jun 2010 at 9:04 AM: Central's [church] new iPhone, iPod touch & iPad app is available for download at the iTunes App Store! Experience services, videos, music & more.

> Greg Laurie (@greglaurie) on 1 Jun 2010 at 10:17 AM: New blog post: Do not be afraid! http://bit.ly/bbokzr

> Joel Osteen (@JoelOsteen) on 15 Jul 2010 at 1:21 PM: Are there things in your heart that you're not pursuing because you're afraid? Read Joel's blog, Now is the Time: http://ow.ly/2c4C4

> Craig Groeschel (@craiggroeschel) on 23 Aug 2010 at 5:23 PM: Just found out Walmart picked up my book "The Christian Atheist" (in 868 stores). Praying it impacts many people!

> Creflo Dollar (@Creflo_Dollar) on 20 Aug 2010 at 10:36 AM: #Free Friday! win a copy of the new book! Post Your #IMWinning testimony. 5 will be RT'ed & post on Creflo's FB fan page. 1 winner an HR!

Clergy tweets serve cross-marketing purposes when microblogging is used to publicize their latest products, including books, newsletters, blogs, and other media. In the same way, tweets are also published to promote related book tours, television appearances, and radio interviews, as evident in the following:

> Kerry Shook (@KerryShook) on 23 Aug 2010 at 7:14 PM: Tonight on NBC local 2 news Chris and I talk about Woodlands Church leadings National Facebook Fast on Aug 25

> Kerry Shook (@KerryShook) on 19 Aug 2010 at 8:01 PM: Just informed LOVE AT LAST SIGHT is #3 USA Today and Wallstreet Journal bestseller list nonfiction.

> Creflo Dollar (@Creflo_Dollar) on 27 Sept 2010 at 12:30 PM: Come join us 4 the New York Book Signing Event for Creflo's new book Winning in Troubled Times this Thursday! 9/30 7pm

Publicity for the clergy brand is further amplified through the visible practice of mentioning or tagging, where highly followed clergy reference the tweets and products of other prominent clergy. This practice maintains the power differential between priest and laity, and it further establishes clergy authority by publicly demonstrating their relationship with, endorsement of, and inspired affiliation to other clergy celebrities. For instance:

> Jonathan Falwell (@jonathanfalwell) on 7 Jun 2010 at 10:17 PM: Working my way through "Surprised by Grace" by @PastorTullian and finding it a great read!

> Ronnie Floyd (@ronniefloyd) on 10 Jul 2010 at 12:26 PM: All Pastors and Church leaders: read "Transformational Church" by Thom Rainer & Ed Stetzer, I just finished it & it is a super read

> Jud Wilhite (@JudWilhite) on 12 Jul 2010 at 12:35 PM: Just sent an endorsement for @kayWarren1 upcoming release "Say Yes to God." Very. Powerful. Love her heart and passion!

> Craig Groeschel (@craiggroeschel) on 29 Sept 2010 at 6:41 AM: Congrats to @AndyStanley on his new book, "The Grace of God!" Life changing book! http://tinyurl.com/2ed15fr

In a related vein, pastors who spend time with other highly followed pastors, famous business leaders, and sports stars also mention it in their tweets, including posting personal pictures and videos of the event. For example:

> Chris Hodges (@Chris_Hodges) on 3 Jun 2010 at 7:23 AM: At a round-table at the Chick-fil-a headquarters in Atlanta. Ed Bastian, Pres. of Delta speaking. http://tweetphoto.com/25248862

> Jack Graham (@jackngraham) on 12 Jul 2010 at 7:38 PM: Watching Homerun Derby and remembering Josh Hamiltons awesome display of power at Yankee stadium 08 and the way Josh honored Jesus.

> Jack Graham (@jackngraham) on 25 Sept 2010 at 1:16 PM: Been a great week with a highlight being hearing and interviewing NFL Hall of Famer Jim Kelly & wife Jill re their faith at PowerLunch

Besides copresence in physical networks, the practice of name-dropping may also work for other pseudo-, imaginary, or inspirational affiliations, as

Religious Authority and Social Media Branding

in this tweet by pastor Andy Stanley: "Steve Jobs [CEO of Apple] forgot to announce the launch of my June Leadership Podcast! I guess he ran out of time." In this way, tweets serve to facilitate a celebrification of these clergy, akin to the interest and attention paid to celebrities in other occupational profiles.

Third, microblogging is performed to encourage "tweetups" and religious services in church or church-affiliated events. Tweets help to promote interactions in physical sacred spaces of ceremonies (e.g., sermons, workshops, regular study group meetings) that amplify social roles in order to legitimize the epistemic status of clergy. These include:

> James MacDonald (@jamesmacdonald) on 4 Jun 2010 at 7:18 AM: Final sermon prep for Revelation 17. Read it before you come to Harvest [Church] this weekend.

> Chris Hodges (@Chris_Hodges) on 4 Jun 2010 at 7:04 PM: Message for Sunday finished. Excited about the new #OnePrayer series and the launch of our summer small groups.

> Ron Carpenter (@roncarpenter) on 5 Jun 2010 at 9:16 AM: Got something for you tomorrow..... I can't wait to preach this one! If you [are] ready for some word, give me a holla!

> Ronnie Floyd (@ronniefloyd) on 5 Jun 2010 at 9:41 AM: Looking forward to preaching Sunday from Galatians 5, hope you are with us.

> Charles Blake (@BishopCEBlake) on 30 May 2010 at 9:18 AM: We are live! Don't Miss the Dynamic Praise & Worship of West Angeles Church! Login & fellowship live!!

> Tommy Barnett (@tommybarnett) on 11 Jul 2010 at 4:14 PM: I am hoping to see you tonight @phoenixfirst when @lwbarrnett gives a powerful dramatic sermon called made alive @7pm

Here, strategic narratives that weave online and offline religious practices counter a sense of deterritorialization by offering a display of clergy's authoritative performances online. Trust in the epistemic authority of church leaders, in turn, is reinforced through the social production and reproduction of religious realities for their members. This creates a sense of epistemic coherence among seekers and followers in highly mediated societies.

Fourth, microblogging allows pastors to perform their authority visibly by strategically reporting "backstage" (Goffman, 1959) and more intimate aspects of their daily work and family life to support the creation of their branded identity. Clergy tweets, for instance, may be crafted to mention or emphasize the spirited, compassionate, and arduous nature of their ministry. These communiqués serve not to only describe and inform but also to impel and perform religious authority. Clergy describe their daily governance and range of leadership activities, within organizational practices to promote social solidarity and recognition of the hectic and challenging dimensions of their work. This practice may be observed, for example, through the following tweets from Jud Wilhite (@JudWilhite; emphasis added):

> On 22 Aug 2010 at 3:41 PM: *Talked to hundreds this wkend.* So many stories of God's grace. 1 word most defines the heart of Central [church] people--gratitude to God & church.

> On 1 Jun 2010 at 12:02 AM: Bedside bk "Lessons from San Quentin" by friend Bill Dallas Grt stuff! *Need a clone to get everything done tomorrow.*

> On 27 Sept 2010 at 11:33 AM: *Long great weekend + late night* with @theideacamp speakers = @Lori_Wilhite [wife] bringing me coffee in bed at 9:30 to gently wake me up!

> On 23 Aug 2010 at 11:09 AM: It's been a while since I had the *weekend hangover after speaking 5 times. Feels strangely good to be wiped out from ministry!*

Here, regular updates on physical and emotional demands of ministry work, including international and cross-country travels for missionary trips, late-night hospital visitations, and frequent sermon deliveries to multiple groups, help portray the pastor as a devoted spiritual leader, compatible perhaps in many aspects with a preferred religious organizational self. Consider another example, of how the following tweet by pastor Jack Schaap is both informative of his overseas mission and performative as it establishes his leadership role in both equipping and teaching the church: "Took 150 'God pods' with me to Ghana. Terrific device: 160 hours of Bible teaching on a solar-powered, waterproof iPod. For use in villages."

Moreover, clergy who post their prayers and intercessions as a form of public communication, as opposed to a more private and personal petition to God, use microblogging to provide another glimpse of their everyday organizing and persona. Examples include tweets like "praying for your family," "Thanks for covering for me. Praying for you," "I will be praying for a mighty move of God's peace in your life!" "So sorry for ur loss. U r in our prayers. Thinking of u in this season." Tweeting prayers like the ones below also reveal clergy attempts to model a prayerful lifestyle in response to personal struggles, as seen in the following examples:

> Eddie L. Long (@BishopEddieLong) on 1 Jun 2010 at 11:07 PM: Dear God, you instill in all your children to forgive. But the pain is in trying to forget. Please heal my memory! Thanks in advance!
>
> Ronnie Floyd (@ronniefloyd) on 15 Jul 2010 at 7:25 PM: Praying..
>
> RT@MattChandler74: There'll b a day when there is no cancer, hurt, fear or death...until then we have 1 place of refuge & hope...

Here, the articulation of their prayers and praises, and intercession on behalf of their church members and followers, affirms their authority, as it situates their guidance and management response in relation to favorable or unfavorable circumstances.

Lastly, clergy-appropriate microblogging for pedagogical purposes, to directly instruct or indirectly impart a lesson, oftentimes quoting famous past Christian thinkers (e.g., Martin Luther and C. S. Lewis) and scripture to increase the legitimacy of their epistemic authority. For example, Rick Warren (@RickWarren) frequently tweets what might be construed as mini-sermons or brief spiritual lessons by accompanying a precept with a Bible reference:

> On 5 Jun 2010 at 4:38 PM: God works when u wait. "The vision awaits its appointed time. If it seems slow, wait for it! It will surely come" Hab 2:3
>
> On 12 Jul 2010 at 8:14 PM: "What I tell you in the dark, tell others when light comes" Mt10:27 If U are in darkness now—listen for God's whisper!
>
> On 11 Jul 2010 at 9:54 PM: Integrity is like virginity. Once you give it up it's gone for good. "The dishonest are ruined by their own duplicity" Pr11:3

As observed above, using all caps for emphasis to capture the audience's attention helps clergy to communicate religious knowledge claims and impose their point of view. In addition, clergy may also engage in individual instruction by using scripture to inspire or boost their teaching, which helps reproduce a communicative framework that facilitates and strengthens expectations of authorization. Legitimation is achieved through the alignment with scriptural authority, often drawing on clergy's skills to apply scripture to new circumstances and to reinforce traditions. Using the DM (direct message) function, clergy can also send messages in the form of prayers and Bible verses to their individual followers to affirm and encourage them.

Furthermore, tweets help clergy to build a notable brand identity by allowing them to preach indirectly. For example, many post rhetorical questions, startling statistics or facts, and catchy, open-ended statements:

> Keith A. Butler (@KeithaButler) on 3 Jun 2010 at 3:00 PM: Examine yourself. Are you obeying God w/your body, finances, relationships? Do you pray for your enemies? Your children?

> Rick Warren (@RickWarren) on 4 Jun 2010 at 4:26 PM: servant leaders constantly ask: How do my actions & words hinder or frustrate those working with me? What's it like for them?

> Ed Young (@EdYoung) on 16 Aug 2010 at 8:39 AM: Life is a sum total of our yeses and no's. What are you saying yes and no to?

Equally significant is how some of these confrontational and provocative tweets serve as "faith memes" (Cheong, 2012b), or replications that spread and enlarge informational networks. By eliciting followers' retweets with a viral-like dissemination across social media platforms, these tweets help clergy gain an even larger following. Such tweets, which appear to be broad and less dogmatic, may help evoke a more reflexive response, in recognition of the need to appeal to followers who may no longer easily submit to ministers as experts with epistemic warrant. Thus, to be of epistemic value, some tweets are phrased as questions with no fixed answer, to increase the probability of their acceptance. This, in turn, enables microblogging clergy to maintain a productive authority role by expanding the scope of their expertise to serve as guides and hosts on the proverbial spiritual journey.

CONCLUSION

The ascendency of digital and social media has profound implications for processes of power, reconfiguring institutional structures and relationships between leaders and members. Communication scholars have, for some time, been discussing the effects of new authorial influence and branding dynamics in corporate enterprises, yet the debate deserves wider consideration in voluntary and religious settings as well.

This essay discussed how religious authority is discursively constructed, illustrating this performative communication approach with microblogging practices by clergy of megachurches. An examination of pastor tweets revealed at least five methods of strategic arbitration whereby social media are appropriated to gain a following and reinforce a distinctive and memorable brand identity. It is observed that tweets work in concert with the larger communication and digital media landscape to sustain pastoral legitimacy and organizational hierarchy. Within a culture of celebrification, tweeting by clergy helps in the continuous authoring of clergy authority, by articulating a preferred self and personal brand.

Yet the construction of a carefully crafted and necessarily condensed version of their brand identity is not without ambivalence and tensions. Potential dialectics operant in the strategic arbitration of microblogging clergy include confession-constraint, differences-similarities, and privilege-disadvantage. Specifically, recognition of the dialectical interplay of confession-constraint highlights the tension of how much clergy can and should be sharing on social media. On the one hand, clergy branding involves frequent updates and a dynamic public sharing of their activities, whereabouts, even personal petitions and prayers. On the other hand, the accomplishment of their authority through the creation of a preferred organizational self necessitates reflective responses that may take time to post and carefully edit (or even censor).

Moreover, it is arguable that scripture dictates that some acts of piety and generosity should be kept private, to glorify God and not to elicit attention to self or public commendation. Matthew 6:1–4 (NIV) reads:

> Be careful not to practice your righteousness in front of others to be seen by them. If you do, you will have no reward from your Father in heaven. So when you give to the needy, do not announce it with trumpets, as the hypocrites do in the synagogues and on the streets, to be honored by others. Truly I tell you, they have received their reward in full. But when you give to the needy, do not let your left hand know what your right hand is doing, so that your giving may be in secret. Then your Father, who sees what is done in secret, will reward you.

The above scriptural excerpt employs hyperbole to highlight how secretive charitable giving should be (i.e., in giving we should not even let our left hand know what our right hand is doing) and seems to suggest that clergy should eschew public displays or expression for social approval. Yet it is interesting to note the differing ways in which some clergy tweet about their actions, engage in self-promotions, and broadcast their good deeds (though it is difficult to ascertain from their tweets alone the extent to which their public declarations are an accurate reflection of their works). Consider these two tweets by Rick Warren (@RickWarren), which reflect this dialectic:

> On 21 Aug 2010 at 2:24 PM: Caution for tweeters & bloggers: "You will give an account on judgment day of every careless word you've spoken"—Jesus Mt12:36

> On 27 Sept 2010 at 9:50 PM: Al, we did! Kay [wife] & I personally paid to print 500,000 military edition of Purpose Driven Life [clergy's book] to give to our troops overseas

Thus, contrary to the marketing discourse that advises pastors to "simply post a Tweet," it may be tricky for clergy to discern the appropriateness of their confession and public shout-outs, in light of scripture-inspired injunctions to maintain a humble profile, even secretive service. Therefore, both the confession and constraint aspects of clergy branding emphasize the need for clergy to strategically arbitrate online and offline texts amid competing needs for disclosure and privacy, as they decide if, when, and how to tweet about themselves and their work.

Moreover, although marketing discourse advocates the creation of a unique brand, clergy identity is characterized by both similarities and differences, in that religious leaders are simultaneously similar to and different from one another and their followers. Recognition of the differences-similarities dialectic highlights that it is challenging for clergy to emphasize only their differences and distinctions while trying to appear accessible and relate to everyday human experiences and struggles. Indeed, for some clergy, interspersed among tweets about their work are quotidian updates on their spouses and children that appear to "humanize" them. In addition, marketing discourse advocates the use of microblogging to communicate a unique persona, but it is ironic how, by following the prescriptions of this literature, clergy social media use may result in similar content—for example, in the manner in which many of them use tweets to elicit retweets and to pose open-ended statements and provocative questions.

Finally, recognition of the privilege-disadvantage dialectic points to how microblogging clergy may be simultaneously privileged and disadvantaged because of their age, race, gender, and other identities that influence the construction of their authority. It is notable that many of the top twittering clergy in the United States tend to be male, white, educated, and middle class. The intersection of their privileged identities allows them, in turn, to compose brands that are aligned with elite or aspirational lifestyles, including globetrotting adventures and hobbies that include golfing, live football game attendance, and family vacations. Future research should consider this dialectic in greater detail, to enhance critical understanding about for whom, and under what conditions, clergy authority is performed on social media, as well as to broaden the examination of the discursive construction of religious authority from the viewpoint of spiritual followers and the extent to which they recognize and respond to microblogging clergy practices.

NOTES

1. To determine which pastors' Twitter feeds would be utilized for analysis, the Hartford Institute for Religion Research was consulted (see http://hirr.hartsem.edu/). This site contains a list of the largest churches (megachurches) in the United States based on average worship attendance. The pastors of the top fifty churches were selected, and of these pastors, twenty-six maintained Twitter accounts. Each pastor's Twitter profile was publicly accessible, and tweets were retrieved systematically from June through September 2010. To provide a diverse sample of tweets, the following rotation was used to select tweets for analysis. For June, tweets from the first week (June 1–7, 2010) were selected; for July, tweets from the second week (July 8–15, 2010); for August, tweets from the third week (August 16–23, 2010); and for September, tweets from the fourth week (September 23–30, 2010). This provided a sample of 1,368 tweets. A thematic analysis of the tweets was then conducted using constant comparative methodology (Glaser & Strauss, 1967). Acknowledgment is made to Jimmy Sanderson for his research assistance.

REFERENCES

Alvesson, M., & Willmott, H. (2002). Producing the appropriate individual: Identity regulation as organizational control. *Journal of Management Studies, 39*(5), 619–644.

Brummans, H. J. M., Hwang, J. M., & Cheong, P. H. (2013). Mindful authoring through invocation: Leaders' constitution of a spiritual organization. *Management Communication Quarterly, 27*(3), 346–372.

Cheong, P. H. (2011). Religious leaders, mediated authority, and social change. *Journal of Applied*

Communication Research, 39(4), 452–454.

Cheong, P. H. (2012a). Authority. In H. A. Campbell (Ed.), *Digital religion: Understanding religious practice in new media worlds* (pp. 72–87). New York, NY: Routledge.

Cheong, P. H. (2012b). Twitter of faith: Understanding social media networking and microblogging rituals as religious practices. In P. H. Cheong, P. Fischer-Nielsen, S. Gelfgren, & C. Ess (Eds.), *Digital religion, social media, and culture: Perspectives, practices, futures* (pp. 191–206). New York, NY: Peter Lang.

Cheong, P. H., & Ess, C. (2012). Religion 2.0? Relational and hybridizing pathways in religion, social media, and culture. In P. H. Cheong, P. Fischer-Nielsen, S. Gelfgren, & C. Ess (Eds.), *Digital religion, social media, and culture: Perspectives, practices, futures* (pp. 1–24). New York, NY: Peter Lang.

Cheong, P. H., Huang, S. H., & Poon, J. P. H. (2011a). Cultivating online and offline pathways to enlightenment: Religious authority in wired Buddhist organizations. *Information, Communication, and Society, 14*(8), 1160–1180.

Cheong, P. H., Huang, S. H., & Poon, J .P. H. (2011b). Religious communication and epistemic authority of leaders in wired faith organizations. *Journal of Communication, 61*(5), 938–958.

Cooke, P. (2008). *Branding faith: Why some churches and nonprofits impact culture and others don't*. Ventura, CA: Regal.

Coppedge, A. (2009). *The reason your church must Twitter: Making your ministry contagious*. Retrieved from http://www.twitterforchurches.com/.

Deetz, S. (1992). *Democracy in an age of corporate colonization: Developments in communication and the politics of everyday life*. Albany, NY: SUNY Press.

Driscoll, C., & McKee, M. (2007). Restorying a culture of ethical and spiritual values: A role for leader storytelling. *Journal of Business Ethics, 73*(2), 205–217.

Fairhurst, G. T., & Cooren, F. (2009). Charismatic leadership and the hybrid production of presence(s). *Leadership, 5*(4), 1–22.

Finke, R., & Stark, R. (1988). Religious economies and sacred canopies: Religious mobilization in American cities, 1906. *American Sociological Review, 53*(1), 41–49.

Fogel, R. W. (2000). *The fourth great awakening and the future of egalitarianism*. Chicago, IL: University of Chicago Press.

Fry, L. W. (2003). Toward a theory of spiritual leadership. *Leadership Quarterly, 14*(6), 693–727.

Giddens, A. (1991). *Modernity and self-identity: Self and society in the late modern age*. Cambridge, UK: Polity.

Glaser, B., & Strauss, A. (1967). *The discovery of grounded theory: Strategies for qualitative research*. Chicago, IL: Aldine.

Goffman, E. (1959). *The presentation of self in everyday life*. Garden City, NY: Doubleday Anchor.

Hjarvard, S. (2008). The mediatization of society: A theory of the media as agents of social and cultural change. *Nordicom Review, 29*(2), 105–134.

Kale, S. H. (2004). Spirituality, religion, and globalization. *Journal of Macromarketing, 24*(2), 92–107.

Lair, D. J., Sullivan K., & Cheney, G. (2005). Marketization and the recasting of the professional self: The rhetoric and ethics of personal branding. *Management Communication Quarterly, 18*(3), 307–343.

Lee, J. (2009). Cultivating the self in cyberspace: The use of personal blogs among Buddhist priests. *Journal of Media and Religion, 8*(2), 97–114.

Lee, S., & Sinitiere, P.H. (2009). *Holy mavericks: Evangelical innovators and the spiritual marketplace.* New York, NY: New York University Press.

Lincoln, B. (1994). *Authority: Construction and corrosion.* Chicago, IL: University of Chicago Press.

Lomborg, S., & Ess, C. (2012). "Keeping the line open and warm": An activist Danish church and its presence on Facebook. In P. H. Cheong, P. Fischer-Nielsen, S. Gelfgren, & C. Ess (Eds.), *Digital religion, social media, and culture: Perspectives, practices, futures* (pp. 169–190). New York, NY: Peter Lang.

Lovheim, M. (2011). Mediatisation of religion: A critical appraisal. *Culture and Religion, 12*(2), 153–166.

Lundby, K. (2009). Introduction: "Mediatization" as key. In K. Lundby (Ed.), *Mediatization: Concept, changes, consequences* (pp. 1–18). New York, NY: Peter Lang.

Miller, K. D. (2002). Competitive strategies of religious organizations. *Strategic Management Journal, 23*(5), 435–456.

Musa, B. A., & Ibrahim, M. A. (2012). New media, Wikifaith, and church brandversation: A media ecology perspective. In P. H. Cheong, P. Fischer-Nielsen, S. Gelfgren, & C. Ess (Eds.), *Digital religion, social media, and culture: Perspectives, practices, futures* (pp. 63–80). New York, NY: Peter Lang.

Serazio, M. (2009). Geopolitical proselytizing in the marketplace for loyalties: Rethinking the global gospel of American Christian broadcasting. *Journal of Media and Religion, 8*(1), 40–54.

Stark, R., & Bainbridge, W. S. (1987). *A theory of religion.* New York, NY: Peter Lang.

Taylor, J. R. (2011). Organization as an (imbricated) configuring of transactions. *Organization Studies, 32*(9), 1–22.

Taylor, J. R., & Van Every, E. J. (2011). *The situated organization: Case studies in the pragmatics of communication research.* New York, NY: Routledge.

Thumma, S., Travis, D., & Bird, W. (2005). Megachurches today. *Hartford Institute for Religion Research.* Retrieved from http://hirr.hartsem.edu/megachurch/megastoday2005_summaryreport.html.

Tracy, S. J., & Trethewey, A. (2005). Fracturing the real-self↔fake-self dichotomy: Moving toward crystallized organizational identities. *Communication Theory, 15*(2), 168–195.

Twitchell, J. B. (2004). *Branded nation: The marketing of megachurch, college inc., and museumworld.* New York, NY: Simon & Schuster.

Twitchell, J. B. (2007). *Shopping for God: How Christianity went from in your heart to in your face.* New York, NY: Simon & Schuster.

White, T., & Yeats, J. M. (2009). *Franchising McChurch: Feeding our obsession with easy Christianity.* Colorado Springs, CO: David C. Cook.

Wuthrow, R. (1994). *God and mammon in America.* New York, NY: Free Press.

PART II

Case Studies

CHAPTER 5

Satellite Publics

Moral Identity and New Media in Moroccan Islam

Bahíyyah Maroon

In the socioreligious production of media space in Morocco, we encounter an Islam that runs counter to both anti-Islamist and neo-fundamentalist mythologies of a rigid and archaic faith. Indeed, the mediatized public sphere of today's Morocco evidences Islam's dynamic doxa. In this essay, I examine the interpretative quality of Moroccan Islam found in every-day viewing practices that contribute to the experience and production of mediatized Moroccan social space. It is important to point out that the meaning and form of the mediatized social practices under consideration are always public in a sense: for in contrast to the privacy accorded a non-believer in a secular public—that one is alone when by him- or herself—no such privacy meets the Muslim believer in solitude. One is, in essence, always a member of the public sphere, for one is ever seen by an omnipotent God. In this essay, both domestic and public sites are considered and both are understood as forms of the public sphere in the Muslim nation-state. The production of media space in the Moroccan public sphere calls us to account for a moral negotiation of social practice situated at the interstices of the individual and the shifting yet structured complex of religion. In what follows I will show that the character of Moroccan media space indicates the negotiated limits and striations of Muslim morality in the country. I suggest that it is a practiced and practical morality informed by citizens' positional relationships to Sunni Muslim principles of reason and moral right.

SATELLITES AND SCREENS AND BROADCASTS, OH MY!

In Morocco's economic capital, the city of Casablanca, hundreds of thousands of satellite dishes meld onto built structures. They are stranded on rooftops and top-floor exterior walls of city buildings. They range from a foot and a half in diameter to the size of small spacecraft. These broadcast objects receiving sound and image are so pervasive as to have become a naturalized element of the cityscape's surfaces.[1] These concave dishes are positioned precisely to receive and project new imaginaries of information. Yet these objects provide the very thing that is said to threaten moral society—globally dispersed broadcasts that can tempt the moral subject with windows onto a morally threatening world. In formal and informal interviews with Moroccans, satellite broadcast television was consistently characterized as a medium that contradicts Islamic morality. The majority of urbanites I spoke with expressed the opinion that many of the satellite-driven programming options degrade the moral sturdiness of Moroccan society. Summarizing the majority's opinion, one young man in his mid-twenties declared, "We get all kinds of bad things from the television now. Everyone likes to have more program options than what we got before, sure, but at the same time it's a problem, because we get all the immoral programs of the Europeans."

Ideas and images censored in the national media networks are readily available via the multinational flood of television stations made possible by satellite. Visuals and sound bites of everything from scintillating music videos to Euro porn, American Christian fundamentalists making pleas for money, and conversion-pandering sermons by Shiite clerics, can all be clicked into view on television screens throughout the Sunni Muslim nation. It is this cornucopia of viewing options that inspires the perception of satellite TV as *haram*—forbidden—and as a harbinger of *fitna*—chaos.

The claim that broadcast objects are morally suspect despite their proliferation as elements of the social environment indicates an intriguing disjuncture between the appearance and the opinion of things. The technological thing is potentially morally dangerous, but everybody's got it and everybody wants more. Casablancans, like all Moroccan citizens, could simply not buy the satellite broadcast option, but they do—and in droves. Thus, in the typical household, censored national channels are accessed alongside the 132-plus stations available via satellite subscription. The same majority that decries satellite television also purchases, installs, and maintains paid subscriptions to access it. In urban centers particularly, satellite dishes or *parabols* are regarded not as luxury items, but as household necessities, like stoves and refrigerators. Satellite dishes are as common as the televisions that receive their signal.[2] The question to ask one's neighbor is not when they will buy a dish, but when they intend to upgrade.

I suggest that this situation is not a matter of hypocrisy. Rather, in the difference between the opinion and the presence of the broadcast object we find an integral aspect of Moroccan Islam: an ardent belief that individuals have the right to self-regulate their social practices in accordance with shared understandings of Muslim morality. The right to self-regulation is fundamental to one's pathway to Allah, because among the many requirements to be met by the faithful, it is incumbent on believers to use their faculties wisely as a form of honoring Allah.

In his book *The Culture of Islam*, William Rosen (2002) argues that cultures throughout North Africa and the Middle East, in which Islam is the dominant religion, place an "emphasis on reason, will, and the responsible exercise of choice," which is evidence of "the belief that humans are reasoning creatures and that it is within human power to control the tendency toward forgetfulness [of rightful conduct] and misguided passion that threatens all society with chaos" (p. 117).

The ability to self-regulate viewing practices in accordance with interpretations of Muslim morality is a core assumption buttressing the space between public opinion and the acquisition of satellite broadcast technology. What is intriguing about the uses of satellite broadcast technology here is the degree to which audiences at home and in public spaces utilize the medium not for the illicit, but rather to view programs that express Muslim morality. Channel selection becomes a tool for broadcasting the use of moral reason in social practice. As we will see, what denotes this morality is by no means homogeneous—reliant as it is on individual interpretations of what constitutes right or good conduct. Yet, although variegated in important ways, the standards of morality at work in the production of Moroccan media space have their limits. It is upholding the limits of acceptability that gestures to the effects and practices of self-regulation, marking Moroccan media space as a location in which the moral finds iteration and careful negotiation rather than explicit subversion.

In the production of media space the Moroccan monarchy plays a delicately negotiated role as the symbolic guide for moral standards rather than a dictatorial regime censoring citizens' reception of international media. While the national channels are clearly monitored, there has been no formal effort to censor access to foreign programs. The nation-state owns and operates the channel RTM—Radio Television Maroccaine—and retains a stake in the private channel 2M. Both are perceived as national and accordingly regarded as symbolic purveyors of a nationalized Islamic morality. The two channels provide media content that adheres to normative understandings of propriety. Programs contain no nudity; contain few if any sexual references; and offer entertainment spectacles, dramatic serials, news, and comedy shows that reflect core social values. Even the content of foreign corporations advertising on the Moroccan channels is highly scrutinized.[3]

The state plays a role in this broadcast scene as benevolent "commander of the faithful" by imbuing programming on the national channels with behavioral prescriptives of moderation, modesty, and respectability. By maintaining a modest image on the national stations, the state upholds its position as a moral authority of Sunni Islam. At the same time, by allowing the proliferation of satellite broadcasts, the state is able to continue crafting its image as a tolerant and progressive government whose citizens are accorded the right to choose their media freely.

SITUATING VIEWING SPACE

Satellite receivers clearly enable the Moroccan public to access media programs from around the world and to absorb broadcast content that is potentially more subversive than the programming from the nation's state-controlled channels. Despite the obvious fact that satellite television requires the cooperation of nation-states in order to exist, the Moroccan state has positioned itself in such a way that it is not viewed as an accountable agent in the potentiality for moral corruption posed by the broadcast object. The expanded capacity for the acquisition of information does not cause citizens to question the moral position of their government. It is, rather, incumbent on Moroccan citizens to make decisions about what they will view and whether it suits their moral sensibilities.

It is, then, in the particularities of people's ordinary viewing practices that we will find the evidence and character of this religious public's shared moral identity. Viewing practices are subject to the limits of individual agency assumed by and placed on citizens through status roles sustained by moralized discourses. Emphasizing the social production of media space demands attention to discursive ideals of morality, but also to the specificity of interface-mediated space as *lived* sites. It is, after all, in social space that culture and belief are most clearly manifested.

With this in mind, I want to turn to the primary sites of the production of media space in Morocco—the domestic salon and the public salon. Through an analysis of the occupation of mediatized space created by the presence of satellite television, the following sections show the experiential character of individual and collective interpretations of Muslim morality. This ethnographic treatment will bring to the fore the dynamics of moral beliefs and practiced understandings of status and gender roles—feminine and masculine—in the production of media space. We will look into two types of audience space in Casablanca—the private home and the public café—and discover how simple acts of channel selection draw out the textured and coherent patterns of morality in practice.

STRIATIONS: THE TELEVISED DOMESTIC SALON

The home of the Abrami family was a short distance from my own. Both of our homes conformed to the conventional layout of servants' quarters found amid elegant flats. These houses were designed to be separate from the luxury of the buildings to which they were attached.[4] Over the course of a year I spent time in the Abrami home on a daily basis. At first, my visits were primarily limited to mealtimes, when the family insisted that I arrive to eat in their company. "Eating alone," they insisted whenever I protested about accepting another invitation, "is bad for one's health and heart. Eat with us whenever you are not eating with others: we are like your family."

When entering the Abrami family's apartment, there are only a few steps before the doorway to the kitchen. On the left-hand side is a step up and a small door to the bathroom. Just six steps past the entry is a door to the only bedroom. If one continues past that door, a short hallway opens to the main room, which simultaneously functions as a dining room, a family room, a study, and a bedroom. All the older children, as well as any guests, sleep in the main room. The small bedroom behind the door is where the father, his wife, and youngest child of three sleep. It is also where all the family members' clothing is kept. There are also small boxes in that bedroom that the older children (and the youngest in imitation) use as places to guard their private notes or prized possessions.

Azhar is the head of the Abrami household and a Berber Sunni from the south of Maroc. His daily life, as I knew it, was a performance of calm piety. Although he is a calm and usually upbeat man, I can't think of a day on which I had occasion to see Azhar that he would not have justification for an attitude of frustration, anger, or simply despair. Each day there were injustices and structural unkindnesses heaped on him. Azhar makes his living by attending to the luxury possessions of Casablancan elites as a building superintendent. He moves between the overly decorated bourgeois theaters of upper-tier homes and the extremely small scale of his own living place on the ground floor of his building. In his modest home, Azhar provides for between six to eight people on any given day. With four children and a wife, he also has to account for the frequent arrivals of family members from the Moroccan countryside. Their stays can last anywhere from a week to several months. The ratio of space to people in the household of the Abrami family is precisely the reverse of that found in the households for which he works.

Azhar demonstrates his conservative interpretation and firm belief in Islamic principles through his everyday practices. He tends not to miss prostrating himself in submission to God, and the evidence of this shows in the slowly darkening circle of marked flesh on his forehead. Azhar also carefully oversees the content of his family's home environment, prohibiting unseemly images on the satellite-linked TV and barring any offensive language on radio broadcasts. The written information and magazine content in the house are always limited to school texts, religious texts, and the only daughter's occasional pop magazine on Arab musicians. A portable radio sometimes appears in the main room, though it is generally kept in the kitchen and only infrequently used. It is in the kitchen that Azhar's second son, Abderahim, spends most of his time in the house. While his siblings, mother, and father all enjoy watching television programs in the main room, Abderahim's interpretation of Islam prevents him from participating.

When I first began spending time in the Abrami home, I was concerned that my presence as an outside woman prevented Abderahim from sitting in the main room. It is true that Abderahim—a Salafiyyah—could not look at me, an unrelated, unmarried woman, directly, being required instead to lower his gaze. However, when I asked his elder brother, SiMohammed, whether I was causing discomfort and forcing him out of the family room, I was told that it was not me but the television broadcasts that prevented Abderahim from being present. While social analysts have long taken the kitchen for granted as the "feminine domain," in the Abrami household the kitchen is at once the feminized site in which the mother cooks the family meals and the appropriated domain in which Abderahim secludes himself in order to assert himself as a pious young man.

Every member of the Abrami household is a Muslim. Each of them practices his or her faith on a daily basis. That is, they adhere to the call to prayer five times a day and fulfill seasonal duties of feasting, ritual slaughter, and fasting. At the same time, however, each member holds onto his or her own particular interpretation of basic Muslim principles such as *halal* (that which is allowed), *haram* (that which is forbidden), and *bid'a* (that which is an invention or, more precisely, a heretical deviation from Islam). The family members' individual interpretations of Muslim principles produce distinctions in the scope of their everyday practices. Here I will look specifically at the practice of occupying broadcast space.

Abderahim, the second-eldest son, believes that in general the images projected into the home via the family's satellite dish are *haram*. He likewise feels that singing and dancing are *haram* and views much of contemporary Moroccan society as immersed in practices that are *bid'a*. His older brother, SiMohammed, on the other hand, a very conservative and studious young man, is prone to listening to and bopping along with hip-hop tapes. In fact, all the other members of the Abrami household thoroughly enjoy music. Yet even there we find subtle but important distinctions in practice. SiMohammed's favorite music genre is hip-hop, but he refuses to watch any hip-hop music videos. According to SiMohammed, he attempted to hear his favorite music without watching television by putting on music video channels from other countries but sitting with his back turned to the screen. He found this solution frustrating, however, as it was, in his words, "too much of a temptation to turn around and look." Whenever we discussed music, the conversation would invariably veer to a frustrated complaint from SiMohammed about the inability of videographers to "make decent videos that people can watch without shame."

While both young men in the family, as well as the father, feel that *all* music videos are a window onto the profane, the women in the household watch Arabic music videos regularly during the hours when the father is not home. For Tilelli, the mother of the house, the music videos are an audio accompaniment as she goes about tasks that take her from one room of the house to another. For her daughter, Saffiyah, the Arabic music videos constitute a vibrant part of her social life. She faithfully follows the ups and downs of her favorite singers on the charts and gathers information on them offered by the commentary of video jockeys, or VJs. She often sings or hums along to songs that narrate love lost, love aspired to, or love found. While Abderahim is never present in the salon room as she watches, her brother SiMohammed can often be found sitting alongside her with a college book in his hand. Although he does not label the Arabic music videos as wholly profane, he views them as devices of temptation that encourage people to embark on paths of wrongful behavior. He chides her for watching music videos, which he says encourage Saffiyah to think of nothing but "a frivolous kind of love that has nothing to do with reality."

The occupation of the main room and the content of what is broadcast through the television are determined by the status of those present in the household at any given point. When the household patriarch, Azhar, is home, he decides whether the channel will be changed if there is something he feels is inappropriate about the broadcast. At the instant, for example, when two actors would lean in to kiss each other, Azhar would clear his throat, cluck his tongue, shake his head, raise his voice, and demand that the program be instantly changed.

Very infrequently, the younger son, Abderahim, occupies the media space of the front room. Abderahim does not generally watch satellite television, but he does occasionally watch tapes of political Islamist sermons. He rarely does this when his father is home, although he does sometimes share the viewing with his older brother. Abderahim's father, who speaks Berber and Dreeja (Moroccan Arabic), would not be able to understand the sermons delivered in modern standard Arabic. His mother, on the other hand, speaks Berber, Dreeja, and modern standard Arabic, and she does watch the sermons with him on occasion. Abderahim's sister is also trilingual and is often home when he watches his sermons. However, she leaves the room, having no interest in anything the Salafiyyah movement has to offer. Similarly, when she is watching her favorite shows, it is Abderahim who leaves the room.

The television is only turned off during times when the whole house is asleep. So long as there are people awake in the home, viewing options provided by the broadcast object swirl through the front end of the home. The family members manipulate the broadcast object's images and determine its programs through choices: clicking a channel, reorienting their bodies to open or foreclose a field of vision, or exiting the room. The decision of what is watched and when is informed by individuals, their collective agreement, and the prioritization of certain family members over others within the status hierarchy of the household. In the Muslim salon saturated with satellite broadcast media, there is a play of forces underwritten by interpretations of morality (*haram, halal, bid'a*). The variances at work in

interpretations of each moral category underpin the experiential occupation of mediatized spaces. Media output informs the cognitive landscape
of individuals, but the specific character of media space is simultaneously
determined and shaped by the beliefs of situated viewers.

STRATIFICATIONS: BROADCAST SPACE IN THE PUBLIC SALON

> What we have learned from twenty years of feminist theory—from
> writers such as Laura Mulvey, Teresa de Lauretis, and bell hooks—is
> that *the eye is connected not only to the mind but also to the heart, to
> an identity constructed across time and space, which shapes, deletes,
> foregrounds, represses, and selects what we see.*
> —Friedman, 1994, p. 575

In the production of mediatized Moroccan public spaces, particularly in
urban settings, satellite-enabled broadcasts on TV are the dominant mode
of information and entertainment reception. In the city of Casablanca, although here and there a neon sign flickers in the dusty sea air, there are
no supersized tickers strapped to the facade of towering buildings flash-
ing minute-by-minute information updates. While billboards have begun
to populate the skyscape, they blare their messages through the silent
medium of print advertising rather than flat-screen "digimercials" or pro-
jector-amplified photographs that change with the weather. The mobile
screens of the city's cell phone users do increasingly provide a unique
means for public interfaces with broadcast media. The urbanscape in Casablanca, however, as in cities throughout Morocco, is first and foremost
beholden to the "media magic" of televised satellite broadcast signals. This
mediatized urbanscape is wholly reliant on traditional modes of public
space for its production—that is, the coffeehouse.

Television sets have staked a critical claim to the atmosphere of public spaces through their placement in the nation's plethora of social cafés
since the early 1960s. As was the case in prior eras, in twenty-first-century
Morocco the majority of city corners are claimed by cafés. In Casablanca,
as in all Moroccan cities, these social sites are so ubiquitous on the ground
floors of buildings that their sprawling terraces have created a third space
in the topography of city streets. The socializing claims of cafés, *les salons
publiques*, are thrust outward such that streets are gobbled up haphazard-
ly with the lingering chairs, table stands, and gangly legs of seated café
goers. Cafés provide the public with the spatial means to participate in

exchanges of everything from political information to collegiality, laughter, mint whisky,[5] gossip, and various household services for barter.[6] It is in the city's prolific café spaces that televisions can be found casting their images onto public audiences.

While cafés are the primary site for satellite television in the public domain, the presence of satellite television is limited to a specific genre of café—*les cafés populaires*. This contrasts with the role of television in family homes, where the broadcast object's commonality surpasses categories of social status or class. In the domestic sphere, a satellite-connected television set is just as likely in a bidonville shack as a sprawling villa in an elite quarter. In public cafés, though, the presence or absence of satellite television signifies the composite class status and gender characteristics of the social space.

Cafés can be divided generally into a few categories. First there are *les cafés populaires*, neighborhood coffee- and teahouses catering to a definitively male clientele. Then there are *salons de thé* and *cafés cosmopolitan*, opulently decorated sites of *haute moderne* design populated predominantly by elite Moroccans and foreigners. Since the advent of the Internet, cyber cafés have emerged as yet another important café type. Television sets are generally absent in the carefully designed environments of upper-end *salons de thé* and *cafés cosmopolitan*. In these spaces the connotation of the television object—precisely its commonality among the masses—makes it an unwanted object. Televisions are also absent in nostalgia cafés (a less frequent café type) and are only rarely found in tourist cafés. Televisions are also absent in the cyber cafés, where the medium for information and entertainment is the web-connected computer screen. Among all these types, it is in the exceptionally prolific men's coffeehouses, *les cafés populaires*, that televisions claim their place in the public domain.

Haute moderne and wired cafés are catalytic social spaces that in certain measures disrupt social and gender hierarchies even as they reify imported, but hegemonic, notions of the "good life." *Les cafés populaires*, on the other hand, carry out the continuities of a familiar moral order by maintaining gender segregation and to some degree distinctions between status groups. It is critical to note that *les cafés populaires* outnumber all other types of cafés put together. In these cafés one will *always* find a cluster of clientele that comprises only men and a droning television.

During my time conducting research in *les cafés populaires* there were only three occasions when I was not the only woman present. Through the segregation of women, *les cafés populaires* function as privatized domains of masculinity within the public. They are spaces of simultaneity, at once private and public. They are salons larger than what most of the men present could afford in their own homes. These coffeehouses are filled stylistically with the familiarity that marks domestic space while also being defined by the perceived right of men to socialize publicly in the company of other men.

IN THE MASCULINE LIVING ROOM

What is shown on television sets in *cafés populaires* is agreed on by consensus. Café proprietors exercise the authority to change programs in much the same way that heads of households do in the home salon. But they are obliged to appease the customer audience; after all, the customer dissatisfied with what is on can always go to another café. Café audience members influence programming by voicing an opinion to the café manager; asking or demanding that he turn up the set volume, adjust the reception, or change the program.

Satellite hookups allow set owners to tune into other Muslim nations' networks. Arabic-speaking stations in Egypt and Qatar, while not the only options, are the most commonly selected when international stations are sought. Satellite television's "real-time" access to transnational television stations gives viewers the ability to choose program schedules that upend the intentions of television industry programmers in various nations. Analysts of satellite television have noted the degree to which broadcast corporations enforce a standardized fare of program formats and scheduling habits. However, the emergence of satellite television has redistributed the power of programming such that viewers can actively construct their own notions of scheduling (Nederveen Pietrese, 2006). The evening news in Qatar is the late-afternoon news in Morocco. Time-zone differences between the receivers and the transmitters of programs and programming slots allow the viewing public to gather news hour after hour from a revolving wheel of local, national, and international sources. One sees this at work in *les cafés populaires*, wherein Moroccan news channels capture midday audience share, but just as quickly as the national program ends the set is changed to another offshore station offering its own news or sports programming.

It is important to point out that all the broadcast channels selected in *les cafés populaires* are Arabic stations. Pan-Arabism may have failed in Morocco as a political ideology, but it is manifest in viewing politics. Satellite broadcasting is used less to "open up" the world and more to affirm the solidarity of an "Arab world" in which viewers share a common language. Through program selection, Moroccan viewers participate in a transnational Arab community. This suggests the degree to which satellite television, rather than marking the triumph of a globalized and globalizing taste in programming, has been instrumental instead in the production of an "Arab world" broadcast audience (Sreberny, 2006).

I spent at least two hours daily in Casablanca's "men's cafés" over a period of one and a half years. On those numerous occasions when two hours became six or seven spent shifting from café to café, I observed a near-seamless continuity in programming on televisions in the spaces. One could, for example, leave a corner café and walk half a block down to another, linger for fifteen minutes, and set off to another *café populaire* on the next block. In all this shifting it is likely that the same *content* type would be on each of the television screens even if the channel itself was different.

Though there are alterations in the two content types of programming (sports and news), they are very rare. For instance, occasionally, in the course of changing from one channel to another, an unexpected choice will arise and the café patron might settle on a nature or science show, though this is not common. Part of what readily distinguishes programming content in public salons from that of domestic salons are the broadcast genres *not* watched. Dramas, comedies, variety shows, and entertainment spectacles are all absent. At the same time, there are absolutely no illicit programs or programs in which any form of sexuality is on display. This is striking in as much as in a secular public sphere a broadcast viewing space made up predominantly of men is likely to include sexualized imagery—one might think here of the female cheerleaders on American basketball broadcasts as the most innocuous of examples. The viewing selection in *les cafés populaires* consists of only two genres—sports and news. Additional genre selections that in another culture might dominate viewing in a perceived masculine public space are not found in this prolific type of Moroccan café.

In Morocco, despite the fact that *les cafés populaires* make themselves an inhospitable domain for women and are defined by their predominantly male clientele as masculine domains, the viewing audience does not utilize this public privacy for the purposes of enabling spaces in which masculinity is bound to expressions of sexual desire. On the contrary, *les cafés populaires* provide spaces in which the viewing practices of participants reify an idealized masculinity that is defined by intellectual and athletic prowess. Manhood here means knowing and doing, before all else. The choices in programming speak to a shared understanding of what it should mean to be a man in Muslim Morocco. Satellite television beams steadily in *les cafés populaires* as a medium for the reproduction of an idealized Moroccan masculinity that appreciates knowledge, assumes the right to generate opinions, and reserves the principle of bodily pleasure for a limited engagement with athletic displays that pose no threat to morality.

Shortly past the final call to prayer in the city of Casablanca, shopkeepers of *les cafés populaires* begin sweeping up as customers finish their last sips of coffee. Only after the doors have been locked and the register counted, just before shutting off the lights, are the café televisions shut off. Shopkeepers and waiters, like their customers before them, return to their homes, where the reliable screens of satellite-beamed television programming await.

NOTIONS OF MUSLIM SPACE: REPLACING THE BINARY

Following the work of Talal Asad (1993), I argue that significations and the performance of morality in Muslim cultures can only be perceived with active contextualization that acknowledges the unfixed yet necessarily iterative nature of cultural practice. Whereas Asad emphasizes historical specificity to give shape to context, I focus on the production of space through everyday practice. In light of this, it is essential to engage the placement of spatial practice in Muslim cultures as it appears in anthropological and sociological studies. Muslim morality and Muslim space ("true" things only in a heuristic sense) have most often been studied with narrow attention to gender segregation and gendered binary distinctions. As is the case with many studies of Islamic cultures across disciplines, we are confronted in these studies with an Islam understood as static. Positioned as a closed system in which the meanings of belief that inform modes of practice are seen as predetermined, Islam writ large is established as not only foundational to cultural practice (a right-enough perspective) but as a fixed, immovable boundary circumscribing the significations of one's existence.

In the work of Pierre Bourdieu (1992), Muslim space is not produced but rather is structured. This is a mystical process inasmuch as Bourdieu assigns little agency of intent or mindfulness to the inhabitants and thus producers of the space itself. The Muslim home, which occupies most of Bourdieu's focus, is a "prefixed" space whose features represent an immutable moral cosmology. Bourdieu's analysis of an Algerian Kabyle home reasonably suggests that there is an *experiential* association of lived space ("the different parts of the house and the different places where things are kept or activities carried out") to the symbolic terrain of belief (Mitchell, 1991, p. 49). The dilemma of fixity emerges in his emphasis on a moral signification of the relation between things—bodies, natural elements, buildings—and where things are placed within buildings. The relation between actors and object has an order, we are told, which relies on "homologous oppositions" (Bourdieu, 1992). The prime axis of these oppositions is the distinction between male and female. According to Bourdieu's cosmological framing, a bed and its immediate area constitute not merely the place in which household residents sleep. The sleeping area surpasses its functional materiality to symbolically represent the feminine essence defined by the theorist as moist, secreted, and entombed in a state of threat.

The anthropologist Combs-Schilling builds on Bourdieu's notion of Muslim social space as defined by fixed homologous oppositions and furthers the notion of the religion as one in which the devaluation of women is naturalized. While one cannot overstate the ongoing forms of oppression experienced by Muslim women in systemic manners within certain nation-states, the notion that the oppression of women is naturalized in, limited to, or worse, unchangeable as a feature of Muslim morality is specious at best and dangerous at worst. In briefly deconstructing Combs-Schilling's argument, it is my intention to reposition theories on morality and space in Islam onto more tenable territory informed by considerations of Islamic texts.

In the book *Sacred Performances: Islam, Sexuality, and Sacrifice*, Combs-Schilling (1989) recounts the story of Abraham and Ishmael in order to support the claim that Muslim cultures function according to static socio-spatial boundaries based on a fixed moral framework. In this framework, a naturalized feminine exists in contrast to a transcendental masculine power. To support this, the author relies on an analysis of the story of Abraham, which

> is pedagogical. . . . The myth verifies that males are the intervening link, the stair step to transcendence, by associating God and men with geographical locations that physically confirm the truth of this invented assumption. The myth depicts men as leaving the world of women, nature, and the plains in order to connect with God on the mountaintops. The myth embeds its cultural assumptions in the topography of the land. It associates women with the temporal realm of nature, with the dry flat plains that in North Africa and the Middle East are dependent upon the high points— the mountains—for water. (p. 237)

This theory, which Combs-Schilling calls the "sexual topography of transcendence," tells us that the mountaintop to which Abraham goes in order to sacrifice his son Ishmael is symbolic of man. Only man, represented by the ideal figure of Abraham, is able to reach the mountain, the domain of communion with God. Ishmael's mother, who does not go to the mountaintop, is said to typify *all* women. As Ishmael's mother cannot surpass the flat line of the woman "left behind on the plains," so are all women rendered ineligible for the experience of ascension.

The dilemma in this assessment of Islam is, as Bourdieu (1995) himself points out elsewhere, that "fluid abstraction is also false abstraction" (p. 112). In Bourdieu we saw an assertion that moisture, wetness, and water are defined as feminine in Muslim cosmology. In Combs-Schilling, water is defined as a symbol of masculine dominion. The point is not which author has the correct interpretation of the gendered meaning of symbolic elements.[7] The issue is that the homologous opposition itself is an abstraction that pushes us toward false positives. I argue that if we are to contemplate a cosmological axis in Islamic cultures, it is not one of male and female, but rather an axis of belief and nonbelief. To draw out this point, I take up the story of Abraham and suggest another reading situated more firmly by the Surah in which it is found.

The narrative of Abraham is quite different in the Qur'an than it is in the Old Testament. Whereas in the Old Testament the story emphasizes Abraham's difficult emotional struggle leading up to his ascent to the mountain and focuses his biographic triumph in the moments on the mountaintop, Abraham's biographic value within the Qur'an derives from a brief life history. In the surah "The Cattle," the significance of Abraham is rendered through a temporal rather than geographic trajectory. The narrative's arc runs between the scene of his willingness to sacrifice Ishmael—a disavowal of the bond between father and son—and the scene of his willingness to turn his back on his own father. In effect there is a repetition—albeit through magnification—of the same disavowal between father and son. The disavowal is based on a judgment of rightful action demonstrating conviction in the presence and law of Allah.

It is critical to our understanding of the cultural meaning of this myth to know that in the Qur'an the story of Abraham is not delivered as a story unto itself, as it is in portions of the books of the Bible. Rather, Abraham's tale is given as an example of rightful conduct set within the surah's narrative structure of a moral sermon. Early on in the surah, the reader is told that Muslim believers must "forsake those who take their religion for a pastime and a jest, and for whom the life of the world beguileth." Abraham is invoked further along in the surah, by the call to recollection: "Remember when Abraham said unto his father Azar: Takest thou idols for Gods? Lo! I see thee and thy folk in error manifest. Thus did We[8] show Abraham the kingdom of the heavens and the earth that he might be of those possessing certainty" (Qur'an 6: 74–75, Oxford World Classics Edition).

The myth of Abraham, as it is rendered in the Qur'an, does not offer us insight into binary oppositions posed as the "existential dilemma" between "God and nature" or, even as it might appear, "between life and death" (Combs-Schilling, 1989, pp. 230–243). Instead, we see that in Islamic scripture the role of Abraham presents the phenomenological character of the will to belief. Abraham is cast as an exemplary worshipper who distinguishes himself from those who do not follow the moral pathway toward God. Belief is not only a conceptual apparatus; it is *a way of being* in the world, which requires judgment, intention, and practice. To work through an analytic frame restricted by gendered binaries negates the complexity of what it means to dwell in the world as such.

What is apparent in the surah "The Cattle," and reiterated emphatically throughout the Qur'an, is that questioning the moral conduct of the self and others is not only a right, but an imperative for followers of Islam. It is incumbent on each believer to follow a path of righteousness, which by its definition compels followers to question what practicing Islam means in the course of their lives. It demands that one judge one's self and others against interpreted standards of being in rightful action.

What is useful about the work of Bourdieu and his students is that it offers social scientists a critical path through which to engage the relationship between what people believe and the manner in which they occupy space. Bourdieu provides us with a means through which to consider the cultural geography of everyday spaces. Yet there are limits to applying his analytical framework. The Kabyle household emerges in the early years of Bourdieu's scholarship, and as such its study carries the remaining strains of structuralisms with which the author was still tarrying. Thus the meaning of dwelling and spatial practices provided is one that revolves around the notion of *fixed habits* that give structure to the shape and meaning of lived space—a space determined and characterized by symbolic representations of belief. In this framing, belief itself becomes fixed to expressions that cannot change. In Bourdieu's Muslim spaces, as in Muslim fundamentalists' imaginaries of Islam and just as well in Islamophobic tracts, we encounter a religion in which there is literally no space for the immutable truth that societies change. In such renderings it is not only belief that is fixed in time, it is the expressions and practices of belief as well that are subject to stasis. But we see clearly, when we look into the home of the Abrami family for instance, or when we sit in the public salons of Morocco's male citizenry, that practical expressions of morality are fluidly presenced by active interpretations of rightful conduct.

MORAL IDENTITIES IN MUSLIM MEDIA SPACE

Considering the broadcast object in Muslim social space illuminates the lived contours of collective belief and individual positionality, which in turn characterize the variations and limitations of media content in social space. Public opinion of satellite television positions it within a moral discourse. In this discourse the media object is cast in terms of the moral negative. Within its universe of streaming images, satellite television contains the heretical, the profane, and the forbidden. This kind of content, though situated amid a host of images and information deemed permissible, is perceived as vesting satellite broadcasting with the power to corrupt the spiritual well-being of society. At its point of danger is the threat of *fitna*: a social chaos birthed in the shadows of a morality subdued by the rising heat of souls frenetically untethered from the calming mores of a rightful and righteous path. I suggest that negative public opinion on satellite television is a recognition of this threat. The proliferation of satellite dishes in light of their perceived threat, however, evidences a willingness to negotiate the potential for harm with the desire for access to choice and the ability of individuals consequentially to "make the right choice."

The public face of this negotiation, the outcome perceivable to the viewer situated within an audience—in the home salon filled with family or the café salon filled with men—is a flow of images comfortably situated within a wide but general aura of the acceptable. The viewing public regularly selects media content that fits within a limited domain of permissibility. As we see in the differing perceptions of *halal, bid'a,* and *haram* held by members of the Abrami household, within that limited space there are still divergences of opinion on where the borders of moral correctness precisely begin and end. The media space created by satellite broadcasting in the home differs from that of the public men's salon, as we've seen. Still, both the domestic and public media spaces of Moroccan salons provide markedly conservative viewing experiences.

There can be no doubt that in the margins of the intimate, those spaces between unmonitored individuals and television screens that are ripe with unlawful options, the threats of satellite television do take root in viewing.

In every city brimming with satellites, there are likewise people clandestinely watching anti-Muslim Christian stations, soft porn music videos, Shiite sermons, and no-holds-barred German porn. Such viewing practices undertaken by the individual have implications for all of society and are undoubtedly widespread enough to warrant study. While we should not undercut the significance of privatized individual practices, when taken together I would argue that the clandestine character of viewing such programs actually evidences the strength of the public will to manifest morality in the mediatized milieu of Muslim belief.

The practiced space between viewers and satellite programs in the cities of Morocco demonstrates the essential roles that interpretation and judgment play in constructions of morality within a predominantly Muslim public sphere. A recognition of how judgment is measured and practiced through negotiated interpretations of the right or the good is necessary to further our understanding of all cultures in which faith among citizens is pervasively experienced in both sociocultural and governmental modes. When confronted with the practiced expressions and habitual facts of everyday life in urban Muslim Morocco, we are compelled to engage with understanding cultures of faith in which expressions of religious belief are dynamic and fluid, even as attachment to tradition maintains both real and symbolic voice.

Drawing on the work of the fourteenth-century Muslim scholar Ibn Khaldun, Timothy Mitchell (1991) argues for understanding culture (in Khaldun's work 'Umran) as a process rather than a schematic plan of "structuring structures" (Bourdieu, 1992). "Umran or culture is to be understood as "activity, bustling life . . . and building . . . [it is] an active, undetermined process, marked in cycles of abundance and decay" (Mitchell, 1991, p. 53). Defined in this manner, the study of culture, particularly the study of religious culture, must analyze the conditions and contexts shaping the experiential realities of what emerges and declines in the normative and transformative qualities of social life.

The shift of conditions brought about by the emergence of new objects of material culture, in this case digital satellite broadcast media, brings to the fore the ways in which the production of space takes the shape of a culture's otherwise abstract moral landscape. The social space of digital media—whether satellite broadcasts or mobile communication technologies—both transforms and is affected by situated understandings of the moral framework that underlies the character of particular cultural paradigms. In Morocco, digital media open up new possibilities of where one might reset a social behavior border or make a judgment call on propriety, while there remain markers of perspective that inform the distance (or not) of redefined sociocultural practices and norms. The lived space of culture is transformed and diversified by new media and its object interfaces, but digital media they are not only a conduit of change. We must recognize, too, the ways in which digital media reshape moral landscapes while it is *also* imbued with the power *to draw out existent moralized practices*. In this sense, new digital media in religious cultures can be accountable for reshaping just as well as strengthening notions of being in belief that are expressed through the exercise of judgment and the use of moral reason in the act of selecting the very window through which one takes in the world. This is evident in the social spaces of contemporary Morocco, wherein the content of glowing screens made by digital interfaces presents us with the interpretive impulse of moral actors whose choices are fluid and dynamic rather than dogmatic and fixed. It is the ongoing valuation of interpretive practice and free will that sustains and propels shared symbolic and practical expressions of morality and of being Muslim as simultaneously circumscribed and transformative.

NOTES

1. At one point during my stay I undertook to count the number of satellite dishes visible from my terrace; the tally came in at 1,357. It took several sessions to generate the final count, whose accuracy is of course liable to the deficiencies of the naked eye.

2. Between the satellite dishes, antennas—projecting metal rods with three or four cross rods—stick out intermittently along the cityscape. The antennas are forgotten remnants of the first years of television in the nation. Broadcast hardware predecessors of satellite dishes, the rust-prone antenna rods uncomfortably pierce the skyline. Derided by urban planners and aestheticians when they first appeared and offering viewers little more than five channels at best, broadcast antennas never reached critical mass—and thankfully so. Still, they tell us something about the history of broadcast TV. They are remnants of television's first

twenty years in the Royaume, when viewers had only two channel options.

3. In fact, foreign advertising was an issue of debate on the Parliament floor in 2002, which was televised on RTM.

4. I suggest that it is precisely in their differential design that the imposition of invisibility is rendered onto the occupation of space by the disenfranchised. Although this design succeeds in removing the poor from the gaze of the economically privileged, it creates at the same time spaces in which the all-encompassing gaze is held precisely by those who are not seen.

5. *Thé de menthe*, an infusion of mint leaves grown in Morocco and gunpowder green tea usually imported from China, is a wildly popular drink. Moroccans often refer to it as "Moroccan whisky," making a joke about the prohibition of alcohol—a known illicit and addictive substance—and the nation's addiction to a favorite drink.

6. Men who work in trades such as plumbing and electrical repair or carpentry, as well as men who make their living through arranging deals, use the café space to solicit and solidify agreements for work.

7. Considering the scriptures of Islamic hadith—the secondary sayings of the prophet—we find that water does indeed have an affiliation with the heavenly in Islam. However, we also find upon close readings of the Qur'an and the hadith that women are decidedly *not* absented from the plane of transcendence that forms the link between the individual believer and the heavenly. Likewise, Bourdieu's cosmological interpretations are not quite borne out by Islamic scripture. For example, his assertion that Muslim women represent the moon is contradicted by numerous passages in the Qur'an that use images of the moon to represent neither woman nor man, but rather the omnipotence of God.

8. In English, the Qur'an's reference to an omnipotent God is translated frequently as "We." Thus God takes on a communal quality in speeches to humankind.

REFERENCES

Asad, T. (1993). *Genealogies of religion: Discipline and reasons of power in Christianity and Islam*. Baltimore, MD: Johns Hopkins University Press.

Bourdieu, P. (1992). *The logic of practice*. Stanford, CA: Stanford University Press.

Bourdieu, P. (1995). *Outline of a theory of practice*. Cambridge, UK: University of Cambridge Press.

Combs-Schilling, M. E. (1989). *Sacred performances: Islam, sexuality, and sacrifice*. New York, NY: Columbia University Press.

Friedman, A. (1994). In this cold barn we dream. *Art Bulletin, 76*(4), 575–601.

Mitchell, T. (1991). *Colonising Egypt*. Berkeley, CA: University of California Press.

Nederveen Pietrese, J. (2006). Globalization as hybridization. In G. Meenakshi Durham & D. Kellner (Eds.), *Media and cultural studies: Keywords* (pp. 658–680). Oxford, UK: Blackwell.

Rosen, R. (2002). *The culture of Islam: Changing aspects of contemporary Muslim life*. Chicago, IL: University of Chicago Press.

Sreberny, A. (2006). The global and the local in international communications. In G. Meenakshi & D. Kellner (Eds.), *Media and cultural studies: Keywords* (pp. 604–625). Oxford, UK: Blackwell.

CHAPTER 6

Examining All the Realms of Nature

Evidence, Insight, and the Quest for Knowledge in Modern Thailand

Emily Zeamer

This chapter looks closely at notions of evidence and proof in various genres of popular narrative in Thailand. I specifically examine Thai supernatural rumors, dharma or religious stories, ghost stories, and newspaper stories about true crime to argue that these narrative genres often share a common theme: they cite a self-consciously modern and rationalist, yet also Buddhist, epistemology, which affirms empirical knowledge as the source of wisdom and insight. Thailand is a strongly Buddhist country, with over 95 percent of the population identifying as Buddhist; and in Thai Buddhist contexts, the practice of examining or analyzing evidence—*phisut* in Thai—is often figured as a spiritual act, as a way that a thoughtful Buddhist can contemplate evidence of karmic nature. Based on this notion, many Thai stories implicitly place the reader, or the observer, in the position of the Buddha-scientist, pious investigator of a world subtly yet profoundly shaped by the work of karma. This notion is often used to suggest that knowledge can be acquired by anyone through the careful contemplation to the empirical evidence at hand.

While I acknowledge the private, spiritual importance of Thai Buddhist tradition in Thai contexts, my analysis here is informed by the understanding (following Foucault) that knowledge and power are co-constitutive, and that power is often an emergent effect of the private and intimate practices of daily life. In this, my work is also a response to Talal Asad's call for an anthropology sensitive to the political dimensions even of private religious practice.[1] My project here is to show how a private, and self-consciously Buddhist, spiritual practice reflects on a broader political and social milieu,[2] and indeed, offers telling glimpses into the features, and limits, of the contemporary Thai public sphere. I do this by examining various discursive uses of the concept of empirical investigation (*phisut*), to explore in each case the way these narratives construct the relationship between an audience and private or public knowledge.

On the one hand, by inviting audiences to judge and analyze the "evidence" for themselves, the narrative genres I discuss here seem to empower the ordinary individual, and even imply the democratization of knowledge by suggesting (based on the Buddha's example) that anyone can attain a deeper understanding through careful observation and reflection. However, as I will explain, by so often identifying the ordinary observer as a source of knowledge—rather than the expert, or the collective—these narratives place an emphasis on knowledge that is produced, often out of necessity, in private, beyond the limits of the public sphere. I argue that this emphasis on private reflection rather than public discourse sheds light on Thailand's broader political and social milieu, in which powerful political agents are often obscure and shadowy figures, and public knowledge about important events is often limited, allowing private speculation and anonymous rumor to flourish.

EXAMINING EVIDENCE

Maio told us that of all the places to visit in Bangkok, she prefers the museum of the Temple of the Emerald Buddha (Wat Phra Kaew), in the historic Grand Palace compound in the old city. She brought me and her friend Dia there on a Saturday, leading us past the throngs of Thai and foreign tourists at the main gate, past the main temple and palace buildings, to a building that only a handful of other visitors seemed to have found. The temple museum is housed in a plain wooden two-story building, tucked into a far corner of the busy complex. We removed our shoes as a sign instructed us, and walked up the polished teak staircase to the second floor, where we found a handful of rooms lined with old-fashioned glass display cases, their shelves crowded with a varied and mostly unlabeled collection of antique Buddha figures and other ceremonial objects that had been left as offerings at some time since the shrine had been built, more than two hundred years before.

One room that was closed to the public stores the delicate gold ornaments used to "dress" the sacred image of the Emerald Buddha.[3] An iron gate secured the doorway, so the three of us—Maio, Dia, and I—paused together to gaze through the bars. The chamber held a single row of glass cases containing the precious gold and jeweled ornaments, each bathed in its own spotlight. The room was carpeted in royal blue, and laid out on the floor alongside the displays sprawled a large white tiger-skin rug, its mouth gaping as if in mid-roar, to show glossy pink gums and shining teeth. Beside the tiger's head someone had placed an ornate gold-colored platter with an offering proper to any shrine: a garland of jasmine and rosebuds and a small glass of water.

Maio touched my elbow as we stood gazing at the scene. You see that tiger, she murmured. See how they have left something for it to eat? It comes alive at night. It comes alive when nobody is around. Maybe they need these gates to secure the doors, she mused. I had had a similar idea, gazing through the stout iron bars at this tiger's shining glass eyes, its sharp white teeth. Standing there, I grew curious. I knew that animals in Southeast Asian legends are often the manifestation of a shape-shifting god or spirit. I also knew that the tiger is a Thai symbol of royal power, and white a sign of magical purity. Surely such a trophy would be a gift worthy of a king. Who had killed it and brought it here? Was this tiger part of history? So I asked Mai: Did you learn about the tiger somewhere? She didn't answer immediately, but my curiosity was growing—maybe I could find a history book in the gift shop that would tell me more about it. Or maybe I really needed to read up on Thai folktales. I asked again: Is this tiger something that people learn about in school? Would the story be written down, in a book somewhere?[4]

Look, said Maio, nodding to direct my attention back to the tiger and the platter set with offerings. They feed/care for it (lieng).[5] It must be a powerful tiger. It is there to protect the Buddha's garments. When no one is around, it becomes a dangerous animal; but it's only dangerous to people with bad intentions, she added, as if to reassure us. Her friend Dia, who had been silent until now, was suddenly irritated. You don't know that, Maio, she murmured. When Maio did not reply, Dia turned and walked to the other side of the room and sat down beside an air-conditioning vent. When I looked over at her, Dia closed her eyes, as if air-conditioning was all she could think about. I guessed that Dia was embarrassed by Maio's unapologetic belief in the spirit world, in the kind of things that Buddhist

Thais from an early age are taught, in public school religion classes and in most modern temples, to view as mere superstition, with only a doubtful connection to "modern" Buddhism.

I realized later that my burst of interest in locating a book that would tell me all about this white tiger was an attempt on my part to locate the "real" story—that is, one authorized by historians, or enfolded in an established literary tradition. A story that would, in other words, put safely in its place Maio's fantastic image of a white tiger springing to life each night. Although surely, somewhere, there must be an account of how this particular white tiger came to guard the Buddha's garments at Wat Phra Kaew, it was not available to us as we stood there that day. And yet, despite Dia's accusatory tone, I realized Maio had never claimed to know for certain whether her idea about the tiger was correct or true, authorized by either tradition or history. Instead, she answered my questions with a gesture, directing my attention back to the scene before us: the room itself, the white tiger, and the precious objects it guarded. Maio offered a reading of the material world based not on the evidence of texts or authorities, but on private reflection. Yet she deliberately stopped short of making an authoritative claim about the "truth" of what she saw. Instead she invited us to follow her example, to examine the evidence for ourselves, and to draw our own conclusions.

PROOF

There are two words commonly used in Thai to talk about proof. One word is *phisut*, which means "to prove the truth/reality using empirical methods."[6] *Phisut* means to prove something through evaluation, as in, "You don't have to simply believe [*cheua*]; [go ahead and] test/examine/ *phisut* for yourself."[7] The word *druat* also means to check or prove, but one can *druat* a fact to see if it is correct without any direct experience, as when a teacher grades a test by comparing answers to a key, or an accountant checks the numbers in a spreadsheet. To *druat* is also to check or monitor on behalf of another authority, as in, "The police checked/*druat* our identification." To check/*phisut* is to verify something on its own terms, without reference to external doctrines or authorities, to seek answers based on the evidence at hand.

Phisut is, on the one hand, used broadly in secular contexts in reference to police investigations, scientific investigations, and legal evidence. However, *phisut* also has a religious aura for Buddhist Thais. A Thai friend, a well-read woman in her late thirties, confirmed that *phisut* often surfaces in Buddhist sermons or dharma talks, often in reference to the Buddha's teaching that the most valuable knowledge about reality is that which is gained firsthand, through reflection on one's own experience.

Phisut is not, as far as I can determine, of Pali origin, nor is it often used in more formal Thai translations of religious scripture. The association between *phisut* and modern Thai Buddhism is notable in the writings of the famous scholar-monk Ajahn Buddhadasa, who notably received his training in the Thammayut monastic lineage, known for following a strict interpretation of Buddhist scripture. Buddhadasa's teachings rose to popularity among more educated and urban Thais in the 1950s and 1960s (see Jackson 2003 and 1988; Swearer 1988) by urging renewed emphasis on meditation as a source of spiritual insight, and promoting the spiritual and intellectual value of renunciant discipline.

Buddhadasa's message has been popularized in Thailand through books and recorded sermons, which emphasize plain-language exegeses of scriptural Buddhism. In one of these texts, available online (tellingly titled "Buddhism in 15 Minutes"), Buddhadasa refers to the value of empirical observation (*phisut*) as a fundamental element of the Buddha's teachings: "The foundation of the Buddhist religion is distinct from all the others, in being a religion based on a form of knowledge that can be developed through the empirical observation [*phisut*] of any individual. That is, any individual [can] make an empirical observation [*phisut*] of all things, as well as everything that arises within themselves, all of it, and reflect upon it. . . . It is said that Buddhist religion is the same, or at least equivalent to, science." While he goes on to say that, contrary to popular belief, science is *not* the same as Buddhism, both are grounded in insight gained from observation, or *phisut* (Buddhadasa, ca. 1976b).[8] Connecting Buddhist wisdom with empiricism, and even with science, may seem unremarkable to readers more familiar with the rationalist Buddhist teachings that have been popularized in the West. While scholars have noted that rationalism and empiricism have been elements of Buddhist teachings throughout the history of premodern Buddhism (see McDaniel, 2008), this analogue between the Buddhist investigator and the scientist is a self-consciously modern development.

The image of the Buddha-scientist is probably grounded in what scholars have called the "Buddhist reformation" in Thailand, which dates to at least the first half of the nineteenth century (Keyes, 1989). Mindful of the spread of European colonial control throughout much of Southeast Asia, the rulers of Siam (the former name of Thailand) set about establishing a bureaucratic state founded on modern rationalist principles, with the aim of preempting Western ambitions to conquer, and thereby "civilize," the country. In the first half of the nineteenth century, King Rama III (r. 1824–1851) would implement religious reforms that would more firmly establish state control over the Buddhist *sangha*, while also purging official Buddhist doctrine of elements deemed incompatible with Western scientific rationality (Reynolds, 1976, p. 211; see also Jackson, 1989).

A key target was traditional cosmology. When Buddhism first spread through India, Ceylon, and Southeast Asia, local animist beliefs were absorbed into a "universal" Buddhist cosmology based on the moral order of karma. As Craig Reynolds (1976) notes, this process effectively "upgraded" local spirits by incorporating them into a single cosmological system (p. 207; see also Kirsch, 1977). A detailed vision of the Thai Buddhist cosmology was recorded during the Sukothai Period (between the thirteenth and fifteenth centuries) in the *Traiphum Phra Ruang*, or *The Three Worlds Cosmology According to Phra Ruang*. The *Traiphum*, which would become a key scriptural text of Thai Buddhism, details a universe consisting of three "worlds" or realms subdivided into thirty-one hierarchically ordered planes, which aside from the human realm included domains of giants and demons, angelic beings, hell realms, and domains of gods and angelic beings. All beings in the *Traiphum*—animals and people, gods and wraiths—are subject to karma; even angelic beings are mortal, though they enjoy lifetimes measured in many eons. The only escape from the endless karmic cycle of birth and suffering, death and rebirth, is by following the Buddha's path to wisdom—by seeking enlightenment. A soul's unique history of death and rebirth thus symbolizes its journey toward enlightenment (Ringis, 1990, pp. 27–28).

Nineteenth-century religious reforms would affirm the central notion of this cosmology—that of karma as the guiding moral force in the universe—while marking many elements as folklore because they were incompatible with Western scientific knowledge.[9] As the national religion, Thai Buddhism throughout the late nineteenth and twentieth centuries has been in some ways aggressively standardized, publicly affirmed as a self-consciously modern, rationalist tradition.[10] This modern Buddhism is taught in the public schools (Wyatt, 1994) and affirmed as the basis of Thai citizenship and nationhood.[11] Yet is important to note that local spirit beliefs and ritual traditions were never actively suppressed, though they are habitually bracketed from official Buddhism, as "local" or "personal" beliefs.

It is in relation to this standardized, modern, and rational Buddhism that the concept of *phisut* can be located. The notion of drawing conclusions based on evidence can be read as a deliberately scientist interpretation of

the Buddha's teaching, which suggests that knowledge of the nature of reality can be cultivated through observation. Blind belief is anathema to this
pursuit. While few of my Thai informants were well versed with Buddhist
scripture that outlines this belief,[12] I found that the core idea was broadly
familiar to the Bangkok Buddhists with whom I worked. More than once,
my Thai informants have pointed out to me that the Buddha did not teach
that the supernatural does not exist. The problem with believing in spirits
is not that spirits do not exist, but that one must believe without proof.[13]
Yet Buddhism teaches that wisdom must be cultivated through the careful
study of sensory evidence.[14]

I also found that many Thais link Buddhist religious insight with
science. A middle-class man[15] I interviewed at a popular religious retreat
center in Bangkok offered this vivid image of the Buddha-as-scientist:

> The world is round, right? Yes, but nobody at Buddha's time knew
> that, there were no scientists. But the Buddha said the world was
> round—how did he know? Because he could see the truth/reality
> [*kwam bpen jing*]. The sky is full of stars, but who knew these
> were suns? . . . The Buddha said that there were eighty thousand
> worlds and a million million suns. . . . What is the origin of this
> amazing capacity of the Buddha himself, to know 2,500 years ago
> all about astronomy when scientists have only recently figured it
> out? To know the nature of the whole universe without having
> anyone tell him about it? How did Buddha know these things?
> Because he had wisdom [*bunyaa*], he cultivated positive karma
> [*bun*]. (Paraphrased from field notes)

Most Thais would agree that while some people pursue wisdom through
formal education, superior wisdom is achieved through the example of the
Buddha himself, by carefully studying and reflecting on the evidence of
experience. In the notion of the Buddha-scientist, an alternative authority
emerges, with insight that rivals or matches that of the secular expert.

PHISUT AND THE LIMITS OF EXPERT KNOWLEDGE

One thing that is compelling about this notion is that it is often used in
ways that seem to invite an alternative or parallel sphere of public discourse, in which an ordinary person can stand alongside experts, to evaluate and judge the "evidence" for themselves. *Phisut* thus offers a legitimate

position from which to challenge, or at least to question, elite and expert authority.

When mainstream television programs engage with popular supernatural beliefs, the apparent aim is often to correct the "backward" ideas of the masses. For example, a news program broadcast in 2004 investigated a popular spirit medium whose followers believed a miracle had caused her breasts to produce milk with curative powers, though she was well past the age of menopause. Several experts had been consulted regarding these claims. The first, a researcher in a white coat and standing in a laboratory, carefully explained that lactation was a natural biological function that could be altered by an abnormal fluctuation of hormones. Next a doctor, in a similarly clinical setting, stated that human milk was simply nutrition for infants, and had no other special powers. In conclusion, as a youthful anchor assured viewers, there is "no need to waste any time in search of that milk." In this case, technical expertise is offered as a guide to understanding the evidence; indeed, a rational and scientific basis of knowledge is affirmed, for it is scientific experts who are called on correct popular belief. Yet by examining each story on its own terms, even this official intervention holds open the possibility that a powerful substance or magical event might one day be discovered that *would* be worth the serious consideration of the public.

In other cases, the actual task of evaluation or analysis of the "evidence" is left up to the audience. For example, in 2011 a television news program discussed an eerie photograph had been taken a few nights earlier in front of a local school. It showed a faint figure passing in front of a lighted sign, yet the photographer claimed that no person had been in the area at the time. Was this a photograph of a ghost? Here as well, various experts were called on to guide audiences through the evidence. An expert in digital imagery was interviewed, who had examined the image and concluded that it had not been doctored. A physicist then explained that light must travel from an object in order to be recorded by the camera's sensor. The camera itself, its make and model, was shown. In conclusion, the reporter suggested that this is something that's up to people to decide whether they believe. Within the framework of *phisut*, even contentious or inconclusive stories may thus be presented and discussed; supernatural rumor and fact can be considered, from the established and respectable vantage of both modern, rationalist Buddhism and modern science.

As this example suggests, the notion of *phisut* as a sort of pious inquiry into the evidence can be used in ways that seem to invite ordinary viewers to develop their own insights, even if these insights run against the grain of expert or official opinion. In the next section I will explain how a range of popular genres of storytelling draw on this use of *phisut*. In doing so they engage directly with the idea of a karmic universe, and encourage audiences to reflect and to speculate on mysterious and even controversial phenomena—and come to their own conclusions.

INVESTIGATING KARMA

Many Thais would define a good Buddhist as someone who seeks to cultivate wisdom and insight, as someone who seeks to understand both human and karmic "nature" (*thammachaat*). The production of karmic knowledge is the goal of a broad subsection of religious stories or dharma tales (*dhamma niyai*), where the term "dharma" refers to the Buddha's teachings or—in a broader sense—Buddhist wisdom. Broadly speaking, dharma tales illustrate a spiritual message by means of narrative example, often framed as a fable and concluding with a line of moral advice, or a *bon mot*. A bookseller I interviewed described dharma tales as "stories for people interested in spiritual/religious/dhammic practice [*pathibhat dhamm*],"[16] who are concerned with learning to do things "properly/accurately [*tuuk dtrong*]." She explained that most people did not have the background to go directly to Buddhist scripture for answers to religious questions, so they "study" (*seuksaa*) by means of story and example. One genre of dharma tale, especially popular with younger and more educated Thais, is the book-length spiritual autobiography, in which the writer recounts personal difficulties, as well as his or her efforts to understand and put into practice the Buddha's teachings about meditation and self-discipline (*pathibat dhamm*). These more secular accounts offer biography as an illustration of karmic and human nature, an opportunity for readers to reflect on the karmic consequences of moral action, or to see for themselves how emotional and spiritual difficulties can be resolved through spiritual/religious/dhammic practice.

Many dharma tales focus specifically on the problem of karma. A popular series of these tales is called *The Law of Karma*, published by the monastery of the visionary monk Luangpor Jarun. *The Law of Karma* series emphasizes true stories of difficulty or hardship—illnesses, personal conflicts, and so on—which are assumed to be karmic afflictions, the result of moral misdeeds (*baap*) committed in this or previous lives. These stories typically show how, by following various techniques of Buddhist disciplinary practice, the crisis is eased, or even miraculously removed, signaling that the karma has exhausted itself (*mot gam*), or been alleviated by the accumulation of positive karma (*bun*). To understand the importance of these stories, it is useful to review the key themes that shape popular views about karma among urban Thais.

1. *Karma is a natural force.* Many of my Thai informants would describe karma as a natural force, one that simply describes the relationship of cause and effect. The difference between karma and physics is, however, that karma describes moral consequences of human actions. I found that my more cosmopolitan informants did not accept the literal realty of the traditional Buddhist cosmology as described in the *Traiphum*, in which the human realm is just one sphere within a many-tiered universe of natural and supernatural, angelic and demonic realms. Yet most Thais do take seriously the notion of karma, as well as the idea that a person's place in the human world is largely shaped by a person's karmic legacy—that is, that unusual luck or misadventure can often be attributed to karma.

2. *Karma explains human differences.* Many Thais believe that karmic inheritance determines a person's status, gifts, and influence in the world. A more secular take on this view is the notion that a person's moral actions shape his or her future life. Wealth and personal attributes (e.g., beauty, intelligence) can be viewed as a consequence of that person's *moral* place in the universe as well, a reflection of his or her karmic inheritance. The most prominent example of this is the Thai king himself, whose power and honor are seen as a reflection of his superior karma or *bun*. Of course, this link between karma and social position has often been used as ideology, to naturalize social hierarchy (Jackson, 2002; Keyes, 1989; Reynolds, 1976; Reynolds & Reynolds, 1982; Tambiah, 1976). Recognizing this, many scholars, and many Thais as well, have equated the popular belief in the "law of karma" (*got haeng gam*) with a kind of fatalism. One well-read Thai man, who described his interest in religion as primarily academic, told me that too many Thai people simply clung to their belief in the law of karma in order to avoid taking responsibility for the negative things that happened in their lives. I have found, however, that most Thais broadly agree that we live in a karmic universe, and that the course of human life is profoundly shaped—often in surprising and unforeseeable ways—by the persistent effects of actions committed in the past.

3. *Karma is mysterious.* And yet it has often been noted as well that, even though the majority of Buddhist Thais believe in the reality of karma, there is no stable consensus on how or whether karma is actively at work in any specific case (Carlisle, 2008; Hanks, 1962; Keyes, 1983). This is because the operation of karma is obscure, worked out over the course of many

lives. One woman told me, for example, about a dream she had, in which she was a Japanese soldier, killing many civilians. This, she implied, could explain her persistent poverty and recurrent health problems. In a karmic universe, each person is enmeshed in a complex and interconnected web of karmic ties to others. One can also be buffeted by the karmic churn of one's own history, even if it is long forgotten. Given the strange—omnipresent yet obscure—nature of karma, Thais are broadly aware of the value of deciphering its mystery.

4. *"Seeing" and understanding karma is a gift, and a skill.* For some, insight into karmic "nature" is developed through spiritual practice: the Buddha taught that skilled meditators would naturally develop insight that might seem surprising, even supernatural, to others. Children (still pure) and experienced meditators alike are sometimes able to "remember" details of past lives or catch visionary glimpses of distant places; and such visions can provide insight into some present karmic state. Others are thought to have inherited a gift of supernatural insight; the power to see into invisible realms may come easily to someone with an extraordinary karmic inheritance. Those with inherited or acquired special powers of insight may become visionary doctors (*mor doo*), who can "see" and, like doctors, diagnose a person's karmic condition. It is often said of the famous monk and meditation teacher Luangpor Jarun that at a single glance he can see a person's karmic history—including all the moral acts committed in this and previous lives—and thus diagnose a person's karmic debts. In accordance with the rules of monastic discipline, he does not reveal what he sees, but his followers hope his insight will nevertheless help them to identify disciplinary practices or ritual acts that will improve their karmic condition. Lacking unusual spiritual gifts, a person's ability to understand karmic nature is erratic and partial. Ordinary people come to sense their own karmic condition like someone fumbling in the dark, without sufficient skill to draw their sensations into a clear understanding of the whole. Given the unique challenges of making sense of a karmic universe, dharma stories bridge the gap between the religious expert and the ordinary person, by presenting an opportunity for a person to contemplate how this dynamic web of karmic relations, though often obscure, profoundly shapes the everyday world.

DHARMA TALES AND THE SUPERNATURAL

Karma stories engage in various ways with the question of invisible forces. Karma is itself an invisible force, yet the agents of karma, too, are often mysterious. Tik, in her early forties, with a college degree, often worked as a tour guide. When I asked her if she knew any "ghost stories," this is the tale she told me:

> It happened to a young Swedish tour guide who worked for my company, and who at the time was new to Thailand and knew very little about Thai culture. The new guide had brought the tour group to the ancient city of Ayutthaya, and they were standing before a beautiful sculpture of the Buddha's face that had, over centuries, become embedded deep in ancient tree roots. As she spoke to the group, the young tour guide crouched down [Tik showed me how the woman squatted with her knees up—a very informal pose]; then she casually put her hand on the Buddha's face! I was shocked—embarrassed, worried that other Thais would see me and criticize me for not teaching her how to treat a sacred object [*sing suksit*]. As soon as I could, I pulled the young woman aside and explained the mistake she had made; she was very embarrassed and apologetic; she hadn't known. We went on with our tour, and later that day we were at a second temple. The Swedish tour guide was standing in the courtyard talking with some people from the group when a temple dog ran up and peed on her. All these people were around, and it stood there calmly with his leg up. [Tik laughed, remembering.] That dog wasn't even quick about it! He acted like he had all the time in the world. (Paraphrased from field notes)

When I asked, naïvely, where the "ghost" was in the story, Tik was momentarily confused. Maybe the dog was possessed by a local spirit who wanted to protect the temple, she explained, but it was impossible to know. The point was that the dog had clearly become an agent of karma. Since the Swedish woman had made an innocent mistake, Tik explained, the karmic retribution for her act was benign, a kind of joke. Tik's ghost story was really a karma story, for it reminds listeners that even careless or thoughtless acts have karmic consequences.

Though dharma tales often (though not always) have supernatural elements—for indeed, karma often works through mysterious agents—dharma tales and ghost stories are considered entirely separate genres, one deliberately religious, the other sensational, even profane. A typical newsstand in Bangkok often has anywhere from five to twenty different magazines on ghosts and the supernatural, clearly targeted at a popular audience. These magazines often feature gory clip-art images borrowed from horror films and tell titillating stories of magic and necromancy, while other magazines may take a more serious and pious tone yet offer no less wonderful tales about famous mystical monks and miraculous events. Uniformly, I found that these magazines were considered lowbrow by my middle-class Thai friends, who would laugh indulgently at my choice of reading material when I brought these magazines home. The bookseller I interviewed laughed when I compared dharma tales to ghost stories, which are "something else entirely," she insisted.

Certainly, dharma tales are quite distinct from these stories in terms of style and presumed audience. The language of a dharma tale is typically polite and formal, and may incorporate words from Pali and Sanskrit, the ancient languages of Buddhist scripture. In contrast, supernatural stories are told in a vivid and often far more colloquial style. Yet popular supernatural stories mirror dharma tales in that they often purport to offer instructive illustrations of the work of karmic nature. The two genres offer, in narrative form, a sort of tour of evidence, an opportunity for audiences to better understand the invisible work of karma.

Well within the more profane pulp/horror genre, a popular late-night call-in radio program called *Shock FM* invited callers to share their "true" ghost stories. The show's host, speaking against creepy background music, continually reminded listeners that there is more to these stories than mere entertainment: they illustrate "the necessary flow of karma" (*gam dtong len bpai*). In one example from *Shock FM,* a listener phoned to tell his "true" ghost story, with periodic interjections from the host:

> *Caller*: This happened to me a few weeks ago. . . . I was drunk, alone in my room, when I saw a figure in white from the corner of my eye, but then it was gone. . . . I heard a sound, it got louder and louder. I looked, could not see where the sound was coming from. Then it stopped.
>
> Later I was reading a book, alone in my room. I looked up, saw a man wearing black. I was so shocked, I did the wrong thing: I ran outside. The elevator wasn't working, so I ran down the stairs until I saw someone, I told him I had seen a ghost. He was surprised, he told me, "That's never happened in this building." . . .
>
> I went to make a meritorious offering [*tam bun*][7] at the temple . . . and when I placed the offering into the monk's bowl [*sai bat*], I said, "You, the person who came to find me, don't return, all right?" . . . Three

days later, I saw a man in a dream, who looked like my friend. He stood [and] didn't say anything, but his expression was pure, clear [*sot sai*].

Host: This must be because you gave a meritorious offering [*tam bun*].

Caller: That building has no history. It must have been the spirit of my friend. (*Shock FM*, recorded April 3, 2005)

As this example suggests, a typical ghost story told on *Shock FM* unfolds like a sort of mystery story. It begins with a startling event: a glimpse of a figure from the corner of the eye, a strange sensation of heaviness, a foul smell, a loud noise. Lacking a natural explanation for the event, the subject wonders if there is a supernatural, karmic explanation. This can have alarming implications: perhaps, knowingly or unknowingly, the haunted committed some wrong in the past, and now an agent of karma has arrived to settle this moral debt. Perhaps this is the soul of a deceased relative or an ancestor, or a malevolent or disturbed soul with unfinished business. In either case, the initial response is anxiety: What does the spirit want? How has my life gone out of karmic balance? Is there a wrong that must be set right? In these tales, the haunted's task is to evaluate the evidence and to find out what should be done to restore the balance of karma.

Analysis is a key element of the tale. When this man hears that this "never happened before in this building," he understands that this is not a chance encounter with a random spirit. This visitation seems personal, a notion that is confirmed when, in a dream, the spirit visits again, and he recognizes it as his friend. Here is where his story engages with the question of karma, for the circumstances suggest that whatever was wrong, the man has helped to right it by making a ritual offering at a Buddhist temple. In the end, caller and host both seem to agree that the haunting was not a case of being in the wrong place at the wrong time. A mysterious encounter is transformed into a story about the curative powers of ritual acts of generosity: a man dies, and his grieving soul appears to a living man, an old friend, apparently begging for help. The haunted man performs a ritual act, presumably giving his departed friend a karmic boost in the right direction. Each haunting thus implies a karmic imbalance, for which a remedy must be sought.

Many hauntings are less personal, yet they may point to half-forgotten histories. A somewhat different story was told on the same broadcast of *Shock FM* by a caller who worked as a night guard at a local high school. He explained that one night he heard strange sounds coming from the area of the bleachers—rough voices speaking in angry tones—but could find no one in the area. When he mentioned the incident to a neighbor, he was told that some years past a body had been found there. This simple story ended here, reminding listeners of the lingering effects of crimes or actions that may be forgotten, or deliberately suppressed. By framing the incident within a broader karmic view of the universe, such stories affirm the reliability of karma as a "natural" force, subject to empirical study, or *phisut*. By tenaciously uncovering clues, the haunted bravely penetrates some of karma's mystery, like a scientist uncovering the invisible operations of a natural process. Such stories remind audiences of the fraught nature of reality, while also demonstrating that an attitude of thoughtful inquiry can help anyone to better understand even uncanny and mysterious dimensions of everyday world—without relying on the advice or guidance of so-called experts.

PICTURES AS EVIDENCE

A pocket book I purchased at a bookstall in an upscale urban shopping center, titled *Paap pii phisut pii* (Spirit photographs as evidence of ghosts), vividly describes an everyday world teeming with spirits and karmic mysteries:

> There are various kinds of truth/reality in this world. There are kinds that have very clear answers, there is no need to prove their reality to make them clear, these are "truer than true." Overlaying this is yet another level. . . . This world is full of high technology able to transform nature in many ways, but that does not affect the ultimate truth, which is the nature of death!!!! . . .
>
> Think about it, after a moment it begins to be frightening. After the heart has stopped [and] the current of karma takes violent hold, where will it carry [you]!? If you are still attached closely to your old home/habits, are still standing still sitting still attached to the people you were close to, [you] will suffer in the condition of a ghost that is just like a breath of wind. How is it possible to endure such a thing!? . . . Feeling . . . heartbroken . . . forlorn, full of feelings of fear, confusion, uneasy in the world. . . . [What if] I were to say that [there are] "transparent shapeless figures" floating, sitting, sleeping, very close, though everything seems normal.
>
> [They] overlay/overlap right here, all the time, everywhere.
>
> They formerly were alive, they have passed through death, became energy, shape/image that inhabits memory—comes to

follow us, and if the power of memory is strong enough . . . Do you believe you might meet each other!!

Perhaps you will meet each other just as a frigid breath of air, a kiss, or perhaps it comes as a smell . . . of perfume . . . of decay [it] may appear as a kind of figure . . . a clear voice . . . a howl . . . however it appears . . . ghost!!! . . . When we go to a funeral, or we read about it in a book, a story, a movie, etc., we are followed everywhere, it is happening, we are "haunted" all the time! (Taypnom, 2004, pp. 12–14; translation by the author, punctuation in the original)

The reality that this writer describes, though filled with uncanny presences, with ghosts and spirits of the deceased, is also significantly a human reality, conditioned by moral or ethical orientations such as love, longing, and desire; a world shaped, in other words, by karma. This writer suggests that to contemplate ghosts and spirits is also to contemplate a karmic universe.

This notion helps to explain a growing popular interest in spirit photographs in Thailand, which now circulate widely on the Internet. These mysterious images are fodder for *phisut*, as a mode of pious inquiry into dharmic "nature." A scholarly young monk explained to me that he and some of his friends had recently become interested in the subject of spirit photographs; he showed me an advertisement he had found for the popular Thai horror film *Shutter* (2004), composed of collage of about a dozen purportedly genuine Thai spirit photographs. He explained that he liked studying these pictures, saying that you can learn something about human nature, even after death. He pointed to one picture of a seated couple with a ghostly, grinning face thrust between theirs. There's a sense of humor, he said with a smile. For him the photographs invited reflection. They also managed to bypass the stigma associated with supernatural beliefs in Thai contexts (White, 2003). Like the dharma tale and ghost story, such evidence invites audiences simultaneously to reflect and to doubt.

Mysterious photographs present a markedly intimate view of the karmic universe, one that stands in contrast to traditional cosmographies. Rita Ringis (1990) notes that traditional murals in Buddhist temples tend to locate the viewer somewhere in the sky, taking the distant, encompassing perspective of a spirit or god surveying a vast scene from the heavens (p. 90). Thus a densely filled universe is ordered and systematized, or miniaturized, taken in at a glance. Such images allow the viewer to share the ideal and penetrating vision possessed by mystics, visionaries, and Buddhas. In marked contrast to what Donna Haraway (1991) has referred to as the totalizing, "god's eye view" (p. 93), the spirit photograph, like many dharma tales and ghost stories, offers a more intimate, and fragmented, perspective. Ordinary observers, without special visionary powers, are invited to examine the evidence for themselves. Such images thus serve as a reminder that insight is always partial, grounded in a particular perspective.

"THE PICTURE OF A STORY"

Photographs need not have traces of supernatural beings to produce the sensation of witnessing evidence of a mysterious reality. The graphic images of accident or crime scenes published in Thai newspapers also seem to invite contemplation on the mysterious work of karma.[18] Images of bodies, including accident victims, murders, or suicides, are frequently published in Thai newspapers with only a small caption, which may include only the name of the victim, if known, the date, time, and location where the body was found, and the cause of death. These photographs often seem to be presented as implicit evidence of a broader phenomenon: a rising suicide rate, for example, or an epidemic of crime in the provinces. Marks of violence on the body are often digitally "blurred" by censors, a sign that works at once to abstract and highlight the wounds, as if they still bear the traces of a mysterious power. In many ways this imagery thus plays into the karmic imagination, for images can very easily be viewed as evidence of bad or careless choices—evidence, in other words, of karma. They often seem to remind audiences that the cause of crime, while often obscure, is seldom truly random.

From such scant information it is usually difficult to draw conclusions. Certainly it is possible this victim's fate is the karmic result of some misdeed in a past life. That is, however, unverifiable. These photographs nevertheless gesture toward a reality shaped by the presence of obscure and often dangerous forces. I have found that, in practice, these photos often remind Thai audiences of a fraught *political* landscape, in which it is all too easy to get caught in the crossfire. This was especially true of many photographs that appeared in the newspapers during and immediately after the violence of associated with the 2003–2004 "drug war" in Thailand. Two years into his first term, in February 2003, Prime Minister Thaksin Shinawatra dramatically announced that he would eliminate Thailand's drug-trafficking problem within an astonishing three months. Over the course of Thaksin's war, which lasted for just over a year, thousands of ordinary and even unknown Thais died violently, an average of thirty a day throughout 2003 (see Mydans, 2003). By the end of the campaign, more than a year later, more than 2,500 had been killed. The link between these extrajudicial killings and the drug war was seldom clear, but a pattern did emerge. A person would be called in by the police for interrogation and be last seen alive leaving the police station. If the body was later found, it was often with a bag of illegal drugs beside it.

Those killed were often villagers, including even children, contributing to rumors that the dead were guilty only of getting in the way of someone more powerful. Critics of the drug war, including Thai and international human rights advocates and foreign diplomats, pointed out that such radical measures could not even be effective, as so many of the dead could not have been big players in the drug trade. Yet during the early stages of the campaign, polls indicated that 90 percent of the Thai public supported the crackdown, even though 40 percent worried about being the target of false accusations and 30 percent about getting killed themselves! (Mydans, 2003). By mid-2004 Thaksin had declared an official end to his war, and many of the people I knew in Bangkok felt that Thaksin had successfully solved the nation's drug problem. At the same time, they were well aware that the war had probably given local "businessmen" (*nak turakit*) and mafia godfathers (*jao por*) cover to consolidate their land holdings or business interests. Yet these allegations did not move far beyond the realm of rumor. After an involved but entirely private conversation with me about corruption in her home village, a young woman laughed and said that she should probably be more careful or she'd "get shot unaware" (*dton ying duay mai ruu dtua*). Her remark mirrors popular sentiment in Thailand, that regardless of who happens to be in power, the elite will continue to do as they please, even if it means eliminating anyone who gets in their way. The wealthy and connected, it is said, can do as they please because they will be protected by their powerful friends; but ordinary people are wise to keep their heads down and their voices low.

In this environment, only an unusually brave (or foolhardy) person makes public accusations, and even journalists will refrain from offering a detailed analysis of a controversial case. Thai journalism, in fact, has often seemed to retreat behind the notion of *phisut*. In an ethnographic study of several Thai-language daily newspapers published in 1991, Duncan McCargo (2002) found that they tended to make a strict distinction between two kinds of content: "news" and "analysis." "Analysis" was conducted by senior columnists, while regular reporters were not considered authoritative enough to "analyze or explain anything" (p. 3). For example, the mainstream *Siam Raht Thai* newspaper had gotten hold of important documents alleging government corruption, yet it failed to translate the scoop into the politically significant exposé it might have been. McCargo traces this failure to the way the story was presented to the readers: journalists simply published the "evidence," including many faxes, and even documents in English, without accompanying analysis that could help readers grasp its significance. The journalists involved insisted that they were not responsible for explaining political complexities; the task of interpretation was up to their readers (p. 91). *Phisut* seems to offer cover for presenting news in this way, for it flatters audiences by implying that they possess the insight to conduct their own analysis, to figure things out for themselves.

Not surprisingly, it is often through fragments, traces, or clues, in images that flash up and then disappear, that Thais struggle to make sense of, and find their way in, a complex political landscape. Consider a story that emerged in 2004, pieced together from fragmentary details presented in a handful of newspaper stories. The evidence, though inconclusive, certainly suggested that a significant conflict was taking place, possibly involving high-level politicians. In July 2004, a house in a rural province was attacked by police, who were reportedly following up on an anonymous tip that drug dealers were hiding there. Two hundred rounds of ammunition were shot directly into the house, yet no drugs were found. Newspaper photographs showed only a confused-looking older couple standing by walls and windows riddled with bullet holes. The couple, and several children who were in the house at the time, had reportedly survived the attack by hiding behind their refrigerator (*Thai Raht*, 2004; see also *Bangkok Post*, 2004a, 2004b; *The Nation*, 2004).

Days passed and no clear explanation emerged, despite signs of some broader intrigue. The couple's son, in jail for a drug-related crime, died in prison a few days later from what was officially reported as a "lung ailment." These clues generated a great deal of speculation. I found that most people I knew in Bangkok privately agreed that the evidence seemed to suggest this was a *reuang amnaat*, which can be translated as a "power story," and also "a matter of power." Many believed that the attack had been ordered not by a provincial official, but by a politician with ties to Bangkok. Perhaps a struggle was going on between two or more politicians; it seemed likely that there was money or property involved. Not long after the incident, representatives from Bangkok reportedly investigated the scene and found no reason to reprimand local officials. Almost as quickly as it had appeared, the story disappeared from the news entirely. Despite calls for an investigation, no government action was taken, so the case remained unsolved.[19]

By the mid-2000s, when I began this research, investigative journalism was gaining ground following new reforms introduced by the 1997

"People's Constitution." Yet Thais I knew complained that journalists were still too cautious. Prasong Lertratanawisute, a Thai journalist who has won awards for investigative reporting, was asked in an interview, "Do you think most reporters lack imagination?" He replied, "I cannot judge them. They must be able to put things together, to draw a picture in their mind by putting information together. They need to see the picture of a story" (*Businessweek Asia*, 2001).

When I visited Thailand in 2011, I found that a cautious attitude toward the press persisted, even though Thais had access to a broader range of media sources with the proliferation of satellite television stations and local radio programs and growing access to the Internet. The political landscape had grown increasingly factionalized in years of instability following the 2006 coup that ousted Prime Minister Thaksin Shinawatra, and both official and unofficial news sources continued to be seen as highly partisan. When I asked one man what newspaper he read, he said quickly that you can't read only one. Journalists, he observed, are too cautious—they know if they write something someone doesn't like, they may get "caught" (*dton jap*). He explained that newspapers "censor" (he used the English word), so you do have to do your own analysis (*wikror*). It is best to read several, he said, and put the information together yourself. He dismissed television news as even less reliable, though he mentioned that sometimes "looking at pictures" can add to your understanding of a situation.

He was most enthusiastic about what the Internet had brought to the story because, as he put it, there's no limit or boundary (*grop*) online. It's open. All the clues, the evidence, can be found there as well, he said; if you can't find a picture in the mainstream news, for example, you can always find it on the Internet. Also, through the Internet, he said, it is possible to join a much bigger conversation. Some bloggers work, anonymously of course, to assemble a whole story from the pieces, while other people join to comment. In the absence of independent investigative journalism, Thais continue to do the interpretive work, assembling a "picture of a story" for themselves.

INTERPELLATING THAI PUBLICS

Following Michael Warner's (2002) observation that specific media publics are called into being by discursive practice, existing "by virtue of being addressed" (p. 50), I would suggest that popular uses of the notion of *phisut* in Thailand serve a discursive function, interpellating the reader or listener as a specific kind of subject. Many of the stories I have considered here are effectively religious tales, which implicitly address a public of pious Buddhists, striving earnestly toward wisdom. They locate the subject as a part of a broader karmic sphere, embedded in a complex and often mysterious realm that is shaped in potent ways by unseen forces and obscure relationships. Under such conditions, it is to be expected that anyone should have a profound and vested interest in learning to decipher it.

Across narrative genres, the inquirer, the investigator, is often a solitary figure. True crime stories, ghost and karma stories, they all present the inquirer as a lone adventurer, a pious yet solitary seeker. These stories tell of mysterious forces and fragmentary evidence: a puzzle to be contemplated in the search for an elusive truth. In the Thai public sphere it is the individual who pursues his or her private, partial, fragmentary understanding of a complex and often dangerous political landscape. Perhaps, with increased access to the Internet, this is changing. Certainly, in the digital realm, it has become possible for larger publics to form, shielded by the relative anonymity that the virtual can provide. The Internet is increasingly seen as teeming with new evidence, and with analysts who are continually expanding the scope and depth of the conversation. Yet there remains a sense that each person must find his or her own way, since many Internet analysts and bloggers are widely seen as partisan, and there is little consensus about whose insight can be trusted. In the years since my research was completed, amid numerous power shifts, as the political elite struggle with one another for power, many public analysts, including journalists and academics, have been forcibly censored, imprisoned, or disappeared. Thus it continues to be taken for granted that a cautious person avoids making allegations that go beyond the private sphere. In this environment I would argue that speculative practices, intrigue, and rumor often mark the limits of Thai public discourse, because public political critique and debate are reasonably seen as too risky for ordinary folk. It is admirable that so many Thais remain deeply committed to the search for truth, despite the difficulties. Many continue to collect and investigate the evidence, to test reality, searching for real insight, even though their conclusions often remain in the realm of rumor, shrouded by privacy and anonymity, an all too easily disregarded realm of public discourse. Certainly conscientious Thais will continue, if often privately and anonymously, to reflect on the nature of the problem and to ask might be done about it.

146

1. Asad (2003) writes, "How have different conceptions and practices of religion helped to form the ability of listeners to be publicly responsive? This last question applies not only to persons who consider themselves religious but also to those for whom religion is distasteful or dangerous. For the experience of religion in the 'private' spaces of home and school is crucial to the formation of subjects who will eventually inhabit a particular public culture. It determines not only the 'background' by which shared principles of that culture are interpreted, but also what is to count as interpretive 'background' against 'foreground' political principles" (p. 185).

2. I draw on Michael Bakhtin's (1981) vivid imagery here: "If we imagine the *intention* of such a word that is, its *directionality toward the object* in the form of a ray of light, then the living and unrepeatable play of colors and light on the facets of the image that its constructs can be explained as the spectral dispersion of the ray-word, not within the object itself . . . but rather as its spectral dispersion in an atmosphere filled with alien words, value judgments and accents through which the ray passes on its way toward the object; the social atmosphere of the word, the atmosphere that surrounds the object, makes the facets of the image sparkle" (p. 277).

3. At the change of each of the three seasons of the Thai calendar, the gold "robes" of the Jade Buddha (*Phra Kaeo*) figure (which resides in a chapel in the temple compound) are changed each season by the king himself, in a royal ceremony. *Pret* are demonic spirits realm described the Thai cosmological text the *Traiphum Phra Reuaung*.

4. Throughout this essay, when I report remembered speech, I do so without any form of quotation. I use double quotations to designate speech transcribed and translated from field notes and field recordings. Though I occasionally received assistance from various Thai colleagues and assistants with many of these translations, any errors or omissions are entirely my own.

5. *Lieng* means to feed or care for a living being with food, or to propitiate or serve a supernatural or other being with symbolic gifts.

6. Thai: *druat sorp hai brajat kwam bpen jing*. This definition is recorded in my field notes, from a conversation with an informant; unfortunately, I did not note the publisher.

7. Thai: *mai dtong cheua si, phisut dtua ayng dai*.

8. This is my own translation of the text; an alternate translation by Grether favors the word "testing" for *phisut*: "The principles of Buddhism are different from those of other religions: it is a religion of knowledge which stands up when tested by anyone. As the Buddha said, 'The truth in Buddhism stands up against testing. That is, it challenges each and all to test everything, until the tester gives up and, changing his mind, is willing to revere Buddhism.' The expression that people use: Buddhism is the same as science, or is in harmony with science—there are those who base this on the ground that statement does not do justice to the real, highest worth of Buddhism. For if one speaks as they do, then anatomy or medicine, which has to do with the examination of parts of the body would become a part of Buddhism. What should in fact be said is that they are alike in that scientific principles can stand proof himself for others to see, or be willing to let anyone scrutinize, text, and cross question as he wishes, and it bears up until no further testing can be done and he must believe" (Buddhadhasa ca., 1976a).

9. The king appointed his younger brother, Mongkut, to implement reform, a man who had a sophisticated religious education, having lived much of his life as a Buddhist monk, and had also acquired a broad Western education, studying science, language, and literature with European and American visitors to Siam. Mongkut assembled scholars to reexamine the *Traiphum* cosmology; under their guidance, many elements identified as pre-Buddhist ("Brahmanic" or animist) were called into question. Mongkut would also establish the Thammayut monastic lineage, emphasizing return to a strict interpretation of Buddhist scripture, which would later give rise to influential reformist monks, including Buddhadhasa. An extensive body of scholarship examines the *Traiphum* and nineteenth-century reforms in detail; see Jackson (2002), Reynolds (1976), and Keyes (1989).

10. Mongkut's religious reforms would establish the foundation of what Charles Keyes has called the "Buddhist reformation," by altering the terms in which political power would be defined in Thailand. Indeed, as king, Mongkut embodied a new ideal, asserting his royal authority on the basis of superior insight and acquired knowledge, rather than on hereditary authority or privileged access to doctrinal texts or ritual techniques (Keyes, 1989, p. 137). A notion of elite power and superior wisdom and insight has endured, however—or rather, it has been reinvented. Christine Gray (1991) notes that the modern symbolism of the monarchy, for example, promotes the notion of the royal elite as possessors of superior karma, and thus superior knowledge, and even visionary insight (cf. Peleggi 2002). Noting that one of the most beloved and ubiquitous royal images is of the king with his camera, Gray argues that the camera has become an important symbol of the king's visionary insight.

11. Noting state involvement in the process of rationalizing Buddhism in Thailand, and promoting Buddhism as the basis of a shared ethical orientation, Frank Reynolds (1976), following Bellah (1988), calls Buddhism a Thai "civic religion."

12. In the scriptural text the *Samyutta Nikaya*, for example, the Gotama Buddha argues strongly against accepting any form of theistic determinism, particularly the notion that any god or external being decides an individual's fate.

13. Among more educated Thais, the pursuit of dhammic knowledge is often a self-consciously secular endeavor. Yet I have found that my informants, regardless of their educational or economic background, broadly accept the view that Buddhism teaches that an attitude of thoughtful inquiry as the key to wisdom (*punyaa*). Also, as I describe below, I have found that most Thais, aware of the dangers of clinging to any belief, accept the *possibility* of the supernatural.

14. In the scriptural tradition of Theravada Buddhism, the practice of meditation is seen as a critical aid in the cultivation of insight because it is a means of studying the complex relationship between cause and effect: "Acceptance of a theory of causal dependence, not only in individual and social life but also in the physical world, enables one to put an end to suffering by removing the causes that produce it" (Kalupahana, 1975, p. 137). One woman, an avid student of Vipassana (insight) meditation, echoed this notion when she explained that a Buddhist seeks to understand of the true nature of reality because this knowledge puts an end to fruitless struggle against the aspects the world that cannot be changed.

15. We met at in northern Bangkok at Sathien Dhammasathan, a Buddhist retreat center run by Buddhist nuns, well known for addressing its teachings to a primarily urban, educated, elite audience.

16. Spiritual practice or "dhammic practice," *pathibat dhamm*, is often used in reference to ascetic and disciplinary practices of renunciant, including but not limited to meditation, though *pathibat dhamm* can also refer more generally to a person who strives to live according to the moral and disciplinary practices of Buddhism.

17. The most common ritual practice from which a layperson can earn positive karma or make merit (*bun*) is by giving a ritual donation of food or money in support of the monkhood or *sangha*.

18. Of course, as such, these images build on a broader tradition—beyond the scope of the present discussion—of meditation on the corpse.

19. This incident is one of a great many unsolved killings and disappearances that occurred while I was conducting research in the mid-2000s and since. Disappearances and unsolved killings are frequently reported on in the local Thai press, yet despite sometimes very active news coverage, such crimes often remain unsolved. Groups inside and outside Thailand frequently call for further investigation into unsolved crimes; see, for example, Human Rights Watch (2004).

REFERENCES

Asad, T. (2003). Secularism, nation-state, religion. In *Formations of the secular: Christianity, Islam, modernity* (pp. 181–204). Stanford, CA: Stanford University Press.

Bakhtin, M. (1981). *The dialogic imagination: Four essays*. (M. Holquist, Ed.) (C. Emerson & M. Holquist, Trans.). Austin, TX: University of Texas Press.

Bangkok Post (2004a, July 9). Police shooting on house to be probed as no drugs found.

Bangkok Post (2004b, July 10). Police could be jailed if evidence was false.

Bellah, R. N. (1988). Civil religion in America. *Daedalus, 117*(3), 97–118.

Buddhadasa Bhikku (ca. 1976a). "Buddhism in 15 minutes." (H. G. Grether, Trans.). Retrieved from http://archives.bia.or.th/.

Buddhadasa Bhikku (ca. 1976b). Rien Buddhasasana Nai 15 Natee. Retrieved from http://www.onab.go.th/.

Businessweek Asia (2001, July 2). The stars of Asia: Opinion shapers: Q&A with Thai journalist Prasong Lertratanawisute.

Carlisle, S. G. (2008). Synchronizing karma: The internalization and externalization of a shared, personal belief. *Ethos 36*(2), 194–219.

Gray, C. (1991). Hegemonic images: Language and silence in the royal Thai polity. *Man*, n.s., *26*(1), 43–65.

Hamilton, A. (2002). The national picture: Thai media and cultural identity. In F. D. Ginsburg, L. Abu-Lughod, and B. Larkin (Eds.), *Media worlds: Anthropology on new terrain* (pp. 152–170). Berkeley, CA: University of California Press.

Hanks, L. M., Jr. (1962). Merit and power in the Thai social order. *American Anthropologist, 64*(6), 1247–1261.

Haraway, D. (1991). *Simians, cyborgs, and women: The reinvention of nature.* New York, NY: Routledge.

Human Rights Watch (2004, July 7). Not enough graves: The war on drugs, HIV/AIDS, and violations of human rights.

Jackson, P. A. (1988). *Buddhadhasa: A Buddhist thinker for the modern world.* Bangkok, TH: Siam Society.

——. (1989). *Buddhism legitimation and conflict in Thailand: The political functions of urban Thai Buddhism*. Singapore: Institute of Southeast Asian Studies.

——. (2002). Thai-Buddhist identity: Debates on the *Traiphum Phra Ruang*. In C. J. Reynolds (Ed.), *National identity and its defenders: Thailand today* (rev. ed.) (pp. 155–188). Chiang Mai, TH: Silkworm.

——. (2003). *Buddhadasa: Theravada Buddhism and modernist reform in Thailand*. Chiang Mai, TH: Silkworm.

Kalupahana, D. J. (1975). *Causality: The central philosophy of Buddhism*. Honolulu, HI: University of Hawai'i Press.

Keyes, C. (1983). Merit-transference in the Kammic theory of popular Theravada Buddhism. In C. F. Keyes & E. V. Daniel (Eds.), *Karma: An anthropological inquiry* (pp. 261–286). Berkeley, CA: University of California Press.

——. (1989). Buddhist politics and their revolutionary origins in Thailand. *International Political Science Review*, *10*(2), 121–142.

Kirsch, A. T. (1977). Complexity in the Thai religious system: An interpretation. *Journal of Asian Studies, 36*(2), 241–266.

McCargo, D. (2002). *Politics and the press in Thailand: Media machinations*. Bangkok, TH: Garuda Press.

McDaniel, J. T. (2008). *Gathering leaves and lifting words: Histories of Buddhist monastic education in Laos and Thailand*. Chiang Mai, TH: Silkworm.

Mydans, S. (2003, April 8). Wave of drug killings is linked to Thai police. *New York Times*. Retrieved from http://www.nytimes.com/2003/04/08/world/a-wave-of-drug-killings-is-linked-to-thai-police.html.

The Nation (2004, July 8). Ayutthaya house hit with 200 bullets.

Peleggi, M. (2002). *Lords of things: The fashioning of the Siamese monarchy's modern image*. Honolulu, HI: University of Hawai'i Press.

Reynolds, C. J. (1976). Buddhist cosmography in Thai history, with special reference to nineteenth-century culture change. *Journal of Asian Studies, 35*(2), 203–220.

Reynolds, F. E., & Reynolds, M. B. (1982). *Three worlds according to King Ruang: A Thai Buddhist cosmology*. Berkeley, CA: University of California Press.

Ringis, R. (1990). *Thai temples and temple murals*. Oxford, UK: Oxford University Press.

Swearer, D. (1988). *Buddhadhasa: A Buddhist thinker for the modern world*. Bangkok, TH: Siam Society.

Tambiah, S. J. (1976). *World conqueror and world renouncer: A study of Buddhism and polity in Thailand against a historical background*. Cambridge, UK: Cambridge University Press.

Taypnom, M. (2004). *Paap pii phisut pii* [Spirit photographs as evidence of ghosts]. Bangkok, TH: Degan Print.

Thai Raht (2004, July 8). Khao Yaa Ba Pit Palaat [Report of drugs mistaken].

Warner, M. (2002). Publics and counterpublics. *Public Culture, 14*(1), 49–90.

White, E. D. (2003). The cultural politics of the supernatural in Theravada Buddhist Thailand. *Anthropological Forum, 13*(2), 205–212.

Wyatt, D. K. (1994). Education and the modernization of Thai society. In D. K. Wyatt (Ed.), *Studies in Thai history: Collected articles* (pp. 219–244). Chiang Mai, TH: Silkworm.

149

CHAPTER 7

Cyber Memorial Zones and Shamanic Inheritance in Korea

Joonseong Lee

It was by chance that I found a Korean memorial website called *Cyber Memorial Zone*, operated by the Seoul city government. (Memorial letters used in this chapter can be found at http://www.sisul.or.kr/open_content /memorial/cyberhome/introduce.jsp. The letters were accessed between January 2002 and August 2006, and the original Korean text was translated into English for an English-language audience.) I was overcome with curiosity. The memory of death and ritual in my mind consisted of scenes such as a small funeral parlor located in a village, a mourning lamp hanging on the gate of a house, but not memorial letters posted in cyber memorial zones. This unfamiliar feeling of a new culture of death came from the difference of time and space. Since leaving Korea in 1993, I had clearly not kept up with the fast-paced changes of Korean society. Despite its unfamiliarity, the cyber memorial zone I encountered that day was so intriguing it became a subject worthy of pursuit. What does such a letter mean to the mourner? What motivated these mourners to write memorial letters in cyberspace? Do they believe that digital space can be a spiritual realm distinct from the secular realm? It seemed that women cyber mourners wrote more memorial letters than did men. Why would this be? As a former Buddhist monk and a current researcher in the field of communications, I came to feel that the study of a new culture of death integrated with innovative technologies was an unavoidable karma.

A cyber memorial zone is a website where people can remember their late loved ones beyond the restrictions of time and space. In this zone, mourners write memorial letters and sometimes post pictures or videos of the deceased. Those who have posted pictures or videos tend to use cyber altars, which feature the photos in frames. The cyber altar with the cross, the Bible, candles, and flowers indicates that it is for Christian believers. Different types of digital flowers appear next to the altars. Moreover, the sample memorial zone created for promotion uses Adobe Flash effects to grab mourners' attention. Many of the mourners in this memorial zone did not use cyber altars; instead, they visited the section where they can write memorial letters. For this reason, I decided to analyze the memorial letters to explore their meanings for cyber mourners.

KOREAN SHAMANISM IN CYBERCULTURES

The memorial letters seem to carry evidence of the distinctive dynamics derived from the shamanic roots of Korean religious culture. This is significant because, in the past, Korean shamans have been framed by cultural authorities as social evils that threaten the social system with their enigmatic power. Even in the modern era, many shaman shrines were removed by military regimes. A negative discourse against shamanism is the logical extension of this legacy of oppression and marginalization.

A modified traditional form of Korean shamanism has reemerged in the digital age. As Kim (2003) points out, "Korean shamanic heritage is indeed surviving in the cyber world and undergoing significant transformation even though it is still in its incipient stage" (p. 280). As an example, shaman publicity websites have flourished in recent years, which are shamanism portal pages where many Korean shamans attempt to promote themselves. Clicking each photo of shamans on these sites allows users to get contact and personal information. Considering the negative discourse against shamans in the past, this is one of the biggest changes in the history of shamanism in Korea; these sites are structured to disseminate information on Korean shamanism. Kim (2003) calls this a new function of shamanism in the Internet age, as shamans present themselves in ways that are both informative and commercialized.

Although shamanism in cyberspace disseminates this tradition in new ways, this does not explain everything about the changing spiritual and religious nature of contemporary Korea. Its advanced Internet culture has influenced the perception of spirituality and religion, paving the way for shamanism in cyberspace to be considered alongside other resources in terms of how it functions as a meaningful spiritual source for Koreans. Therefore, analytic emphasis should be placed on the dynamics of shamanism as something that is intrinsic to Koreans since the founding of the nation. Traditionally, shamans in Korea acted as mediators between human beings and higher beings. While performing *kut*, the Korean term for a shamanic ritual, shamans channeled the revelation of divinity to enliven the living and appease the dead. These two aspects were seen as different expressions of one quality: the threshold between this world and the other world. On the edge of these two worlds, shamans helped the living experience the exulted spirits and vitalize their lives, while managing the rite of death to lead the deceased to the other world.

When death occurred, shamanic ritual helped the deceased and the bereaved soothe their *han*, or the multilayered complex of deep sorrows and pain intermingled with resentment, regret, spite, or grief. Whether *han* is individually accumulated or is the agony of the entire village, the shamanic rite of death was an important method for Koreans to handle the sorrows and pains of the *han*-ridden death, the experience of unexpected or unjust situations or those beyond one's control. The experience of appeasing *han* in the shamanic rite of death produced distinctive dynamics that have been embedded in the Korean ethos.

We can think of the memorial writings in cyber memorial zones as a new shamanic rite of death. Embedded within the various levels of inherited shamanic dynamics, cyber memorial zones now partly substitute for the roles of traditional shamans, who helped the Korean populace to appease their *han*. Visitors to the zone attempt to relieve their *han* by writing memorial letters to their loved ones, particularly late family members. These letters address the individual sorrows and pains that accompany the separation and loneliness brought about by the death of loved ones.

Cyber memorial zones do not limit their functional ranges only to appeasing an individual's *han*; they also seek to relieve the collective *han* of a populace, accumulated through political, social, and cultural marginalization. As Seo (1981) has suggested, the collective *han* of the populace, or *minjung*, is the "suppressed, amassed, and condensed experience of oppression" and "the sense of unresolved resentment against injustice suffered," which "forms a kind of lump in one's spirit" (p. 65). The collective *han* becomes social and political as well as personal, making these cyber memorial zones operative on both levels. Whenever socially unacceptable, tragic events result from the mismanagement of the government or other civil authorities, these cyber memorial zones can become the forum where these tragedies are publicly mourned and intolerable public mishandlings denounced.

Cyber memorial zones as an apparatus of Korean cybercultures are not thus individually oriented and representative of sociopolitical change, link- ing the religious or spiritual register to the political ones. Cybercultures comprise the formation of political, social, and cultural discourses in cyberspace, which reflect everyday life (Bell, 2001). From the view of cybercultures, the division of cyberspace and real space becomes obsolete. The term "inside and outside of cyberspace" more appropriately represents the quality of cybercultures. This characteristic of Korean cybercultures profoundly corresponds with the dynamics of the traditional shamanic inheritance, namely, its function as a mediator between this world and the other world.

DIFFERENT CATEGORIES, VARIOUS DYNAMICS

This ambiguous, contested, and aspiring shamanic inheritance, which has been present in the ethos of the Korean populace since the beginning of the state, has thus created distinctive dynamics in Korean cybercultures. On top of this, the emergence of cyber memorial zones in Korea reflects the distinctive dynamics derived from this shamanic inheritance on different levels. The various levels of dynamics express themselves in cyber memorial zones, which fall into four categories: individually oriented zones, sociopolitically oriented zones, commercially driven zones, and celebrity-driven zones. Although each category has one or more distinguishing characteristics, these characteristics intermingle with one another. No single characteristic is exclusive to any one zone. In my study, I have found it useful to look at zones according to a merged set of categories. In the following section, I will focus on three categories of memorial zones—individually oriented zones, sociopolitically oriented zones, and celebrity-driven zones—and analyze how the writings in each zone function for their writers to release their *han*, as well as how the memorial writings from different categories are interrelated.

INDIVIDUALLY ORIENTED ZONES

To examine the individually oriented cyber memorial zone category, I looked at four sites: *The Post Office in Heaven, Ocean Funeral Café,*

I.Missing.U, and *C Park Café*. *The Post Office in Heaven* is the memorial-writing site of *Cyber Memorial Zone*, which the Seoul city government created for the purpose of promoting cremation. As of the time of my analysis, visitors have posted fifty-six thousand writings in the zone. *Ocean Funeral Café* is also a memorial-writing zone for the bereaved, who use a local cruise line that owns this site to scatter the remains of their late families into the ocean. This cruise company utilizes its web presence to advertise its ash-scattering service and has placed it in *Daum*, one of the biggest web portals in Korea. *I.Missing.U* is an individual memorial-writing zone for *D Sangjo*, a prepaid funeral service. As a private and commercial crematorium, *C Park* provides its memorial-writing zone, *C Park Café*, for the survivors whose late family members' remains were interred in its ossuaries. As *Ocean Funeral Café* does, the company used the *Daum* web portal to set up the café. In addition, *C Park* creates one more individual writing zone, *Letters to Heaven*, which is linked to its home page.

Mun-kyu and His Wife

Mun-kyu lost his wife to cancer. He found *The Post Office in Heaven* when he cremated his wife and placed her remains in the enshrinement park established and managed by the Seoul city government. Since the funeral, he has written almost six hundred letters to his wife, which amounts to a letter every five to seven days. A former businessman, he has now retired to a rural area. He also set up a family cyber memorial zone for the rest of his family who are scattered across the world. Mostly the family cyber memorial zone gives Mun-kyu a place to remember times with his wife, but his family members also visit the memorial zone to put digital flowers on their mother's picture, particularly on *sul*, the first day of the first lunar month, and *chu-suk*, the Korean harvest moon day.

Noticeable in Mun-kyu's memorial letters is his remorse that he should have departed this world earlier than his wife but did not. He told me that all the memorial letters reflect memories about his wife that he wanted to write to her. The letters include his various feelings of regret, remorse, longing, nostalgia, and so on. For this reason the cyber memorial zone for him offers him the space to vent his *han*. On a winter day with a heavy snowfall, the longing for his wife becomes sorrow.

> The snow can be romantic with you,
> But it is only sorrow to me without you.
> They [children] don't know how much I love you.
> If they get old, they may understand the half of it.

On this windy and cold day, I am thinking of you playing with
   angels in a garden.
I have loved you, am still loving you, and I miss you.
Am I strange to say, "Love you and miss you"?
Is the old man not qualified even to say that to the one that he
   loved?
I was young at some time in my life . . . So sad . . .

In this letter, his desperate yearning for his late wife and the feeling of impermanence that he has in the twilight of his life intermingle. Seemingly the more he yearns, the more the feeling of impermanence grows and the angrier he becomes. One day his anger explodes and he blames God and the church in a very critical manner:

As a human being, I cannot see your soul now.
When I die, can my soul recognize your soul? Can soul see soul?
Is it because they hatefully captivate people and make a story that
   you and I can recognize each other and meet again in heaven?
Anger swells in me and is about to flare up. Saving soul?
Then why do they have more than one hundred sects?
Does that mean that more than one hundred gods can save a soul?
Then how can we as the foolish find the right god?
How fraudulent they are . . .

Reading this letter, I wondered what made him turn so against the Christian community. I later found an answer. Mun-kyu's wife was a dedicated Christian. When she was alive, she wanted him to believe in God as sincerely as she did. When she learned of her cancer, she relied more on her belief in God than on treatment with medicine. Although he insisted that she needed medical treatment, she refused. Mun-kyu explained his anger about his wife's faith by discussing his views on her beliefs:

You confused belief in God with superstition.
As you say, medicine and medical skills are given by God.
If so, you could receive the treatment as well as believe in God.
However, you crossed the bridge of no return without yielding to
   my wish.
How come such a reasonable person like you had such supersti-
   tious belief?

*That's why it is said that religion is a necessary evil that was creat-
ed by bad eggs.*

This letter helped me understand Mun-kyu's anger against Christianity. In addition, as he expresses his frustration about his wife's refusal
to receive medical treatment, his sorrow, regret, and spite increase. In that
sense, writing letters in a cyber memorial zone can be an instrumental tool
for Mun-kyu to vent the forlorn air of anguished despair. However, this
zone does not only offer him sorrow and pain; after venting his anguished
despair, sometimes he seems enlivened. As the family celebrated the lunar
New Year without his wife, he wrote:

> *The lunar New Year is closing.*
> *I am so anxious about the family gathering this year.*
> *How can I spend the day without you?*
> *Can I take care of the family even half of what you did last time?*
> *As a widower, I don't know what to do.*
> *I miss you and I need you. Help me . . . Help me . . .*

Mun-kyu said that writing a letter to his wife affords him some consolation. As he ends his letter, calling for help from his wife, one sees her
as a source of his comfort. Different from other letters, here he tries to
understand that his wife is not in this world anymore and seeks to create a
positive connection with her. By doing so, he asks her to help him to take
care of his family:

> *Dear Sweetheart,*
> *This morning I feel much less depressed and much more refreshed.*
> *Is it because of bright and warm weather?*
> *Or are you caring for me?*
> *Well . . . tears blur my vision again.*
> *I need to go. I do not want to show my red eyes to you.*
> *See you again.*

Although he bursts into tears in this entry, his tears this time seem
not to come from sorrow and pain with the anguished despair of *han*.
Equating bright weather with his wife's care for him, his tears play a role
of catharsis. The consolation that Mun-kyu feels in this zone may come
from the purging of his emotion. But the moment of his catharsis does not

last long, and his striving for consolation may be one of the reasons he has posted letters in the zone almost six hundred times.

Jung-sun and Her Father

Jung-sun's father passed away from liver cancer a few months before she went to college. I was fortunate to conduct e-mail interviews with Jung-sun and to learn more details about her memorial letters. Among his survivors were his wife, Jung-sun, and her eight-year-old sister. After the funeral, she learned that the funeral company that had helped her family scatter her father's remains offshore had established an online bereavement site called *Ocean Funeral Café*. A few days later, she decided to post her memorial letters in the zone. Her first memorial letter starts with sorrow and regret:

> *It's been a week since you left me, Dad.*
> *How have you been?*
> *It wrings my heart to think of how you suffered from pain and*
> *   loneliness after you knew you had liver cancer.*
> *Although I knew about it, I could not fathom how much your pain*
> *   would be.*
> *I was always sorry about that.*

In the e-mail interviews, Jung-sun said that she and her father had a very close relationship. He was considerate, quick to understand, and, above all, loved her very much. She felt free to vent her anguish and sorrows to her father, as a result of which he knew almost everything about her. That's why, she said, losing her father created such terrible sorrow for her.

As the eldest daughter, Jung-sun also feels that she carries the weight of supporting her mother and younger sister. She must care for her family now, filling in for her father. Because of this sense of responsibility, she keeps any of her difficulties and worries from her mom and younger sister. As she said in an e-mail interview, "When I write a letter to my dad in the [cyber memorial] zone, although I am not able to see him, I can feel him and talk to him about whatever I need just as I did when he was alive. I feel like I write it to myself, but it helps me calm down. I don't know if I can say that the writing 'helps' my life or not, but at least I feel that my inner anguish is being released."

Seemingly, Jung-sun becomes happier by writing a letter to her father in the cyber memorial zone. In order to determine how these memorial writings helped relieve her anguish and appease her *han,* I asked her to specify their role in her grieving process. She said that when her father was alive, she was childish and immature, though the eldest. However, her father passed away, and suddenly she realized that she had a responsibility to support her family. But she initially had difficulties putting herself in her father's position. Even though things went wrong, she did not ask for others' help. Instead, Jung-Sun said in the interview that she wrote a letter to her father because she believed that if she did so her anguish could be released: "It depends on the individual, but it works for me. When problems are entangled, I am under a lot of stress but have no one to talk with, and then I try to calm down myself while writing a letter to father. By doing this, I figure out what made them tangled and how I can deal with them."

However, memorial writings do not always work for Jung-sun. Sometimes she is depressed and writes a letter to her father, but she remains sad throughout her writing:

> *Suddenly, today, you are so hateful to me?*
> *Why did you have to go to heaven so suddenly?*
> *I know it is useless complaining but . . .*
> *You make me mad . . . You could have lived with me longer than*
>   *this . . .*
> *Then why . . . why . . . why . . . why . . . please come back . . .*
>   *please . . .*

Despite her varied emotions in this letter, her memorial letters primarily show balanced emotional flow, which means that although she starts a letter with sorrow and pain, as she writes she becomes relaxed. One of the features of her memorial letter is that she ends it by calling for the help of her father, saying, "Dad, please help Mom, my younger sister, Jung-su, Grandma, and me not to get hurt anymore. As the eldest one, I'll do my best for my family." Or she says to her father, "I pretend that everything is OK without you and try to help Mom not to think of you, but it seems difficult for her to accept your absence. Help us from the heavens!!! OK? Bye~" Once she had a stomachache, and she left a message for her father: " I think I caught enteritis . . . so painful. I have to go to Daejeon tomorrow . . . Dad, please pray for me to get well soon!!"

I asked Jung-sun if she felt like her father was giving her help when she asked for it. As a Catholic, she believes that her father was incorporated with God after going to his rest, and therefore her father can help her: "We believe that God listens to us and fulfills our wishes. In this difficult time, I also want to count on such a religious belief that my father, who became one with God, responds to my call for the help. However, thinking realistically, I don't think it works. It is I, myself, who encourages me to overcome the situation while reading the memorial letters that I wrote."

Although she acknowledged the difference between the religious belief and realistic thinking, what comforted her in the web zone stems from her religious beliefs. In addition, the fact that many of her letters to her father end with a request for help shows her belief that her father possesses the same powers as an omniscient and omnipotent God to help and protect her. The above interviews with Jung-sun show how a young woman used cyber memorial zones to release the difficulties in her life and to achieve redemption. Many Korean women use cyber memorial zones for the same purpose. This is one of the sites' unique features. Given women's marginal role in traditional Korean funeral culture, the level to which memorial zones serve as an open space for women to grieve deserves exploration.

Individually Oriented Zones as Women's Spaces
Individual memorial space in cyber memorial zones is special for Korean women because, traditionally, women rarely had any space to offer these memorials. Men stood at the center of the funeral process, and a woman's normal role was as a marginalized supporter or witness to the ceremony. Although women worked hard to prepare the ceremony, they then became almost invisible in the process. And the gender inequality of the funeral culture did not end at the funeral event.

Conventional norms prevented married women from involving themselves in the affairs of their maiden homes. Married women, therefore, often encountered resistance if they wanted to visit their own families to express their condolences at a death, even for the death of a parent. When she married a man, a woman became no better than a stranger to her family of origin. Once married, a woman was expected to live and die in the home of her husband. This marginalization of women was based on the relations of gender power in the home, where possession of domestic space was considered as a primary male privilege (Park, 2001). These special inequalities evolved from the dominant social ideology, Confucianism.

Industrialization and modernization brought social change and accelerated the decline of patriarchal power. The cybercultures in Korea thus exhibit signs of the changing dynamics of gender inequality. According to B. J. Park (2001), with industrialization and modernization the abridgment of the male space has continued, and eventually the emergence of the information society may lead to even the reduction of the perceptual space of the patriarch in the family. Although the patriarchy in Korean society still influences the Korean family in general, the emergence of the digital era may symbolize, or even support, a shift in the Korean perceptions of gender and space.

Reflecting on the history of Korean women's social status and cultural space, we might argue that the high rate of women participants in writing memorial letters represents an improvement in women's social standing. In the case of *The Post Office in Heaven*, which is managed by the Seoul city government, women participants wrote about 85 percent of memorial letters posted on the zone from 2002 to 2005. As with the case of Jung-sun, many Korean women have their own memorial space in cyber memorial zones and use it for the purpose of releasing *han* and managing the difficulties in their lives. Women creating this private grieving space is a new cultural phenomenon unimaginable in the traditional funeral culture. With cybercultures, men no longer have exclusive possession of memorial space. Not only can women occupy this space, but they now have access to nearly boundless memorial space in cyber memorial zones.

A poster with the nickname "Your Daughter Beauty" (YDB) has written hundreds of memorial letters to her mother on *The Post Office in Heaven*. Most of YDB's letters include personal episodes from her daily life. One interesting story involved a time that YDB went to a public bathhouse with her mother. In contrast to Western culture, Korea has a tradition of public bathing, both indoors and out, and bathing together is not uncommon, so YDB bathing with her mother in a public bathhouse and the two of them helping each other to rub off dirt would be a common practice. The public bathhouse story showed up a few times in her memorial letters. One day in late winter she wrote:

> Whenever I have a bath, I remember you, Mom.
> Before you got ill, you would rub off the dirt on my back and say, "My daughter's skin is the texture of *sundubu* [uncurdled tofu]. Very beautiful." I was so angry to hear that . . . do you remember? Then you became ill, so I had to give you a bath, which sometimes made me tired and vexed. But Mom . . . now I desperately miss the time.

In addition, when YDB was tired and exhausted, she yearned for the time she had a bath with her mother: "Recently, I had not got enough sleep. So tired. Because of being tired, I tended to show a temper with ease. At such a moment, I want to take a bath with you. If I could not, I would just be with you. That's all I want."

These two excerpts about YDB's longing for the public bath with her mother suggest that she had, in particular, a "body memory" of her mother. According to Casey (2000), body memory refers to "memory that is intrinsic to the body, to its own ways of remembering: how we remember in and by and through the body" (p. 147). In this view, YDB remembers her mother "in and by and through the body," washing her or being washed by her.

Considering Casey's (2000) proposition that "the body is of central-most concern in any adequate assessment of the range of remembering's power" (p. 147), YDB recalling her mother through body memory seemed to make her experience in the cyber memorial zone more intensive and complete. The following letter supports this conclusion: "Mom, I want to plead my difficult situation today. I think you will allow me to do that. Why is it so difficult? I think you know already about my situation. . . . When can I throw off this yoke? I also want to come near you. . . . Hold me in your bosom, please." As most people have memories of how comfortable it was in their mother's embraces, YDB expressed her desperate need for her mother's consolation while encountering a difficult situation in her life. In her memory, her mother represents not only the person who raised her but also the origin of energy to fight against difficulty. When YDB said, "I think you know already about my situation," the strength of her body memory of her mother filled the void between this world and the other world.

Another body memory is shared between this world and the other world in the following letter. This time a woman, nicknamed "Ms. Unknown," wrote her late father about an abortion that left a traumatic and indelible memory. But during this very difficult time in her life, Ms. Unknown's father greatly helped her overcome the problem and recover. This traumatic memory provided the catalyst for establishing an immanent connection to her late father in the other world: "Dad, whenever I think of you, I can remember your bright smile. When I let you know [of] my premarital pregnancy, you comforted me instead of scolding me. I was too young to realize how much you cared for me then. . . . Daddy, while you are there, please take care of my baby I aborted because of my immature mistake. . . . Daddy, now take a comfortable sleep. Don't worry about me because I am now grown up. I love you with my heart." The delicacy of the subject in this letter makes disclosing this memory to the public very difficult, especially considering that Korea remains under the influence of a male-dominant sexual ideology in which virginal purity is considered a necessary virtue for a woman. In that sense, I wonder how her body memory encouraged to share her story with the public at large, albeit anonymously.

The next letter, from "Wife"—a bereaved woman—to her late husband, presents a slightly different scenario from the previous two examples. While the two letters of YDB and Ms. Unknown showed strong longing for the imminent connection with their late family in the other world, Wife's posting shows a weak attitude and does not demonstrate confidence based on sharing the memory with her late husband: "My dear, how are you? We are so-so. Sometimes happy, sometimes sad . . . Although my life always looks bare without you, time is just flying. Today while I listened to your favorite songs, my eyes swam with tears. Miss you so much. Kids have grown up remarkably. I think you are watching us. It's been just one year since you left me . . . When can I be with you again?" This letter suggests that after her husband's death, she has felt a sense of constant emptiness. The letter also shows that her husband's favorite music reminds her of the happy hours shared with him. The rhythm of the music became lodged in her body as a good feeling. In the case of Wife, music was the main element of body memory, linking Wife and her late husband.

At the end of the letter, Wife asks her husband when she could be with him again. Her feelings of emptiness without her husband appear to influence her negatively and make her think about life in the other world instead of living here in this world. Wife's attitude is quite opposite to that of YDB and Ms. Unknown, who use their body memories to work positively on their lives in this world. Wife likely relied a great deal on her husband when he was alive, which would not be strange given the social structure. Wife's case, however, makes me reluctant to jump to the conclusion that this new phenomenon of cyber memorial zone necessarily implies the emancipation of Korean women from conventional social norms. Granting that women could acquire their own personal memorial space in cyber memorial zones, when memorial letters are sent to their late husbands, the letters mainly show women struggling to survive under the influence of these same social norms.

Nevertheless, the discussion of cyber memorial zones as a space for women confirms the initial assumption that these zones do allow Korean women to transcend some conventional funeral practices, perhaps leading to their decline. Online, Korean women can perform memorial services on behalf of whomever they want to without the restrictions of time and space. We see this in the case of a poster nicknamed "The Youngest One!" (TYO!).

TYO! lost her brother a few years ago. Like Jung-sun, TYO! contacted the funeral company that helped scatter his ashes at sea and found out that the company maintains a cyber memorial zone. Since her brother's death, she has written more than 1,100 letters in this memorial zone. Because she has written a letter almost every day, and even three or four letters on some days, the entries serve as a memorial diary. In an e-mail interview, she told me how she feels when she writes a memorial letter to her brother: "This kind of Internet memorial culture helps me to soothe the sorrows of my mourning. [While writing,] I feel like talking to him, and he appears to be with me. Whenever and wherever the Internet is connected, I can see him." Because her memorial site was like a diary, it included the minutiae of her life and other personal episodes. And she wrote the letters in a colloquial style that seemed to reduce the estrangement between this world and the other world. TYO! added that her brother, who died in a traffic accident, was young and single. Because he died unmarried, TYO! thought that no one would plan and oversee his memorial service. In addition, he died away from home, something that should be avoided in the Korean tradition. The circumstances surrounding her brother's death made it more lamentable. As an office clerk, TYO! can access the memorial zone and care for her late brother every day, giving her some relief from the grief she feels. Without this opportunity to care for her brother, she would continue in her life of *han*.

As the cases above have shown, cyber memorial zones, as a space for women, are significant because women in Korean funeral culture are no longer marginalized, but instead have become active participants. Although the memorial zones are not a perfect utopia through which women can achieve complete emancipation, they certainly give women a space to release their personal *han* and to redeem themselves.

SOCIOPOLITICALLY ORIENTED ZONES

Sociopolitically oriented and individually oriented cyber memorial zones differ primarily in the respect that the former focus more on social and collective memory. Because sociopolitically oriented zones derive from participants' free will, seek no financial profit, and deal directly with sociopolitical issues, the zones lack the fancy facades and decoration that mark the individually oriented zones sponsored by funeral companies. Instead, in the sociopolitically oriented zones, declaring issues clearly takes precedence. In addition, most memorial letters in these zones are written to the deceased involved in tragic occurrences, while persons writing letters in individually oriented zones address them to their late family members.

Another interesting difference between these two categories is the continuance of memorial writings. More often than not, sociopolitical zones become vigorously activated with the occurrence of an incident. Hundreds or thousands of memorial writings appear in these zones over a very short time period, which indicates the intensity of the public's response to the event. This intensity does not last, however, and as time goes by the heightened attention drops drastically. Years after the event, few visit these memorial zones, most of which appear deserted. On the contrary, individually oriented zones continue to receive new memorial letters for a long time. Some of the sociopolitical memorial zones rely on audiovisual materials, but they focus on delivering the reality of what happened in the occurrences.

Hyo-soon and Mi-sun Memorial Zones

Hyo-soon and Mi-sun, two fourteen-year- girls, were hit and killed by a U.S. military armored car in June 2002. The memorial zones established after their deaths sought to mobilize prayers for their repose. Their miserable deaths and the Korean government's lukewarm attitude about the incident infuriated the Korean people. With the creation of many cyber memorial zones for the two girls, memorial letters flooded these sites. One memorial zone, named *Memorial Gathering for Hyo-soon and Mi-sun* on the *Daum* web portal, bears portraits of Hyo-soon and Mi-sun on its front page.

Memorial letters to this zone reflect the tension and increased attentiveness of the Korean people to these deaths at that time. In the letters posted in the Hyo-soon and Mi-sun memorial zones around June 2002, the collective *han* of feeling sorry for their tragic deaths was poured into the web spaces. Many young mourners were especially sorry for Hyo-soon and Mi-sun because when they were brutally killed, young Koreans were too excited by the Korean soccer team's advancement in the 2002 FIFA World Cup to notice their deaths. A young woman, nicknamed "Rain & Snow," wrote, "So sorry . . . so sorry . . . cannot but be sorry . . . The day you were killed . . . I really did not know you trudged along the way where you could not be returned, with your hope brutally shattered by a U.S. armored car. At that time, I just enjoyed watching people who chanted *dae-han-min-kuk* [great Korea]. Yes . . . I did not pay attention to the story about you. So sorry . . . forgive me my apathy. I will never forget the meaning of your death."

As the incident developed, the zone mirrored the grief of people in a small and weak country that has no jurisdiction over the U.S. soldiers stationed in their territory. The mourners ranged from teenage students to middle-aged housewives and businessmen, which suggested that Hyo-soon and Mi-sun's death became the collective *han* of most Koreans. A poster with the nickname "Yanki," slang for the Westerners in Korea, sent them the following letter:

> *Because we are powerless, the superpowers despise us.*
> *We have to build up our national strength, not to be ignored.*   165
> *This kind of tragedy should not happen again. . . .*
> *Dear Hyo-soon & Mi-sun,*
> *If you are born again in this country, we should be a superpower.*
> *And no American forces anymore.*

In November 2002 national anger reached its peak when a U.S. military court acquitted the two soldiers involved in this incident of negligent homicide charges. The web zones swelled with memorial letters pouring out resentment about the injustice. In addition, these memorial letters showed the broad consensus that the U.S.–South Korea Status of Forces Agreement (SOFA) unfairly advantaged the United States, making an acquittal unavoidable. A writer nicknamed "Loveangel" noted, "We hardly say anything. When the two girls were killed, we only chanted the shameful term of *dae-han-min-kuk* in vain. When the mass media gabbled that Korea is the pillar of Asia and the hope of the region, the two lambs of God were sacrificed. Under SOFA, we allowed the two soldiers to live, who deserve to die. Shame on us."

From this reasoning, the Hyo-soon and Mi-sun memorial zones became the public forum to discuss the unequal relationship between Korea and the United States, and furthermore, to criticize America's reckless foreign policy. Finally, the efforts to release the collective *han* of people went beyond the boundaries of cyber memorial zones and allowed a million Koreans to hold a massive rally in December 2002, where they mourned the death of the two young girls and demanded the revision of the unfair SOFA. This represented a clear moment where the discursive formation of death grew into a political discourse through the will of the people.

CELEBRITY-DRIVEN ZONES

Jung Eun-im Memorial Zones
Jung Eun-im's memorial is an example of a sociopolitically oriented and celebrity-driven zone. Jung Eun-im was a famous radio/television host who died in a traffic accident at the age of thirty-six. She started her career in 1992 hosting a radio show called *FM Film Music*, which made her quite

Cyber Memorial Zones and Shamanic Inheritance

popular. In that sense she was a celebrity. However, Eun-im differed from other celebrities. She broke from the practices of previous hosts, who had remained mostly apolitical and indifferent to various political and social issues. She became actively engaged in sociopolitical topics of the day. Eun-im would begin the show with controversial statements, such as that the government's house-demolition order against the destitute should be stopped, or that she would pray for the repose of innocent Koreans in Cheju Island, who were massacred by our army under the name of ideology. She also played a famous *minjoong gayo*, or resistance song, titled "A March for Comrades." The more she rebelled against social norms, the more her popularity grew.

However, Eun-im had to leave the show for no known reason. Many suspected that she could not continue under the pressure from authoritative powers. Although brutal military regimes lost their power at that time, Korean society still suffered in the aftermath of tyrannical reigns. The fans of the show demanded that the radio station bring her back, but their request was ignored. From this point of view, her departure from the show could be seen as the result of power tension in the transitional period from military-led autocracy to people-led democracy. Jung Eun-im finally came back as the host of the show, a midnight program, in fall 2003. The show ended the following year because of budget cuts.

When she started the show again, she created and maintained a personal blog in the *Cyworld* web portal. There she interacted with her fans, discussing political and social issues. In this blog, named *Eun-im's Attic*, she made comments on controversial topics, like the following: "As soon as I came to the office, a shocking comment from a colleague waited for me: 'How foolish the Assemblymen are in speaking up against dispatching troops to Iraq!!' The term 'national interest' seems to have a strong power. In front of the national interest, the act against dispatching troops becomes foolish."

Eun-im implies that national interests should not align themselves with supporters of the unjustified war. The alignment may provide Korea with an economic advantage in the short term, but eventually the nation will face the criticism that it volunteered as a puppet of the United States in the name of national economic interests. Eun-im wrote this comment three weeks before the fatal accident in June 2004. After her death, many of her fans replied to this comment. Among the replies, one woman said, "What you left behind made me miss you more and more. Please have peace in heaven." A man replied, "Why did God need to take such a righteous woman with him so early?" A young woman dropped a line that read,

"I do not want to cry anymore, Sis. There are so many people who love you. Cheers!!" As seen here, one unique quality of Eun-im's zone lies in her fans' perfect sympathy with her aspirations for social justice and better treatment for the helpless, the weak, and the abandoned.

Another distinguishing feature of this zone is that in the wake of her death, her personal blog and her other cyber fan cafés became cyber memorial zones as her fans continued to post memorial letters. After the accident, Eun-im was in a coma for three months before she died. When the accident was reported, fans flocked to her home page, praying for her fast recovery. A fan nicknamed "Brian," who listened to her film music show as a high school student and is now a doctor, also wished her a full recovery. He wrote that he learned empathy and passion for the world from her. Like Brian's, many letters show that Eun-im's pure sensitivity and aspiration for social justice with music touched them and made them miss her earnestly.

In addition, Eun-im personally cared for the blog when she was alive. Fans consider the zone as the other Eun-im or the incarnation of Eun-im. While visiting the blog, they can hear songs like "The Chokin' Kind" by Joss Stone and "The Closest Thing to Crazy" by Katie Melua. And fans post Eun-im's photos or the compressed files of her programs so that they can see and feel her in the zone although she is no longer in this world. Hey-kyung, a dedicated fan of Eun-im, said to me:

> This is the space where Eun-im and I can be together.
> Whenever I missed her insanely or faced difficulties, I logged into her blog, as I seek for God when I need him. I don't think that my relationship with her is over due to her death. I can still see and feel her. Although she's gone, she's still alive in me.

Because Jung Eun-im genuinely dealt with various controversial issues in Korean society during her broadcasts, fans attempt to share in her love for the world. Given this, although her cyber memorial zone appears to be a celebrity-driven one, it certainly incorporates sociopolitically oriented characteristics.

INTERPRETATION

So far I have explored how shamanism, the indigenous belief system in Korea, has been revived in the dynamics of shamanic inheritance with the advancement of cybercultures in Korea. Cyber memorial zones, as an apparatus of Korean cybercultures, testify to the rebirth of shamanism in the form of digital spirituality. With the historical consideration of Korean shamanism, which the ruling classes have oppressed and marginalized, I have attempted to understand the rebirth of shamanism as the empowerment of the Korean populace. For that purpose, I have outlined the characteristics of different categories of cyber memorial zones and in this essay classified them into three basic categories: the individual oriented, the sociopolitically oriented, and celebrity driven. More often than not, each memorial zone shares some characteristics with the others, and the discussion above has focused on the modified categories of memorial zones.

In examining these zones, I have discerned the ways that inherited shamanic dynamics are constructed. Above all, when individual *han* is released through writing a memorial letter, the dynamics of shamanic inheritance are constructed. They are also constructed when the collective *han* is released in sociopolitically oriented zones. The experience of appeasing *han* in the memorial writings in cyber memorial zones, whether individual or collective, can be explained as an example of the category of "words against death" (Davies, 2002). Davies contends that people can cope with unacceptable situations in life, such as the death of loved ones, by forming words against death "in a wide variety of ways, from asserting belief in an immortal soul to emphasizing the continuity of identity through heirs and successors" (p. 5). Considering memorial writings as a type of "words against death," these writings can help people to appease their *han* and overcome pains and sorrows. The notion of "words against death" provides a tool to understand the construction of inherited shamanic dynamics in cyber memorial zones.

As memorial letters in sociopolitical zones demonstrated, dynamics of shamanic inheritance influenced the participants' aspirations to a communal relationship. Hyo-soon and Mi-sun memorial zones evidently contained the dynamics that allowed the participants to release the collective *han* of the public, inspired the aspirations of communal relationship, and provided a forum to defy unjust and inappropriate government policies. When cyber mourners in Hyo-soon and Mi-sun memorial zones gathered outside cyberspace and demanded the revision of the unfair SOFA, it was apparent that the discourse that had been isolated to cyberspace had spread and created a wider and more powerful form of public discourse through the dynamics of shamanic inheritance.

The role and function of these zones is significant. The establishment of Korean cybercultures has included a specific role for these zones, as they have extended to various controversial sociopolitical issues. Even if the venting experiences of the populace in the memorial zones lack a strong, immediate impulse toward sociopolitical and cultural action, the zones remain noteworthy for their potential to empower the populace through their invocation of the dynamics of the shamanic inheritance. In other words, the inherited shamanic power expressed in new ways in Korean cybercultures, symbolic of a desired triumph over a long-enduring marginalization of the Korean populace, or *minjung*, provides the shamanic heritage with the chance to openly dissolve the collective *han*, thus confirming the consolidation of a newly achieved power for this tradition.

REFERENCES

Bell, D. (2001). *An introduction to cybercultures*. New York, NY: Routledge.

Casey, E. S. (2000). *Remembering: A phenomenological study* (2nd ed.). Bloomington, IN: Indiana University Press.

Davies, D. J. (2002). *Death, ritual, and belief: The rhetoric of funerary rites* (2nd ed.). New York, NY: Continuum.

Kim, S. (2003). Korean shamanic heritage in cyber culture. In M. Hoppál & G. Kósa (Eds.), *Rediscovery of shamanic heritage* (pp. 279–295). Budapest, HU: Akadémiai Kiadó.

Park, B. J. (2001). Patriarchy in Korean society: Substance and appearance of power. *Korean Journal, 41*(4), 48–72.

Seo, N. D. (1981). Towards a theology of han. In Y. B. Kim (Ed.), *Minjung theology: People as the subjects of history* (pp. 51–66). Singapore, SG: Commission on Theological Concerns, Christian Conference of Asia.

CHAPTER 8

Baadaass Mamas

Race, Sex, and Afro-Religiosity in Sankofa

Montré Aza Missouri

This essay centers on the transformation of the "tragic mulatto" in signifying a black nationalist identity in *Sankofa* (Gerima, 1993). The film
is directed by Ethiopian filmmaker Haile Gerima, who is most noted for
his part in the L.A. Rebellion of the 1960s and 1970s, grounded in "third
cinema" ideology, as well as for being a pioneering member of FESPACI,
the Pan-African Federation of Filmmakers. As argued in this essay, many
of the themes in Latin American and Caribbean third cinema—specifically
the use of Afro-religiosity as a means of political resistance—are expressed
in the later works of L.A. Rebellion filmmakers, including *Sankofa*.

In reading *Sankofa* it is important to understand the film in terms
of postcolonial third cinema, which is centered in a Fanonian notion of
the filmmaker as the "native-poet" who has an obligation to use his or
her craft for the social, political, and psychological liberation of colonized
people and in an effort to build national culture separate from that of the
colonial oppressor.[1] The postcolonality of *Sankofa* speaks to the idea of
African Americans as a "colony" within a nation-state, or at the very least
an oppressed people who, like a former colonized people, seek to construct
an identity beyond that of the oppressor.

"Sankofa" is the name of an Akan[2] symbol embodying the idea that an individual must return to whence he or she came in order to move into the future. The concept of "Sankofa" is characterized by the Adinkra[3] symbol of the bird perched with its head turned backward to its tail. Instead of flying, the bird stops and looks back to examine where it started its journey. The symbol is a malleable one and open to black nationalist meanings for an African diaspora seeking to lay claim to its cultural roots in Africa. The film *Sankofa* uses this theme, as well as the signifier of the bird, as a means of "passage" across time and space—from past to present, and from West Africa to the Americas.

The film narrative follows the journey of a black fashion model on a photo shoot, curiously at Elmina Castle in Ghana, the oldest slave castle in West Africa. While the model, Mona, playfully performs before the lens of a white male photographer, the ghosts of the past, as embodied by an elder Ghanaian drummer named Sankofa, warn against her frivolousness. Mona eventually drifts into the male slave dungeon and is surrounded by black maleness—elders, young men and boys, all enslaved Africans. There is clear air of disapproval as the contemporary character of Mona within this dungeon is transported in time and space to a nineteenth-century Southern plantation, where she is now Shola, a house slave. By the end of the narrative she suffers a series of rapes and unthinkable brutality at the hands of her white slave master and the local Roman Catholic priest. After being encouraged to join a slave rebellion by her partner, Shango, Shola is killed in the midst of a fight and transported by a large bird from death back to contemporary time and Elmina Castle, the time and space of the fashion photo shoot. The character returns as Mona emerges from the men's dungeon, now too enlightened to bother with her white photographer and instead joining the elder Ghanaian drummer Sankofa along with a group of seemingly African American tourists who sit fixated on the Atlantic Ocean, looking toward the west—the Americas.

Cinematic themes in *Sankofa* as examined in this essay are black nationalism, which informs every aspect of the film, along with the black matriarchy alternating as symbol of—threat to—black nationalism. Throughout this film there is an overall discomfort with black femininity outside the frame of black masculinity. The black woman is not imagined as a separate identity from black manhood; when in the film miscegenation jeopardizes that dependency, this is framed as an encroachment on black male territory by white men and is met with anger and frustration by virtually all the black male characters. The ultimate solution to the problem of black female victimization is death. As the film suggests when black women die having suffered as the property of white men, they can be reborn and take their rightful and appropriate place as dutiful partners to black men in the struggle for black nationalism.

Although I would argue that *Sankofa* is important as a project produced, distributed, and exhibited independent of the Hollywood industry, thereby remaining committed to a third cinema model, the film is highly problematic in its representation of gender, sexuality, and religion. In *Sankofa* there is an erasure of black femininity that makes the film difficult to categorize as empowering the womanist gaze. I will explore these issues in terms of race, sex, and religion from a womanist perspective. I will begin with the notion of "Oshun as Sister-in-Distress," examining the black female character Mona/Shola as embodying aspects of the Yoruba deity Oshun despite the film's uneasy representations of black women and sexuality. I introduce here a comparative discussion of *Sankofa* in reference to another film, *Xica da Silva* (Barbosa et al., 1976), a classic example of Brazilian third cinema which tackles similar questions of race, sexuality, and religion framed with a black woman slave protagonist, yet departs from *Sankofa* in its approach. In the final argument here, "Afro-Religiosity and Third Cinema," I will use third cinema theories to focus on how Afro-religiosity is used cinematically in the production of postcolonial identity premised on the elevation of folklore and popular memory.

OSHUN AS SISTER-IN-DISTRESS

According to Kara Keeling in *The Witch's Flight: The Cinematic, the Black Femme, and the Image of Common Sense* (2007), the film *Sankofa* is a "construction of a revolutionary black nationalist subjectivity . . . [and] is exemplary of common-sense black nationalism's negotiations with what it considers to be versions of 'black femininity'" (p. 45). Keeling argues that *Sankofa* "dramatizes the violence with which common-sense black nationalism tends to confront black femininity." While interrogating images of "common-sense black nationalism," Keeling defines "common sense" as "a collective set of memory-images that includes experiences, knowledges, traditions." She suggests that these "common-sense" "memory-images" are formulated as clichés that exist to maintain a status quo within the African American community.

One draws from Keeling's reading that "common-sense black nationalism" is embedded in patriarchal notions of race and sex as widely held "norms" within the African American community. Again, she argues that *Sankofa* prescribes an "erasure" of sexuality and femininity for its female characters in order to ascend to "black humanity," yet there are no similar requirements placed on its male characters in terms of sexuality and masculinity for achieving "blackness" (Keeling, 2007, p. 66). In *Sankofa* this "erasure" is not simply that of the sexual black woman but specifically of black women and miscegenation. The narrative insists that the reasonable outcome for black women who have been raped by white men, in order to regain their feminine purity, is death, either as matricide committed by a son or murder at the hands of white male slave overseers. Nonetheless, death is symbolized as a transformation—a metaphysical "rebirth" for the black woman to achieve an ideal of Afrocentric womanhood.

With this transformation, there is a purging of "whiteness" that miscegenation represents, which allows for the film's black women characters to transcend to a state of Afrocentric enlightenment. Keeling (2007) suggests that *Sankofa* examines how "common-sense black nationalism secures consent to dominant conceptualizations of gender and sexuality and thus to the forms of domination and exploitation those conceptualizations rationalize" (p. 45). Keeling specifically regards the black female characterizations in the film as deeply embedded in a gendered black nationalist agenda that frames these characters within the conventions of dominant mainstream cinema.

In *Sankofa* the representations of black women are from a puritanical view of femininity and sexuality, despite the film's reliance on the Yoruba deities for its characterizations. The film's double protagonist, Mona/Shola, exhibits the flirtatious and sexual confidence of the Yoruba deity Oshun as contemporary fashion model Mona. Similarly, as nineteenth-century house slave Shola, the character also demonstrates alternate sides of Oshun as caregiver and as female warrior. Of the three Oshun paths presented here—the "seductress," the "charitable mother," and the "warrior"—the aspect perhaps most problematic in this film is that of the "seductress." Images of Shola as a charitable house slave who saves the master's food for field slaves or, eventually, as a rebellious field slave who helps start a slave insurrection rest comfortably within the black nationalist construction of black femininity. This construction is reminiscent of notions of ideal black femininity projected by the Black Panther Party of the 1960s and 1970s. In contrast, the concept of a sexualized black female character such as Mona appears to challenge black nationalism, as Mona uses her feminine sexuality to negotiate within a white male power structure.

The other significant female character in the film is Nunu, who represents the black matriarchal figure that encompasses African and African diaspora historical elements. Nunu exists within the realm of Yoruba-Atlantic Iyalode,[4] a female commander, as well as historical references to the Ashanti warrior queen Yaa Asantewaa, who during the late nineteenth century, in what is now Ghana, fought against the British colonial forces but was ultimately captured. The characterization of Nunu also appears to be influenced by Harriet Tubman, again as a gun-toting historical female figure committed to the freedom of her people. However, with Iyalode and Yaa Asantewaa, there is a regard for the sociocultural, political, and also the spiritual domains that these two positions embody in terms of Yoruba and Ashanti spiritualities, respectively. This is further emphasized as Nunu is presented as an Akan priestess.

The relationship between Nunu and Shola, like that of other female characters discussed in this research, is one of "insider" and "outsider." Nunu is a leader within the slave community but also, more important, is a respected elder among the maroon society,[5] while Shola is an "outsider" in the field slave community, since she is a house slave, and is introduced to the maroons and Afro-religiosity by Nunu. There is a naïveté in terms of the slavery system apparent in Shola's voice-over, but it is not clear in the film as to why. Perhaps it is because Shola is in fact Mona, who has been transplanted into this nineteenth-century Southern plantation—traveling back from the future.

With contemporary fashion model Mona, the film plays on the notion of the black woman as the subject of the white male gaze in scenes of Mona performing for the white male photographer and his camera. Mona consciously flirts with an infectious laughter of Oshun as she seduces the camera. In *Sankofa* the fashion photographer's camera is used similarly to Mr. Snead's camera in *Daughters of the Dust* (Dash, 1991), as both films draw an association between the photographic lens and male power. However, the films also illustrate that the one being looked at and photographed also possesses power. Mona appears to understand this point as she uses her own sexuality to assert a degree of power over the camera and her white male photographer.

In *Sankofa* there is a focus on the dynamic of black women coded as beauty in the fashion world and the white male gaze, something also seen in other films, including the 1975 film *Mahogany* (Ballard, Cohen, & Gordy), starring singer Diana Ross. In the case of *Mahogany*, Ross plays Tracy, a young woman from the Chicago projects who leaves the United States to become a famous fashion model in Europe. Tracy seemingly enjoys the glamorous life with her fashion photographer boyfriend, played by *Psycho* star Anthony Perkins. Tracy is forced to question the superficiality of her world when she goes back to her old neighborhood and falls for black community activist Brian, played by Billy Dee Williams.

Donald Bogle (2003) refers to characters such as Tracy as the "sister-in-desire," a variation on the "tragic mulatto." The 1970s blaxploitation female figures featured in such films as *Cleopatra Jones* (Tennant & Starrett, 1973) are "tragic mulattoes" rebranded as baadaass mama, further discussed in this essay within the context of the "strongblackwoman."[6] However, both the "sister-in-distress" and the baadaass mama are presences intended to address pressing socioeconomic and political issues facing a black community. *Sankofa* and *Mahogany* proposes similar messages to black women, urging them to abandon superficial Westernized beauty and the fashion industry in favor of affirming the more serious endeavor of black patriarchy.

Another film that examines an interplay between the white male gaze and black female subject as centered in a black women's narrative with the political intention of third cinema is *Xica da Silva*. *Xica* stands in stark contrast to *Sankofa*. On the surface, *Xica* appears to rely heavily on worn stereotypes of black women as oversexed prostitutes. From such a reading of *Xica*, typical constructions of black women characters might be apparent. However, the farcical images of sexuality employed in *Xica* aim at subverting the often patriarchal notions of black women and sexuality such as those presented in *Sankofa*.

Sankofa and *Xica*, both set during the nineteenth-century era of slavery in the Americas, focus on black women's struggles to navigate the slavery system. The two films also explore slavery in relationship to sex and power. While *Sankofa* focuses on the rape of black women by white masters as a means of racial terrorism, *Xica* blurs the lines between "slave" and "master" in terms of sexual and sociopolitical power. I do not mean to underplay the reality of the widespread practice of raping black women as a socioeconomic phenomenon of antebellum slavery. Violence toward black women at the hands of white men during slavery functioned as a means of intimidation in the black community even during Reconstruction. Yet in terms of black resistance against white oppression, Robert Reid-Pharr (2007) argues that throughout American history, black people have "cajoled" the white establishment for their survival. Reid-Pharr asserts, "The Black American has utilized sex and sexuality as a means by which to ensure the survival of black individuals and communities to a *much* greater extent than he has utilized violent confrontation" (p. 4). This is an important point, as *Sankofa* offers violence only as a means by which a slave woman can negotiate her existence but which at the same time ensures her death, whereas *Xica* examines how black women used sexuality as a means of survival.

As in *Sankofa*, both Catholicism and Afro-religiosity are represented in *Xica da Silva*. Xica embodies the boldness, arrogance, sexuality, and desire for wealth, as well as for freedom, indicative of the Yoruba-Atlantic deity Oshun. Again, like the deity of sexuality and wealth, Xica's approach to interacting with her master reaffirms an amoral worldview in which she uses sexuality as a commodity for personal freedom. The film stresses this connection between Oshun and Xica with conspicuously lavish costuming, décor, food, and a personal wait staff linking to the abundance, beauty, sexuality, and wealth of the Afro-religious deity. Further, on the elaborate boat built for Xica to sail on the river, she acts as a queen overlooking a sexual orgy of sorts performed by her servant. Here again, the river is significant, as Oshun is a river deity.

Notions of gender and sexuality in *Xica* parallel arguments made by African feminist Oyeronke Oyewumi in *The Invention of Women: Making an African Sense of Western Gender Discourses* (1997). The character Xica reveals two distinctly non-Western perspectives on gender and sexuality that permeate this film and thereby provide African feminist representations from a white male director. First, Oyewumi asserts that sexuality from a non-Christian, African context is *not* moral. Therefore, monetary exchange based on sexual favors is *not* a question of morality. Rather, sexuality is amoral. However, Oyewumi's argument does not condone rape, since rape is the violation of one's personhood and ability to control one's own body. Second, Oyewumi contends that African women within precolonial societies were not linked to one another simply by virtue of their "bio-logical" characteristics. In other words, the whole notion of "feminism" itself within an African context is necessary in addressing the patriarchal systems put in place as a result of colonialism. Instead, what can be assessed from Oyewumi's assertions is a rethinking of Western mores regarding women and their sexuality.

Although Xica may appear to be a caricature of the sexualized black woman, her character symbolizes a source of feminine resistance by black women—a resistance to the "common sense" of black patriarchy that Keeling describes. Although Xica does not initially attempt anything like the massive slave resistance of Shola on the Lafayette plantation, she does demand ownership of her body and even the conditions of her enslavement. Xica transforms her body from a source of white male pleasure into a means of distinctive, irresistible torture, as framed by the screams of pain heard from the bedrooms of her white male prey.

With its quirky and seemingly clichéd attempts to conceptualize black female sexuality as a means of resistance, the film attributes agency to Xica as the character who has masterfully elevated herself beyond a victim. She is not a male's toy, but rather men are her toys that she chooses to manipulate at will, even to the benefit of Teodoro, a black Robin Hood–like figure who steals gold and diamonds from the local and colonial government and whose wife is being held as a slave by João Fernandes. The scene of a secret meeting between Xica and Teodoro in a far-off cave stands in stark contrast to the exchanges between Shola and Shango in *Sankofa*. Whereas Shango is a constant reminder for the audience of Shola's perpetual "sin" of being the master's sexual prey and of not being revolutionary, Teodoro and Xica's encounter is one of equals, as Teodoro recognizes that her means of resistance is through sexual power, while his is through the stealing of gold and diamonds. Neither is presented as immoral; rather, it is the slavery system itself that forces individuals toward these extremes as means of resistance that are projected as fundamentally immoral.

Conversely, *Sankofa* invites the uneasy perception that Shola is a willing victim in these continual rapes by her master. It is only at the hands of black nationalist Shango that Shola can be cleansed of the transgression of rape, which is presented in a bathing scene by a river in which Shango gently cleans and in effect heals her body and spirit from the impact of sexual rape of the slave master and the spiritual rape of the local Catholic priest. Shola is at a crossroads between the white patriarchy of slavery and Western Christianity and the patriarchy of black nationalism. Perhaps the only alternative to these choices is the world of Nunu, who provides a feminine space to which Shola can retreat. Within that geography there is an emphasis on Afro-religiosity and the remembrance of a pre-slavery African past. Yet that centering of Afro-religiosity is not solely the domain of Nunu and her knowledge of spiritual forces.

In fact, *Sankofa* references the significance of Obeah, an Afro-Jamaican religion, in the daily slave life with Shola's insistence that Shango, a Jamaican-born slave, provide her with a potion to force Joe, a mulatto slave overseer, to fall in love with Shola's friend, fellow house slave Lucy. Although the potion does not create the sought-after romance between Lucy and Joe, it does force Joe to come to terms with his hatred for his mother, Nunu, and his unresolved issues with being mixed-race and the product of rape. This reliance on Shango strengthens Shola's positioning with him, as Shango relentlessly scolds her for seemingly not being "black enough." Likewise, throughout the film, Shango's beliefs and Nunu's religion construct a continuity between the Obeah system of the Americas and the Akan religion of Africa, specifically embodied in the culture of Jamaica, and demonstrate how each working together invokes daily resistance and a mass slave uprising on the Lafayette plantation.

In comparison to the mass uprising presented in *Sankofa*, *Xica* also provides a reading of black women's survival and even resistance in terms of reclaiming a sense of control over their bodies. It is this survival and the ultimate desire for freedom that motivates Xica, and yet the film's theme—like *Sankofa's*—is centered on a national cultural identity constructed through the narrative of a black slave woman. In the case of *Sankofa*, it is the transformation of Mona, an unconsciously sexualized woman, into Shola, a sexually abused house slave who finds her true revolutionary self through the Akan folklore of slave elder Nunu and the Afro-Caribbean knowledge of roots and spirituality of Shango, that results in an empowered field slave who is willing to die in order to kill her white slave master and torturer, Master Lafayette. Again, in the final act of *Sankofa*, Shola's spirit is transported from the Americas back to the slave castle in Ghana by a bird, where she travels through space and time from the past to the present, presumably after she has been killed on the plantation while attempting to the kill the master. This transformation is what the film proposes to its audience, to go back and remember in order to resist as well as to be transformed, adopting an Afrocentric, black nationalist cultural identity.

In *Xica da Silva*, by the end of the film João has become possessed by his efforts to satisfy Xica's insatiable desire for signifiers of wealth—Parisian clothes, luxurious boats, servants, and so on—all seeming substitutes for the freedom from slavery which João refuses her. With his excesses, João is investigated by a Portuguese inspector and is ultimately sent back to Lisbon, a town now distraught at the return of the Portuguese official. The white townspeople blame Xica for João's fall. With nowhere to go, Xica escapes to the monastery where José, the son of Xica's original slave master and another one of her sexual conquests, has remained in exile. José, without the wealth of his father, and Xica, without the luxurious lifestyle that João afforded her, denounce the cares of the bourgeois elite. Their playful declaration and flirtatious banter signify a far deeper message of revolution, intertwining the cry for slave emancipation with Brazil's independence movement. Through the sexual union at the end of the film, there is a symbolic link of the political history of resistance in Brazil to the story of Xica, a black slave woman long dismissed as merely a sexual object, who can instead become the symbol of national identity based on resistance. However, that resistance is not simply one of violence but also one of survival.

However, unlike *Sankofa, Xica de Silva* intermingles both Afro-religious symbols and Catholic references as Xica, in a sign of respectability and a testament to her imminent liberation, wants to attend the local Catholic church for Mass, a privilege exclusive to the white elite. After she is ejected by the church's priest, João insists that he will build Xica her own church. In the final scene of the film, it is again a Catholic monastery to which Xica and José escape as paupers in exile, vowing to fight the elite bourgeois. It is there that Xica is sexually aroused by José's call to freedom, and she initiates an Oshun-like sexual advance. Within these scenes, the film presents a religious hybridity in a far more comical way than in *Daughters of the Dust* but still proposes that beyond the African past, the experience of the Americas has been one of intermingling cultural and religious signs in the process of forming a distinctive cultural identity.

Despite black female protagonists and questions of female sexuality, Afro-religiosity, and power, as well as complex scenes that critically examine the gender relationship, it is difficult to position *Sankofa* as a womanist film. Rather, it is a third cinema call to action—a cinematic push toward the nationalist struggle like that of *Xica* which envisions the postcolonial existence of the nation within the symbolic narrative of a black woman and slavery. Different from *Xica*, the characterizations in *Sankofa* rely on version of a disempowered "tragic mulatto," including the "sister-in-distress" and baadaass mama, that turns black female victimization into black nationalist rage. According to the film, the inherent problem with the black community is the presence of femaleness and the female form. As imagined in this film, it is through the transformation of feminine frailties into masculine assertions that true black liberation is born.

AFRO-RELIGIOSITY AND THIRD CINEMA

In *Soul Power: Culture, Radicalism, and the Making of a U.S. Third World Left*, Cynthia A. Young (2006) argues that the L.A. Rebellion "addressed many of the dilemmas posed by the sixties: the cultural roots of identity, the possibility of black freedom despite political alienation, and the similarities between the ways that the U.S. nation-state secured local and global domination of nonwhite peoples" (p. 213). According to Young, L.A. Rebellion filmmakers not only relied on but also transformed the techniques and aesthetics in a turn that is known as third cinema. This is significant, of course, as director Haile Gerima, an adherent of the L.A. Rebellion, has continued to rely on the movement's ideological basis in his production up to even his most recent work, *Teza* (Gerima, 2008).

The L.A. Rebellion manifesto shared basic characteristics with Fernando Solanas and Octavio Gettino's "Towards a Third Cinema" (2000), by identifying third cinema as an alternative voice to the imperialist Hollywood system and the camera as the means of liberating previously unheard communities and nations. The black independent films of the L.A. Rebellion, made by figures such as Haile Gerima, Charles Burnett, Larry Clark, and later Julie Dash, are grounded in a third cinema framework.

In defining "third cinema," it is essential to understand "first cinema" as the dominant Hollywood system as well as other commercial industries based on the notion of the cinema audience as passive consumers. Such industries would include Bollywood and Nollywood. By contrast, "second cinema" represents those European film movements that sought to counter the commercial Hollywood system. European "arthouse" cinema, influenced by Italian neorealism and French new wave, presents counterimages that challenge the ideology and mechanics of the Hollywood system.

Yet second cinema, despite its resistance to the dominant global system, according to third cinema theorists, embodies a narcissism and preoccupation with the individual. Instead, third cinema is an approach to film that encourages audiences to be active participants propelled toward actions as a result of watching the film. Unlike first cinema, in which the audience is expected to be passive spectators consumed by the "magic" of film, third cinema disrupts the illusion by reminding its audience that they are watching a film and that the film is simply the beginning of a larger sociopolitical dialogue and an invitation to social action.

Likewise, new modes of production which may require defying the conventions of Hollywood production, such as members of the crew taking on multiple roles (a practice that would be prohibited on Hollywood productions), is permissible and perhaps encouraged in third cinema filmmaking. Even the means of exhibition vary from those of first and second cinema. Although one may watch a third cinema production in a theater, the ideal is that the film, as a call to action, be accessible in nontheatrical spaces in order to reach the wider community. Third cinema may share stylistic aspects of film with second cinema, such as neorealism in terms of using nonprofessional actors and shooting entirely on location, but again, there are central differences, the main one being to approach film not simply as entertainment for consumerism or solely for social commentary but instead as a call for sociopolitical action.

Toni Cade Bambara (1993) uses the mission of the L.A. Rebellion as the means of positioning the social and political significance of Dash's *Daughters*, which explicitly relies on Yoruba spiritual traditions for the film's image systems and characterization. By referencing Yoruba orishas such as Obatala, Ogun, and Yemoja in the historical context of a post-Reconstruction, black American South, *Daughters of the Dust*, like *Sankofa*, places the African American experience within the Yoruba-Atlantic phenomena and therefore provides a historical and cultural basis for a shared African diaspora identity with Latin America and the Caribbean.

Beyond the realm of cinematic aesthetic, from a historical perspective the relationship between Afro-religiosity and resistance in the Americas is apparent in various emancipation and national independence movements, and in defining national identity. Attribution of the successful 1791 Haitian revolution to the practice of Vodou; the connection between African religion and the establishment of Palmares (a separate nation of runaway slaves in northeastern Brazil during the seventeenth century); and the continued sociopolitical power of Afro-Brazilian priestesses of Yemanjá and Oshun in Salvador, Bahia, are all prominent examples of the intersection of Afro-religiosity, resistance, and national identity.

Even within the history of enslavement in North America, Afro-religiosity has been linked with slave revolts, according to Walter Rucker (2001). He argues that Akan religious conjurers were pivotal to a 1712 uprising of slaves in New York City, in which ten whites were killed and which caused fear throughout the British colonies. Rucker cites similarities between the New York City uprising in 1712 and another slave revolt in Jamaica in 1760, in which Akan-based, Obeah religious conjurers were instrumental. In both cases, white powder was rubbed across the slaves before the revolt as a means of spiritually empowering them with the belief of invincibility.

Rucker (2001) argues that the influence of Afro-religious conjurers served the purpose of leading and aiding slave revolts and uprisings throughout the North American colonies both by empowering slaves with talismans for invulnerability and through intimidation tactics, as most slaves feared the perceived spiritual powers these conjurers possessed. Rucker also identifies the spiritual conjurer as acting as a cultural conduit between Africa and America by preserving the cultural/spiritual practices of West and Central African communities. Finally, in the highly mixed slave communities of the American South, slaves from the French and British Caribbean, American-born slaves such as the Gullahs, and African-born Akan-, Mande-, Igbo-, and Bantu-speaking slaves found a common bond in their admiration and fear of the Afro-religious conjurer, who operated without fear of the white master's power and who could devise remedies and portions that encouraged daily resistance by ordinary slaves.

Returning to the question of cinematic aesthetics, *Sankofa* and other productions by L.A. Rebellion directors, including *Daughters of the Dust* and *To Sleep with Anger* (1990), project Afro-religiosity and folklore as cultural memory. Film theorist Teshome Gabriel (1989) suggests that "historians privilege the written word of the text—it serves as their rule of law. It claims a 'centre' that continuously marginalizes others" (p. 53). However, Gabriel recognizes within films of Latin America and the Caribbean the importance of an "unofficial history" that informs third cinema aesthetics in its empowerment of the disaffected and the disenfranchised. Examples include African folklore and oral tradition with the auteur filmmakers in the role of the "griot,"[7] as used to describe third cinema or the works of Senegalese filmmaker Sembène. In Latin American third cinema this "popular memory" and "oral history" inform the "slavery films," focused on historical moments of black resistance that act as a metaphor for continued struggles of a postcolonial nation. bell hooks (1992) echoes the call for elevating the oral and visual text as the cultural and historical narratives of a people by arguing, "As red and black people decolonize our minds we cease to place value solely on the written document. We give ourselves back memory. We acknowledge that the ancestors speak to us in a place beyond written history" (p. 193). Yet the aesthetics of L.A. Rebellion filmmakers again construct the "memory" of a people as much as it reflects. These memories find their origins as much within a Latin American and Caribbean independent filmmaking aesthetic as they do within the oral traditions of Africa.

In addition to a reliance on popular memory, in "Post-Third-Worldist Culture: Gender, Nation, and the Cinema" Ella Shohat (2003) argues that Latin American and African third cinema seeks to counter the mainstream Hollywood style of filmmaking by sharing "a certain preoccupation with First-World feminist independent films which sought alternative images of women" (p. 55). Shohat continues by suggesting that the "digging into 'herstories' involved a search for new cinematic and narrative forms that challenged both canonical documentaries and mainstream fiction films, subverting the notion of 'narrative pleasure' based on the 'male gaze.'" Similarly, L.A. Rebellion filmmakers focus their efforts on subverting the Hollywood style by giving prominence to black female characters and by centering on black women narratives. This emphasis on black women informs the work of L.A. Rebellion filmmaker Julie Dash (e.g., *Daughters of the Dust*). And the experiences of black women are central to the narratives of L.A. Rebellion filmmaker Haile Gerima with his first feature,

Bush Mama (Gerima, 1974), and his most celebrated film, *Sankofa*. Like Latin American and African third cinema films, *Sankofa* aims to engage a postcolonial discourse by questioning Hollywood aggrandizement of a white male hero.

Instead, by presenting black women at the center of the narrative, L.A. Rebellion third cinema challenges the Western meta-narratives of racial and gender hierarchy and, in so doing, according to Shohat, finds commonality with so-called first world feminist filmmakers. What makes the L.A. Rebellion even more compelling is the premise that the African American community is a socially, economically, and politically third world space located within the first world of the United States. Therefore, a cinema that subverts the conventions of mainstream American film does so by answering back to its own neocolonial condition.

I would argue that L.A. Rebellion filmmakers borrowed not only from the political ideology of Latin American third cinema filmmakers but also from an aesthetic that centers on constructing a postcolonial national culture and identity based on a shared heritage of Afro-religious cultural history. Brazilian and Cuban filmmakers have used Afro-religiosity as a means of forging national identity through their audience's acceptance of a national culture based on a shared spiritual heritage with Yoruba people. Cinematically, Yoruba-derived religions have formed a backdrop for exploring Marxist ideology in films such as Glauber Rocha's *Barravento* (Netto & Rocha, 1962) that set into motion the Cinema Nôvô movement. In keeping with Rocha's Marxist convictions, he is critical of Yoruba-Atlantic religion despite his affinity for his native Bahia, Brazil, which is commonly thought of as the center of the Yoruba-derived religion Candomblé. However, the work of Brazilian filmmaker Carlos Diegues, including *Xica da Silva*, incorporates signifiers based on Candomblé in order to explore historical accounts of Afro-Brazilian slave resistance as a call for Brazilian national resistance to global capitalism and American imperialism. More recently, documentaries such as *Odô Yá! Life with AIDS* (Cypriano, 1997), on Candomblé rituals providing healing and hope for Brazilians living with AIDS, and notably Walter Salles's *Central do Brasil* (de Clermont-Tonnerre & Salles, 1998), both present the practice of Candomblé as a central aspect of the Brazilian national character.

Similarly, productions like the Cuban film *La Vida es Silbar* (Herrera & Pérez, 1998), directed by Fernando Peréz, use the Yoruba orishas allegorically, whereby the main character, a follower of Shango, the deity of thunder and male sexuality, is in search of his mother, the aptly named Cuba, who is a devotee of Yemayá (Yemoja), the deity of maternity and resistance. In this film the protagonist runs through the streets of Havana in the rain, in search of Cuba. It is not coincidental that Yemayá is also the deity associated with the Middle Passage and the patron of those incarcerated, enslaved, and oppressed. Just as the nation of Cuba seeks to be free from the dominant power just to the north, the United States, the main character seeks to be free from the torture of childhood memories, and, at the same time, he searches for the protection of his mother, Cuba.

Additionally, the 1995 Cuban comedy *Guantanamera*, directed by Tomás Gutiérrez Alea, utilizes the Ikú, the Yoruba force that is death, within the context of the road trip film. Solimar Otero, in "Ikú and Cuban Nationhood: Yoruba Mythology in the *Guantanamera*" (1999), further examines the role of Afro-religiosity as represented in post-revolutionary Cuban cinema and in constructing a Cuban national culture and identity with respect to images in *Guantanamera*. In discussing Oscar E. Quirós's work, Otero states, "Quirós points to an important assumption that Cuban filmmakers are counting on: that Cubans will identify African religious culture as their own. Along with this assumption comes the hope, the desire to trigger a connection between these cultural forms and national identity" (p. 122). Otero goes on to discuss films that specifically depict Yoruba-Atlantic religion, as she recognizes that "African religion in Cuban revolutionary film takes on a social meaning, usually one of resistance" (p. 123).

From politics to cinema, Afro-religiosity plays an essential role defining Cuban national identity. Like those of the Brazilian cinema, Cuban films have relied on slave narratives with depictions of black resistance and Afro-religiosity to construct films that galvanize national audiences, specifically white audiences. These films fall within the theoretical framework outlined by Gabriel in that they elevate "popular memory" to the level of the dominant discourse of "official history." Films such as Tomás Gutiérrez Alea's *La última cena* (Llapur, Vives, & Gutiérrez Alea, 1976), like *Xica* and Carlos Diegues's *Quilombo* (1984), construct images in which there is an identification with the struggle for liberation by black people within the historical context of slavery and the present-day struggle by maintaining a post-revolutionary Cuban society amid mounting global socioeconomic pressures. In these films the historical resistance of black people and the part that Afro-religiosity played in these struggles act as signifiers and rallying cries for a continued commitment to socialist ideals.

Nelson P. Valdés (2001) attributes Fidel Castro's appeal as a charismatic populist leader to a communicative relationship between him and the Cuban people grounded in a set of predetermined references based on the Yoruba-Cuban religion Santería.[8] Valdés correctly identifies the beginning of this complex dialogue between Castro and the nation as Castro's first televised speech to the Cuban people, one week after the fall of former Cuban president Fulgencio Batista. According to Valdés, Castro's assumption of power on January 1, 1959, is significant timing since, within the Santería calendar, the date signifies the day of Eshu-Eleggua, who in Yoruba religion is the messenger of all the deities and the ruler of crossroads and pathways. In Valdés's account, Castro's victory on that day was the first of several signifiers for the Cuban people that he was the "chosen one."

In his address at the presidential palace in Havana, a nervous Castro spoke to the nearly one million people crowded before the building. Castro, in the middle of his speech, asked for an affirmation from one of his commanders sharing the stage with him. As Castro asked, "How am I doing, Camilo?" the answer came in the apparition of two white doves flying over the crowd and circling over the podium where Castro spoke. Based on Valdés's assessment and documentary footage from *Fidel: The Untold Story* (Steven & Bravo, 2001), one dove landed on the podium and the other perched on Castro's shoulder. To historians, the doves were quickly understood by the crowd and the millions of Cubans across the nation watching the speech on television to be the affirmation from the Yoruba deities that Castro was the divine leader of Cuba.

Although Valdés recognizes the doves as messengers of the Yoruba deity of human creation, Obatala, in the documentary film *Fidel* the doves are identified as symbolic of the island's patron, Ochún. The symbol was viewed as a divine endorsement of Afro-Cubans' abolitionist fight, the Cuban people's fight for independence against Spanish rule, and now a Castro-led fight against a pro-American Batista dictatorship. Historically laden and politically charged, the appearance of these two white doves in the black of night, hovering and landing on the new Cuban leader, was perhaps not only great televised theater but also legitimation of Castro's regime within the shared conception of Afro-Cuban culture and Afro-religiosity as a historical basis for social and political resistance.

However, returning to the question of Afro-religiosity in Latin American third cinema and, in particular, the use of Santería in post-revolutionary Cuban film, Castro's efforts to claim a Afro-religious divine mandate for his rule of Cuba is clearly seen in the films of the Instituto Cubano de Arte e Industria Cinematográficos (ICAIC). The ICAIC is the Castro-backed national film school in Havana, headed by third cinema filmmaker and cofounder Julio García Espinosa. By concentrating on filmmaking that represents both Afro-religiosity and Marxist ideology, ICAIC filmmakers have created a harmonious relationship between otherwise uncomfortably juxtaposed concepts of Marxism and religion.

For Cuban and Brazilian cultural and political resistance, figures from Yoruba-Atlantic culture and religion reign as symbols of national identity regardless of race or class: in Cuba it is again the figure of Oshun, the Yoruba deity of love, wealth, and female sexuality, as manifested in the Catholic visitation of La Virgen de Caridad de Cobre as a beautiful mulatto woman. This racial and cultural hybrid as a New World incarnation of the Yoruba deity is recognized as embodying the essence of Cubanness with historical significance to the Afro-Cuban slave rebellions, Cuba's fight for independence from Spanish rule, and, generations later, the Cuban Revolution. The representation of the Yoruba-Atlantic deity Oshun as a mulatto woman embodies the national identity of the Cuban people across racial lines and, as a symbol, is characteristically linked to the Cuban people and their resistance.

Likewise, for Brazilians, national identity is personified within the image of the Yoruba deity of maternity and the ocean, Yemanjá (Yemoja). Similar to Cubans, Brazilians across racial and class lines identify with the Yoruba deity, manifested in a mulatto woman as symbolic of the racial and cultural hybridity of Brazilian people. For both countries, which are highly racially and culturally mixed, Afro-religiosity and culture engender national unity and cultural identification through a common set of codes. These mystical and exotic African-derived religions are a means of proudly distinguishing the nations from their former European rulers and the contemporary neocolonial power of the United States.

By incorporating characterizations based on Yoruba deities and folklore, Latin American third cinema filmmakers use Afro-religious symbols as cinematic shorthand for national unity and cultural resistance, as representations of social concerns from classism to homophobia, and as a consistent theme of globalization. The mulatto represents the marginalized segments of the population, since, despite her light skin, she is not white and therefore does not enjoy the privileges of the ruling class. Imagining the Yoruba female deity as the mulatto woman in symbolizing the state, I would argue, suggests that this figure is seen as being somewhat different from her black or indigenous ancestry.

The mulatto woman represents all three of the major races of the Americas while seemingly not belonging to any one of them. A cultural and racial mix, her spiritual powers are from Africa and her sexual charm is the racial blend of the Americas—she can be the prostitute, the loving mother, or the fierce warrior who fights for liberation and resistance. As opposed to the United States, a nation personified more by the ethnocentric, machismo conquests of film star John Wayne than the request for the "huddled masses" of Lady Liberty, the mere presence of this fragile yet fierce female form as embodying the nature of the national character is a point of resistance from the positioning of Euro-America.

L.A. Rebellion filmmakers' appropriation of Afro-religiosity and the black woman, specifically the figures of the mulatto as Mona/Shola in *Sankofa*, takes on even greater significance as the filmmakers direct their audience to confront questions of blackness and of cultural roots as a racially and culturally hybrid African American community. In this regard, the mulatto woman comes to symbolize something more than simply an eroticized image empowered by the mystical knowledge of the "dark continent." Instead, this figure is a framing of the African American experience as one of hybridity, a positioning between Native American, European, and African ancestry. Additionally, L.A. Rebellion filmmakers Haile Gerima, Charles Burnett, and Julie Dash utilize Afro-religiosity as means of crafting an U.S.-based third cinema.

For example, *Sankofa* remains committed to the aesthetic tenets of Latin American third cinema in terms of the manipulation of time and space, as shown by *El otro Francisco* (Giral, 1975), and revisiting the history of slavery in order to provide critical commentary on contemporary social and political issues, as seen in *La última cena* and *Xica da Silva*. However, *Sankofa* stands apart from *Daughters of the Dust*, which is politically progressive not simply in terms of its representations but also in its cinematic style, forging a distinctively womanist approach to filmmaking. A more recent example of the continued tradition of weaving various times and spaces within Latin American and Caribbean third cinema is the documentary work of Gloria Rolando, notably *The Eyes of the Rainbow* (Rolando, 1997). Here the director recounts the life of black revolutionary Assata Shakur, her escape from the FBI, and her decades-long exile in Cuba. Rolando brings together the folklore of the Yoruba female deity of lightning and the female warrior Oya with the musical form and images of the American South and Shakur's own stories of her grandmother. In retelling her grandmother's dreams of Shakur's eventual escape from prison after being accused of murdering a New Jersey police officer, Rolando, like Gerima with *Sankofa*, constructs a connection between African Americans and Afro-Caribbeans through a shared heritage of Afro-religiosity and political resistance.

The challenge for a film such as *Sankofa* is how to subvert the narrative, style, and structure of dominant cinema. As previously discussed, undermining the "usual" nature of Hollywood storytelling does not simply involve a change of cinematic character or plot but also the deconstruction of the "normative" way of seeing and knowing. *Daughters of the Dust* meets this challenge by not only abandoning the conventional single protagonists and the racial, sexual, and religious conventions of the Western hero, but also by disregarding the standard structure and visual style of mainstream cinema. Conversely, *Eve's Bayou* (Amin et al., 1997) has less lofty political intentions and therefore remains committed to the traditions of Hollywood storytelling, albeit centering its narrative on a space, a time, and characters normally unseen on film screens. *Sankofa* stands at a crossroads between two diverging ideological spaces. This is a political film with intentions best expressed in Shohat's reading of third cinema filmmakers as redressing the racial and gender discourse; however, it attempts to achieve this goal by reasserting male domination centered on black nationalism.

Locating a space for a black nationalism in the midst of a female narrative is an approach tackled at several intervals in the film career of Haile Gerima, whose debut feature and the first of the "Watts films" of the L.A. Rebellion, *Bush Mama*, featured a female protagonist. Throughout Gerima's more than thirty years of filmmaking, he has focused much of his energy on telling the story of the African American experience. In his most recent work, *Teza*, he returns to his mother's village in Ethiopia to present a seemingly autobiographical story of lost innocence and the struggle for identity after years of migration. In *Teza* there is a sensibility toward Afro-religiosity, in this case with regard to the Ethiopian Orthodox Church and its regenerative effect on a community at the brink of collapse. This very personal story unravels as the protagonist struggles with notions of belonging and home that are potentially lost to him forever. In the midst of violence and corruption, the central theme of *Teza* is how an individual and a nation reconstruct their identity with a sense of rebirth and renewal.

Although *Teza* frames a greater sense of humanity within the female characterizations, there is still a necessity for death in framing motherhood. Rather than the matricide seen in *Sankofa*, *Teza* depicts infanticide, as the protagonist Anberber's lover takes her infant baby boy and smashes him to death over something as seemingly trivial as watching her husband wooing another woman. In the film, the child is sacrificed in front of his father as means of revenge. As with the death of Nunu at the hands of her own son, this scene is very difficult to understand, as it is driven by the behavior of a female character otherwise presented as rational. The final scenes of the film become more problematic as this same woman who killed her baby son in an earlier period of her life is now giving birth to the protagonist's son. Perhaps, as in *Sankofa*, death is the ultimate erasure, as a possible resolution to the apparently problematic coexistence of black male and black female. Any black women characters that stand outside of black male authority, specifically in terms of sexuality, require erasure. It is through death that black women characters, both Nunu and Shola, can transcend to become acceptable members of the nationalist Pan-African community.

In *Sankofa*, black women characters are limited to actions that have more to do with postcolonial male anxieties and frustrations than with womanist erotic intentions of blackness as beauty and of giving pleasure to the womanist gaze. The images in *Sankofa* may be powerful, but they are not necessarily empowering to black women, despite the emphasis on black women's experiences. Instead, *Sankofa*, although squarely grounded in third cinema, stays within the space of dominant, mainstream cinema in terms of framing the female subject and its preoccupation with serving the male gaze. In this regard, *Sankofa* does not question the white male status quo in terms of furthering projecting patriarchal systems. The images do not disrupt business as usual but instead affirm it with the subjugation of black women within the use of black nationalist "common sense."

189

NOTES

1. Frantz Fanon in *The Wretched of the Earth* discusses the importance of the artist in the construction of national culture. This notion of art as part of the postcolonial project informs "third cinema" and the push for film as an apparatus for decolonization.

2. Akan is the family of ethnicities to which the Ashanti belong. In this context, the term "Akan" refers to the cosmology and indigenous spiritual practices of the Akan.

3. The Akan in Ghana use Adinkra symbols in artwork as well as to adorn items with great significance like a royal stool or materials for regular use such as bowls or T-shirts. Adinkra symbols are designs like ancient Egyptian hieroglyphics as images signifying broad concepts.

4. According to Oyeronke Olajubu in *Women in the Yoruba Religious Sphere* (2003), Iyalode is one of the most powerful chieftaincy titles given to a woman in a Yoruba town. At times in Yoruba history, the Iyalode ruled the military and may have competed with male chiefs for goods (p. 26).

5. Maroon societies initially were secret compounds populated by runaway slaves in the Caribbean, South America, and the American South. These compounds were often the destinations for other runaways in an escape to freedom. Maroon societies were primarily self-sufficient but were also known for conducting slave raids on plantations, stealing food and taking slave women.

6. The term "strongblackwoman" is used by Michele Wallace in her 1978 work *Black Macho and the Myth of the Superwoman* (1999), in which she examines black matriarchy as constructed during slavery and as a continued notion that dehumanizes black women and underestimates the experiences of oppression that black women face.

7. "Griot" is a West African term with French and Portuguese origins. It is the name given to a storyteller or oral historian.

8. Valdés states that the Roman Catholic Church acknowledges the enormous influence Santería has in Cuban life, especially among that country's large Catholic population.

REFERENCES

Amin, M. (Executive Producer), Bennett, M. (Co-executive Producer), & Lemmons, K. (Director). (1997). *Eve's bayou* [motion picture]. USA: Trimark Pictures, ChubbCo Film, & Addis Weschsler Pictures.

Ballard, J. (Producer), Cohen, R. (Producer), & Gordy, B. (Director). (1975). *Mahogany* [motion picture]. USA: Motown Productions, Nikor Productions, & Paramount Pictures.

Bambara, T. C. (1993). Reading the signs, empowering the eye: *Daughters of the dust* and the black independent cinema movement. In M. Diawara (Ed.), *Black American cinema* (pp. 118–144). London, UK: Routledge.

Barbosa, J. (Producer), Correa, A. (Producer), Ferraz, H. (Producer), Oliosi, J. (Producer), & Diegues, C. (Director). (1976). *Xica da Silva* [motion picture]. Brazil: Enbrafilme & Terra Filmes.

Bogle, D. (2003). *Toms, coons, mulattoes, mammies, and bucks: An interpretive history of blacks in American film* (4th ed.). New York, NY: Continuum.

Brown, E. (1992). *A taste of power: A black woman's story*. New York, NY: Anchor.

Cypriano, T. (Director). (1997). *Odô Yá! Life with AIDS* [motion picture]. (Available from Filmmaker Library, 3212 Duke Street, Alexandria, VA, 22314.)

Dash, J. (Producer & Director). (1991). *Daughters of the dust* [motion picture]. USA & UK: American Playhouse, Geechie Girls, & WMG Films.

de Clermont-Tonnerre, M. (Producer), & Salles, W. (Director). (1998). *Central do Brasil* [motion picture]. Brazil: Canal+.

Diegues, C. (Producer & Director). (1984). *Quilombo* [motion picture]. Brazil: Embrafilme.

Dunn, S. (2008). *"Baad bitches" and sassy supermamas: Black power action films*. Urbana, IL: University of Illinois Press.

Fanon, F. (2001). *The wretched of the Earth*. New York, NY: Penguin.

Feitshans, B. (Producer), & Hill, J. (Director). (1974). *Foxy Brown* [motion picture]. USA: American International Pictures.

Friedan, B. (2001). *The feminine mystique*. New York, NY: Norton.

Gabriel, T. H. (1989). Third cinema as guardian of popular memory: Towards a third aesthetics. In J. Pines & P. Willeman (Eds.), *Questions of third cinema* (pp. 53–64). London, UK: BFI.

Gerima, H. (Producer & Director). (1979). *Bush mama* [motion picture]. USA: Mypheduh Productions.

Gerima, H. (1989). Triangular cinema: Community, storyteller, activist. In J. Pines & P. Willeman (Eds.), *Questions of third cinema* (pp. 65–70). London, UK: BFI.

Gerima, H. (Producer & Director). (1993). *Sankofa* [motion picture]. USA: Channel Four Films.

Gerima, H. (Producer & Director). (2008). *Teza* [motion picture]. Ethiopia: Negod-Gwad Productions.

Giral, S. (Director). (1974). *El otro Francisco* [motion picture]. Cuba: Instituto Cubano del Arte e Industria Cinematográficos.

Grayson, S. (2000). *Symbolizing the past: Reading "Sankofa," "Daughters of the* dust," and "Eve's bayou" as histories. Lanham, MD: University Press of America.

Gross, J. (Producer), & Van Peebles, M. (Producer & Director). (1971). *Sweet Sweetback's baadasssss song* [motion picture]. USA: Yeah.

Haley, A. (Writer), Lee, J. (Writer), Chomsky, M. J. (Director), Erman, J. (Director), Greene, D. (Director), & Moses, G. (Director). (1977). *Roots* [television series]. Burbank, CA: Warner Bros. Television & David L. Wolper Productions.

Herrera, F. (Producer), & Pérez, F. (Director). (1998). *La vida es silbar* [motion picture]. Cuba: Instituto Cubano del Arte e Industria Cinematográficos & Wanda Films.

Hobson, J. (2005). *Venus in the dark: Blackness and beauty in popular culture*. New York, NY: Routledge.

hooks, b. (1992). *Black looks: Race and representations*. Boston, MA: South End Press.

Keeling, K. (2007). *The witch's flight: The cinematic, the black femme, and the image of common sense*. Durham, NC: Duke University Press.

Lauretis, T. de (2007). *Figures of resistance: Essays in feminist theory*. Urbana, IL: University of Illinois Press.

Llapur, S. (Producer), Vives, C. (Producer), & Gutiérrez Alea, T. (Director). (1976). *La última cena* [motion picture]. Cuba: Instituto Cubano del Arte e Industria Cinematográficos.

McClintock, A. (1995). *Imperial leather: Race, gender, and sexuality in the colonial contest*. New York, NY: Routledge.

Netto, B. (Producer), & Rocha, G. (Director). (1962). *Barravento* [motion picture]. Brazil: Iglu Filmes.

Olajubu, O. (2003). *Women in the Yoruba religious sphere*. Albany, NY: SUNY Press.

Otero, S. (1999). Ikú and Cuban nationhood: Yoruba mythology in the film

Guantanamera. *Africa Today, 46*(2), 117–131.

Oyewumi, O. (1997). *The invention of women: Making an African sense of Western gender discourses*. Minneapolis, MN: University of Minnesota Press.

Pottersman, V. (Producer), & Shabazz, M. (Director). (1981). *Burning an illusion* [motion picture]. UK: British Film Institute.

Reid-Pharr, R. (2007). *Once you go black: Choice, desire, and the black American intellectual*. New York, NY: New York University Press.

Rodríguez-Mangual, E. M. (2003). Santería and the quest for a postcolonial identity in post-revolutionary Cuban cinema. In S. Brent Plate (Ed.), *Representing religion in world cinema: Filmmaking, mythmaking, culture making* (pp. 219–238). New York, NY: Palgrave Macmillan.

Rolando, G. (Director). (1991). *Oggun: An eternal presence* [motion picture]. (Available from AfroCubaWeb Online.)

Rolando, G. (Director). (1997). *The eyes of the rainbow* [motion picture]. (Available from AfroCubaWeb Online.)

Rucker, W. (2001). Conjure, magic, and power: The influence of Afro-Atlantic religious practices on slave resistance and rebellion. *Journal of Black Studies, 32*(1), 84–103.

Shohat, E. (2003). Post-third-worldist culture: Gender, nation, and the cinema. In A. R. Gunaratne & W. Dissanayake (Eds.), *Rethinking third cinema* (pp. 51–78). London, UK: Routledge.

Solanas, F., & Gettino, O. (2000). Towards a third cinema. In R. Stam & T. Miller (Eds.), *Film and theory: An anthology* (pp. 265–286). Malden, MA: Blackwell.

Steven, S. (Producer), & Bravo, E. (Director). (2001). *Fidel: The untold story*

191

[motion picture]. USA: Bravo Films & Four Point Entertainment.

Sundiata, I. (2003). *Brothers and strangers: Black Zion, black slavery, 1914–1940*. Durham, NC: Duke University Press.

Tennant, B. (Producer), & Starrett, J. (Director). (1973). *Cleopatra Jones* [motion picture]. USA: Warner Brothers Pictures.

Valdés, N. P. (2001). Cuba's Fidel Castro (b. 1920): Charisma and Santería: Max Weber revisited. In A. Allahar (Ed.), *Caribbean charisma: Reflections on leadership, legitimacy, and populist politics* (pp. 212–241). Boulder, CO: Lynne Rienner.

Wallace, M. (1999). *Black macho and the myth of the superwoman*. London, UK: Verso.

Weinstein, H. (Producer), & Berry, J. (Director). (1974). *Claudine* [motion picture]. USA: Third World Cinema & Twentieth Century Fox.

Young, C. A. (2006). *Soul power: Culture, radicalism, and the making of a U.S. third world left*. Durham, NC: Duke University Press.

192

CHAPTER 9

Techno-Vodou

Transnational Flows in the Spiritual Marketplace

Alexandra Boutros

Vodou is an official religion of Haiti, practiced by the majority of the population[1] in Haiti and throughout the Haitian diaspora. Sometimes classified
as a Neo-African religion (Bellegrade-Smith, 2005) and closely tied to the
history of Haiti (Dayan, 1995), Vodou is also highly misunderstood—particularly in North America, where a legacy of Haitian-American relations
(Renda, 2001) has shaped stereotypes that form the mythos of "Voodoo"
in the North American popular imagination (Browning, 1998; Hurbon,
1995a). Vodou involves multiple forms of ritualizing, from large-scale communal ceremonies that involve the interplay of dance, song, drumming,
and food, culminating in what Brown (2001) has called possession-perfor-
mance—the arrival of the gods and goddesses of Vodou in the bodies of their
practitioners—to smaller, interpersonal rituals that occur between ritual
specialists and individual practitioners, or "clients." Clients go to the priests
and priestesses of Vodou for help with specific and personal problems, and
their existence should signal something about the spiritual economy of
Vodou. Clients pay Vodou priests and priestesses (*houngans* and *mambos*)
to help them gain employment, find success in love, mend a family rift, heal
a persistent illness, and solve or resolve a host of other personal problems.
These clients give money or gifts to a *mambo* or *houngan* and leave with

herbal "baths," talismans, or other *wanga* (spells). The client-specialist relationship is an intrinsic part of Vodou, constituting an extended community of practitioners and contributing to the financial (and spiritual) well-being of priests and priestesses. As Vodou is integrated into what some might call the spiritual marketplace, the reach of the client-ritual specialist relationship—at least in some instances—has become diffused, no longer bound only to the geographic space of a local *peristyle* (or temple). Scholars like Wade Clark Roof (1993, 1999) have observed that boundaries between institutional religions seem to be becoming less rigid and religious identities more malleable. This has led to a generation of what Roof calls "seekers"— individuals whose religious affiliation shifts throughout a lifetime (p. 204). Although Roof is speaking specifically about the American religious (and spiritual) landscape, the way in which spiritual seekers access new religious traditions and spiritual practices exceeds the national boundaries of the United States, intersecting with and affecting preexisting patterns of transnational exchange. Arguably, forms of digital media, including the Internet, can facilitate the shifting of religious affiliation by "seekers," providing easy access to forms of digital religion. This essay explores how digital media and technology intersect with the client-specialist relationship in the context of newcomers to Vodou. It examines both continuities and ruptures, acknowledging that while mediated ritual practices and interpersonal communication appear to be forging new religious experiences, such new experiences arise not solely from mediated interactions themselves, but from a network of social, cultural, and economic forces.

Because Vodou is so vastly misunderstood in North America, it is subject to a host of stereotypes that have given rise to a plethora of popular-culture Voodoo that encodes a colonial historicity, a history of Haitian-American relations, and particular forms of transnational racisms. It can be difficult for North Americans to "know" Vodou outside of this context. This analysis is part of a larger project that takes as its starting point how Vodou comes to be "known" by those outside the religion. Since the turn of the twentieth century, anthropologists and social scientists inside and outside Haiti have taken Vodou as a subject of focus (Courlander, 1973; Deren, 1983; Desmangles, 1992; Herskovits, 1937; Hurbon, 1995b; Hurston, 1990; Métraux, 1959; Price-Mars, 1983; Rigaud, 1969). While more recently some scholarship on Vodou in the North American diaspora has emerged (Brown, 1991; Laguerre, 1984, 1998; McAlister, 2002; Richman, 2005a), little scholarship has focused on those who could be called newcomers to Vodou. These individuals are often derided as "new agers" whose adoption of historically, culturally, and geographically specific religions, such as Vodou, is part of a long history of cultural appropriation. Any analysis of newcomers to Vodou must negotiate a particular colonial and postcolonial history of consumption that shapes the appropriation of Vodou in the West. If we accept the premise that religion is part of what some call a spiritual marketplace (Roof, 1999; Hanegraaff, 2001; Carrette & King, 2005), then considering how that marketplace aligns with older patterns of consumption of Haiti in particular and the Caribbean in general is essential to understanding the ways in which online Vodou and those who engage with it are shaped by particular histories. As Sheller (2003) explains, "Contemporary consumer cultures are directly connected not only to the wealth generated by slavery, but also to the contemporary inequalities between the 'underdeveloped' Caribbean and the 'modern West'" (p. 3). While it is easy to dismiss newcomers to Vodou as having little to tell us about "authentic" Vodou practice, mapping their journeys to and from Vodou illuminates a complex set of transnational and intercultural relationships. This analysis examines how forms of digital networked communication intersect with these transnational and intercultural relationships.

Vodou, like many religions, has a visible online presence. This visibility provides portals to the religion in the form of informational and educational websites, listservs, chat rooms, and online stores. On the one hand, online Vodou can function as representation, becoming part of a searchable compendium that contributes to how Vodou is both known and misunderstood within the North American popular imagination (Boutros, 2012, 2013). On the other hand, online Vodou facilitates networking among a diversity of practitioners (both Haitian and newcomers) living in geographically dispersed places who use Internet networks to communicate and organize, as well as to perform and attain religious services. Communication technologies combine with travel and the circulation of goods and cultural signifiers in the maintenance of social, national, and religious connections over vast distances. Forms of digital communication are not explored here as determining factors in religious change, but as components in processes of negotiation that shape religious community, practice, and identity. How the practitioners discussed in this analysis engage with the circulation of information and artifacts through online religious practices offers a snapshot of how practitioners of online Vodou accommodate or negotiate issues such as cultural appropriation, popularization and commodification, religious tourism, and the increased public visibility and accessibility of online Vodou.

Although ostensibly an analysis of online Vodou, this is also an exploration of the ways that online experiences and practices intersect with offline religious engagement. Although early understandings of "virtual worlds" imagined them as places apart from the "real" and the everyday, contemporary theories of Internet-based communicative practices acknowledge that the online and the offline have a more symbiotic relationship. Online experiences and events affect offline lives and vice versa. As Campbell (2013) explains, digital religion can be defined as a "technological and cultural space that is evoked when we talk about how online and offline religious spheres have become blended or integrated" (p. 4). In addition, online Vodou also affects the lives and practices of those who do *not* use computer-mediated communication technologies on a regular basis. For instance, the marketing of Vodou initiations online, often by non-Haitians, brings a host of "spiritual tourists" to urban *peristyles*, or temples, in Haiti affecting an economic, social, and cultural environment that reaches beyond the online world. Like other forms of media, digital media have an impact that reaches beyond the direct experience of Internet use. And, like other forms of media, digital media are shaped by the cultural valences into which it is "born" and deployed. While accounting for the digital divide is essential in any discussion of online communication practices, it is also important to guard against an analysis that conflates those factors that may circumscribe access to digital venues with prevalent assumptions about digital uptake in certain populations.

Scholars such as Nelson (2002) and Everett (2009) have pointed out that one of the founding and enduring myths of the digital era—one that positions cyberspace as bodiless and, ultimately, raceless—constitutes a place where blackness is variably positioned as surmountable or exceedable in narratives of technological progress. Technology is not simply a series of innovative but neutral objects, parading through the story of progress, making our lives better and better. Instead, as scholars such as Latour (1993) and Gitelman (2006) have observed, the materiality of media technology is one component in a complex set of relationships that manifest in a particular culture at a particular time. While this analysis looks closely at the relationship between Vodou and digital technology, it is situated in a broader understanding that how we imagine technology in relation to a particular time and place, a particular culture and community, is as important as understanding how technology actually works. Access, whether to digital or Internet technologies, or to the Vodou religion itself, is as central a concern of this analysis as is an accounting of the social and cultural factors that impede or encourage experience of Vodou online. For new practitioners to Vodou, online experience can be a means of getting to actual community and ritual practice. The processes of territorialization and deterritorialization by the traffic of (and in) Vodou online constitute routes to and from Vodou websites that need to be scrutinized in order to understand the interconnection between the visibility of online Vodou and its offline counterparts.

"NOW MY HOUSE IS THE WORLD": GOING FROM OFFLINE TO ON

Although the Internet may have provided a point of access for interested religious seekers, it has also enabled Vodou practitioners to maintain both religious community and forms of religious practice despite geographic separation. The Vodou Magic listserv, for instance, was initiated by the owners of a botanica—a retail store that sells ritual objects—in Philadelphia. This botanica was opened in 1998 by Mambo Sandrine, who identifies as African American. She was first initiated in Vodou in the early 1990s by a Haitian priestess in Port-au-Prince, Haiti. She had been directed to this priestess by a Haitian neighbor she had met when she was living in Brooklyn, New York. Although initiation is not, strictly speaking, necessary to practice Vodou, it is often recommended, particularly for those who seem to be struggling or enduring an unusual string of "bad luck," which is frequently attributed to a failure to properly honor, either the "spirits" (*lwa*) of Vodou or one's own ancestors. At the time of her first initiation Sandrine had recently been laid off from a long-term job, had seen the dissolution of a significant relationship, and was suffering from a host of minor but plaguing health conditions. Once in Haiti, the priestess who performed Sandrine's first initiation (*kanzo*) suggested she undergo further initiations, which Sandrine did (traveling back and forth between Brooklyn and Haiti) over a period of four years before her final initiation (*asogwe*) as Vodou priestess. Sandrine felt that initiation was a positive force in her life. While in Haiti she met her husband, Patrice, who moved with her to Philadelphia and helps with her religious practices. Sandrine is herself a newcomer to Vodou. However, she does not conceptualize herself this way. Instead, she understands her journey to Vodou as, in part, a spiritual reclamation of a forgotten past; "Vodou remembers Africa," says Sandrine. As an African American, Sandrine was raised in a black Evangelical religious community from which she removed herself at a young age because, although the church offered a strong social structure and moral guidance, it never felt like a good "fit." Like many other "spiritual seekers" (Roof, 1999, p. 206), Sandrine had broken with one religious tradition and was exploring new (often "alternative") religious and spiritual practices and ideas before her neighborhood friend introduced her to Vodou. Sandrine's motivation, however, was at least in part determined by her own understanding of her identity as an African American woman. Sandrine felt that while the African American religion she encountered in childhood was "rich" and "deep," it did not fulfill her because it was too divorced from what she understood to be the African roots of her identity. In "remembering" Africa, Vodou healed a rift that Sandrine perceived in her cultural history. In this way, Sandrine's narrative aligns with the stories of other newcomers I have interviewed who see Vodou as a way of reclaiming a past fractured by the brutal history of slavery. Vodou becomes a way of reaching through the experiences of the "New World" and touching an African past that was lost during the Middle Passage that brought African slaves to North America and the Caribbean. While Sandrine's journey is commensurate, in some ways, with the journeys described by Roof in *Spiritual Marketplace* (1999), her engagement with the "spiritual marketplace" is constituted at least in part by a racial identity. Sandrine's own understanding of Vodou as a type of spiritual "home" undoubtedly tempers her engagement with other practitioners, many of whom are also newcomers.

From the outset Mambo Sandrine and Patrice used their small botanica as a space for ritual. Although large-scale Vodou ceremonies could not be held in the small shop, Sandrine performed readings (divinations) and other forms of spell work in the back of the store, where she also housed small altar spaces. By 2002 Sandrine's services had garnered significant word-of-mouth attention in the Philadelphia area, and she was seeing more clients. Many of these individuals were newcomers from diverse ethnic, religious, and class backgrounds and expressed to Sandrine a wish to become more informed about the religious tradition they had newly discovered. Sandrine decided to hold formalized "workshops" on Vodou in her shop. For a nominal fee (which was often waived if practitioners could not afford it), individuals could come to Sandrine's botanica and learn about the history of Haiti, the complex and extensive pantheon of Vodou gods (*lwa*), and how each different *lwa* could be ritually served and honored. A short time after initiating these workshops, Sandrine observed that, because of family or work obligations, many of those who signed up for the duration of the workshop were unable to attend all of the sessions. Feeling strongly that these individuals should still "get their money's worth," Mambo Sandrine began to search for a solution to this problem.

In 2002 Mambo Sandrine and Patrice launched a small website to advertise some religious products for online purchase. The website was not initially successful and soon went offline. Later in 2002 Sandrine and

Patrice started a listserv. The electronic mailing list was easier to maintain and did not rely on random surfers for an audience, but rather drew
on members of Sandrine's small botanica community who signed up to
the online forum. Initially, the listserv was a way for Sandrine to provide
material to those who may not have been able to attend her workshops.
After each session, Sandrine would summarize what had been discussed
and circulate this summary online. Gradually, the list came to function as
a way for Sandrine's clients to keep in touch between workshop sessions
and ritual events. Sandrine explains:

> Of course, a lot of people didn't have a computer. Some would
> come here [to the store] whenever they could and use the com-
> puter here. Patrice had to switch from dial-up to cable because
> we started to get lineups! We also set up a computer exchange.
> People would bring in monitors, old computers, hard drives, parts,
> anything they had. Patrice would go through it all. He was always
> tinkering with computer parts back then. We got another comput-
> er set up from that, and then we started to give computers away.
> Most people just had a dial-up, but that was OK for the listserv,
> I guess.

In a way typical of Vodou ritual specialists, Mambo Sandrine sought to
look after the practitioners who congregated around her (Brown, 1991). For
Mambo Sandrine, that social responsibility extended to helping her practitioners—many of whom she identified as lower middle class—maintain
their religious education despite hectic work schedules and unpredictable
family obligations. Mambo Sandrine's botanica, already a gathering place,
became a much-needed (and free) Internet café. Not only did the Vodou
Magic listserv emerge from a particular and socially situated geographic
locale, it also fostered connection to that same locale as practitioners came
in to use the computers housed at the botanica.

When it first started, the Vodou Magic listserv had less than thirty
members. Within eight months its membership had swollen to just under
one thousand. Four years later (2006) it had grown to approximately three
thousand members, one quarter of whom were active on a daily basis.
Much of the list's success had to do with Sandrine's growing reputation.
By 2006 there were several websites advertising Vodou services by different ritual specialists. Surfers seeking Vodou had to negotiate and evaluate
these different sites. Some of those drawn to Sandrine's site identified with
the story of her journey to Vodou (which had been "pinned" in one of the

listserv forums so that it was always visible). Several of the practitioners Sandrine worked with through the botanica were African American, as were a proportion of those who only used the electronic mailing list. As one user who identified as African American explained, Sandrine modeled access to the religion through her own journey to Vodou: "I feel as if I am following exactly in her footsteps. I will *kanzo* [initiate] this summer in Haiti and it just feels right, something I have been looking for a long time." Whereas in Haiti priests and priestesses derive their religious authority, in part, from a lineage (often based on kinship) through which ritual and spiritual power is passed along generations, in the context of an electronic mailing list community largely constituted by newcomers, it is a story of discovery, combined with a story of spiritual healing through the reclamation of a precolonial "African" past, that lends authority to Sandrine. Although for a time the Vodou Magic listserv maintained a connection to its original geographic locale (the botanica web page was reinstated, and list members often purchased ritual supplies online) and quite a few of the original members remained active, many members communicate with one another only through the Internet. For these members, the Vodou Magic listserv, although seldom their only connection to a Vodou community, was an important aspect of their religious identity. The list allowed practitioners to exchange information and ideas about Vodou and to share advice about personal problems (many of which were conceptualized in religious terms). It also allowed for a form of geographically dispersed religious practice, as Sandrine not only conducted teaching about Vodou on the listserv, but also provided spiritual advice and private divination consultations for practitioners who contacted her "off-list." Some of these practitioners eventually traveled to consult with Sandrine in person and sometimes to undertake initiation in Haiti under her guidance. Many users, however, did not connect with Sandrine's offline community. Practitioners whose contact with Mambo Sandrine is virtual rather than physical are engaged in a form of long-distance Vodou. While the Internet seems to generate this type of long-distance interaction, it is not the only vehicle for geographically dispersed religious practice. In *Migration and Vodou* (2005a) Karen Richman observes how Haitian migrants who are unable to attend important ritual ceremonies in Haiti become long-distance participants using cassette and video recorders. Such participation inevitably reshapes Vodou practice. As Richman explains, "Creative use of cassette tape and, increasingly, video recorders [has] resulted in a reconfiguration of the boundaries of the ritual performance space, allowing migrants to continue to serve their spirits on the inalienable family land" (p. 25). Arguably, the Internet also reconfigures the boundaries of ritual space when, for example, practitioners and ritual specialists engage in a long-distance exchange of spiritual services, much as Mambo Sandrine does with members of the Vodou Magic listserv.

When first introduced to the Internet, Houngan Boniface, a ritual specialist living in Port-au-Prince, saw it as a way of expanding the parameters of his religious enterprise and practice: "I love my web page. It is always there, even when I can't see it, even when the Internet is down, even when I am in the countryside, it is there working for me." This *houngan's* web page was created for him by a newcomer to Vodou, a young technophile living in New York who met Boniface at the time of his initiation in 2002. With minimal effort and cost Houngan Boniface was able to advertise himself as a ritual specialist to a much wider audience than he was able to attract locally. Boniface's website disseminated rudimentary knowledge about Vodou and suggested that those interested in learning more about Vodou, or requiring Vodou services, could contract him via e-mail. Thanks to the young initiate who sent the *houngan's* web address to many Vodou-related listservs, Boniface's web page got many "hits" and interested individuals began to correspond with him via his e-mail address. Of course, Internet communication differs from face-to-face communication in numerous ways, not least because it can remove content from its context. In Port-au-Prince, Boniface generally encountered people who understood Vodou and its situatedness in the history of Haiti. Online, Boniface was more likely to encounter individuals who carried sometimes problematic assumptions about Vodou generated by being removed from its historical and cultural situatedness and constituted through exposure to popular-culture representations of "Voodoo." Boniface soon learned that he had to act as a filter: "At first, it was young people wanting to know about magic. Some of them wanted to know about 'left hand'[2] work. I told them I don't do this kind of work and many of them stopped e-mail[ing] me." After filtering out those whose misconceptions of Vodou made him uncomfortable, Boniface began to build a more regular correspondence with a group of individuals who were, as he put it, "dedicated."

These practitioners were "from all over, France, [La] Norvège, Canada, New York City." When I asked Houngan Boniface if these individuals were mostly white, he vehemently disagreed: "Not just *blans* come to me. I see people of all colors, Jamaicans, Africans, some [second-generation, diasporic] Haitians even, and Chinese, one red Indian[3] even." As a Haitian, Boniface was accorded a certain religious authority. Indeed, Boniface suggested that he was often sought out because he was one of the few "true" (or authentically Haitian) ritual specialists of Vodou who advertised online.

And yet Boniface expressed no hesitancy when it came to incorporating non-Haitians into his practice and, to some extent, his ritual community.

Some of these individuals traveled to Haiti to meet Houngan Boniface and have services and initiations performed by him. Many, however, did not travel to Haiti, but remained in their homes, behind their computer screens. These individuals had a long-distance relationship with Houngan Boniface. They spoke with him about the practice and rituals of Vodou, and, perhaps more interestingly, they struck up a form of long-distance Vodou. There has not been, nor does there seem to be, an inclination toward the transferring of major Vodou rituals, such as the ceremonies honoring the feast days of particular *lwa*, into a cyberspiritual form. In fact, most practitioners (both Haitians and newcomers to the religion) emphasize the embodied and actual affective aspects of the religion, stressing that there is no substitute for "real-life" rituals. There does exist, however, a lot of small-scale interpersonal ritualizing that makes use of the Internet as a means by which to connect ritual specialist and practitioner. In the Vodou tradition it is common for ritual specialists to provide services to their congregation (both initiated and uninitiated). This spiritual work most often encompasses divination readings and spell making (or *wanga*), and most often rituals specialists are paid for their work in this area.

Online practitioners—separated from Houngan Boniface by sometimes-vast geographic space—interact with the faraway priest in much the same way that they would interact with a ritual specialist face to face: they tell Houngan Boniface their problems and he proposes spiritual solutions. After reading their e-mails and familiarizing himself with the specifics of their particular situation or "condition," Boniface conducts "readings" (or divinations) for these distant clients. Although he initially corresponds by e-mail, Houngan Boniface usually conducts actual readings over the phone because, as he explained, "it is easier to read over the phone. I hear the person's voice and the spirits help me to see what they need. By e-mail it is harder; all the words look the same. Voices are all different." Houngan Boniface takes it upon himself to call these individuals, often out of the blue, sometimes weeks after they e-mailed him with problems or questions. Boniface conceptualizes the difficulties he encounters with spontaneous long-distance communication in religious terms, feeling that communication barriers are the spirits' way of ensuring that he conducts his spiritual work at efficacious times. He explained his system by saying, "I would just pick up the phone at my sister's house and call [so and so]. If the phone line was not working, then I should not call them that day. If they were not answering, then it was not a good day [for spiritual work]." Once contact is made, the practitioners are always glad to hear from Houngan Boniface and, aware of the instability of telecommunications in Haiti, usually make time to speak with him right away. At the end of the phone call, Houngan Boniface recommends a course of action to help the practitioner with his or her particular problem. Often this involves things the practitioner could do on his or her own, including, for example, leaving small offerings of food and money at a crossroad or intersection near their homes. Sometimes, however, Boniface needs to intercede more directly in the lives of his practitioners for his spiritual work to be effective: "Usually people need a 'bath' or a 'drink' or a *pakèt*, and I can do this for them." Baths, drinks, and *pakèt* are all part of Houngan Boniface's repertoire of spiritual work. Usually made from a combination of herbs and other substances, these items are meant to be used by practitioners to clear negative energy or to bring good luck. Baths and drinks are, as their names imply, herbal recipes invested with ritually charged items and ingredients, which practitioners must either ingest or apply directly to their bodies. *Pakèt*, for Houngan Boniface, is a generic term for a host of small talismans made by enclosing herbs, soil, and other objects in cloth that is then bound tightly with string. After a divination session with one of his long-distance practitioners, Houngan Boniface—who is an accomplished *medsen fey* (or leaf doctor, someone who is knowledgeable about the healing properties of plants)—then prepares a ritual bath, drink, or talisman for his faraway practitioners. Later his sister mails these packages, the baths and drinks often disguised as local shampoos, to practitioners around the world.

In return and in payment, these long-distance practitioners send packages back to Houngan Boniface. These packages are often filled with jams and other nonperishable food items, "foreign" cigarettes, expensive perfumes (which he uses for ritual purposes), and often items of clothing (for him and his relatives). Sometimes "they send money, too," Boniface told me. In this way, practitioners reimburse Houngan Boniface for his costs (of long-distance phone calls and postage) and pay for the ritual services he provided them. Even though Boniface often spends long periods offline, away from computers, for work or religious reasons, or because he is unable to "connect" due to the sometimes-poor Internet services in Port-au-Prince, he is still able to sustain long-distance religious relationships, sometimes with practitioners he has never met in person. "Now," Boniface joked, "my house is in Europe, America, Africa, China, the whole world!" In the social networks of Vodou, "house," much like "family," refers to those Vodou practitioners who have been initiated by or who work with the same ritual specialist. In Houngan Boniface's case, his house has a tangible, geographic foundation in his *peristyle* in Port-au-Prince but, as he points out, also reaches far beyond that to include the home bases of those practitioners from "faraway places" whom he has initiated and worked with long-distance. Through communication, travel, and the transportation of goods, Boniface is able to extend the scope of his religious community and arguably the parameters of his ritual practice. For Boniface, the mediation of Vodou through the Internet and other technologies does not remove Vodou from its cultural specificity and social networks. It does, however, reshape how cultural specificity and social networks are accessed by practitioners. The stories of Mambo Sandrine's Vodou Magic listserv and Houngan Boniface's long-distance *travay* (ritual work) speak to how online Vodou is closely linked to offline practices and geographic places. In both cases, the Internet facilitates not only communication with geographically dispersed practitioners but also a form of spiritual enterprise. Both Houngan Boniface and Mambo Sandrine have capitalized on the power of the Internet to advertise their goods and services to a wide audience. Some may see this as part of the increasing commercialization of religion, which leads, inevitably, to the dissolution of cultural specificity, authentic religiosity, and efficacious religious practices. Nevertheless, the work of spiritual entrepreneurs such as Mambo Sandrine and Houngan Boniface is continuous with the practices and discourses of Vodou. While the Internet directly affects the social conditions of Houngan Boniface in Haiti and Mambo Sandrine and her practitioners in Philadelphia, the practices of long-distance Vodou also affect those at a geographic remove from these places. The Internet facilitates a form of virtual social interactivity, but it also facilitates the circulation of goods. When religious goods circulate, in part because of the Internet, then ritual meaning, investment, and energy are also put into circulation.

Unlike some religions where money is seen as a corruptible and tainting presence, economic exchange has always been part of the Vodou tradition. *Houngans* and *mambos* are paid for their *travay*, and they, in turn, pay (or feed) the *lwa* (gods and goddesses) who make this work possible. As is the case with Houngan Boniface, payment is not always made through money, but may take the form of an exchange of goods and services. The economic exchange that structures the give-and-take between practitioners and between practitioners and their spirits is part of a system of currency that includes good luck (health and success), spiritual power, and the favor or blessings of the spirits of Vodou. In Vodou, as in many other Afro-Caribbean religions and African-influenced religions in Latin America, material success is representative of spiritual success and power

(Romberg, 2003). Seeking out more clients is a way for ritual specialists to ensure both financial well-being and spiritual success. For some, this search takes them, via technology such as the Internet, into a spiritual marketplace that exceeds Haiti and its diaspora. Their participation in this marketplace shifts the locus of spiritual exchange but does not entirely re- move it from its social, cultural, and historical context. Vodou practitioners such as Houngan Boniface and Mambo Sandrine maintain the social sit-uatedness of their Vodou communities despite the ways that networked digital communication, consumerism, and globalization contribute to the dispersion of that same community. Romberg (2003) notes that the eco-nomic exchanges that are such a part of religions such as Vodou "cannot be characterized by the 'disembedding' of social relations and a disregard for social responsibility. Intimately associated with being blessed by the spirits, consumerism fits rather into a morally grounded personal and civil local ethos" (p. 13). Similarly, while the Internet is also charged with "dis-embedding" social relationships (Giddens, 1991), Daniel Miller and Don Slater (2000)—whose research explores Internet use as a component of Caribbean, and specifically Trinidadian, culture and identity—challenge this idea. Instead, they argue that the Internet, like other technologies, is situated in social space. Miller and Slater explore how "members of a specific culture attempt to make themselves a(t) home in a transforming communicative environment, how they can find themselves in this envi-ronment and at the same time try and mould it in their own image" (p. 1). Practitioners like Mambo Sandrine and Houngan Boniface use the Internet to communicate and advertise, to maintain religious community, and to garner new spiritual clients, but they never use the Internet exclusively for these things. Instead, the Internet is a useful component of a diverse interpersonal religious practice that employs multiple communication and ritual technologies.

Marshaling a host of technological and cultural resources, these prac-titioners have carved out long-distance religious interactions that are commensurate with locally and culturally specific Vodou practices. When Houngan Boniface creates ritually charged objects for his oversea clients, or Mambo Sandrine insists on the maintenance of community and social networks, they are engaging in activities that have always been part of the Vodou tradition. For them, networked, digital communications are part of an everyday religious practice that builds and enhances interpersonal rela-tionships. If the Internet is assumed to perpetuate a disembedded, rootless, virtual cyberculture without social consequence, this may be because of the types of Internet use on which this study focuses. As Miller and Slater

(2000) explain, an ethnographic exploration of Internet use in the Trinidadian context revealed that research participants did not set it apart from their everyday experiences and interactions, but rather sought to integrate it into already existing social relations. Miller and Slater observe that there exists an "attempt to assimilate yet another medium into various practices (email complements telephone for family contact, websites supplement TV for religious evangelism, etc.)" (p. 6). They argue that the Internet is not a "particularly virtual phenomenon when studied in relation to Trinidad," although virtualness may be an important component of the Internet in other contexts. Instead, the Internet, for some, can reinforce connection to place and specific identity. Miller and Slater found that "Trinidadians took to the new media in ways that connected to core dimensions, and contradictions, of their history and society" (p. 3), and in so doing, "entered into the transcultural networks of the Internet from somewhere, as people who felt themselves encountering it from a place, as Trinidadians" (p. 7). A similar situatedness can be seen in the ways that Houngan Boniface combines e-mail, phone, and mail, or how Mambo Sandrine's listserv maintains ties to a particular locale and community.

But while Internet practices are integrated into and even enhance the practice and spiritual economies of some practitioners, the ways in which digital media shape and reshape the flows of meaning, practice, and signifiers of Vodou between North American and Haiti need to be understood in a broader context. Mambo Sandrine is herself a newcomer to the religion, and the majority of her clients are as well. While Houngan Boniface is Haitian, many of his clients—acquired via the web—are newcomers as well. In these instances, digital religious practice reshapes the boundaries of Vodou not only by enabling a form of long-distance religious practice, but also by facilitating access for outsiders to the religion. This analysis has explored how, at times, that access, and the influx of newcomers it brings, is conceptualized as a spiritual boon in the context of the spiritual economy of Vodou. Certainly, Boniface conceptualizes his popularity overseas as both emblematic of and enhancing his own spiritual power. At the same time, a particular understanding of racial identity shapes Sandrine's engagement with Vodou. These examples are not simple instances of cultural appropriation or spiritual "seeking," but instead demand a reconsideration of both concepts that understands the flows of the spiritual marketplace as multidirectional. Here, we do not have a simple one-way exchange of spiritual seekers appropriating Caribbean religiosity for their own purposes, but a complex set of relationships, often transnational, that frame identification with Vodou.

NOTES

1. Until recently the two dominant religions in Haiti (both with official status) were Vodou and Roman Catholicism, and many Haitians identified with both concurrently. Inroads by Evangelical Christianity have changed the religious landscape in Haiti somewhat, although Vodou remains a majority religious practice. For more in-depth discussion of Evangelicalism in Haiti, see Richman (2005b).

2. "Left-hand" work generally refers to malevolent spiritual practices aimed at extreme forms of control (of other individuals). It carries with it a certain cultural and social stigma among some Vodou ritual specialists. Boniface was using this term to categorize requests he received via e-mail to cast "curses" or negative spells.

3. Boniface uses this term to refer to a Native American individual.

REFERENCES

Bellegrade-Smith, P. (2005). Introduction. In *Fragments of bone: Neo-African religions in a new world* (pp. 1–12). Urbana, IL: University of Illinois Press.

Boutros, A. (2012). Virtual Vodou, actual practice: Transfiguring the technological. In J. Stolow (Ed.), *Deus in machina: Religion, technology, and the things in between* (pp. 239–260). New York, NY: Fordham University Press.

Boutros, A. (2013). *Lwa* like me: Gender, sexuality, and Vodou online. In M. Lövheim (Ed.), *Media, religion, and gender: Key issues and new challenges* (pp. 96–110). New York, NY: Routledge.

Brown, K. M. (2001). *Mama Lola: A Vodou priestess in Brooklyn*. Berkeley, CA: University of California Press.

Browning, B. (1998). *Infectious rhythm: Metaphors of contagion and the spread of African culture*. New York, NY: Routledge.

Campbell, H. (2013). Introduction. In H. Campbell (Ed.), *Digital religion: Understanding religious practice in new media worlds* (pp. 1–22). New York, NY: Routledge.

Carrette, J., & King, R. (2005). *Selling spirituality: The silent takeover of religion*. New York, NY: Routledge.

Courlander, H. (1973). *Haiti singing*. New York, NY: Cooper Square.

Dayan, C. J. (1995). *Haiti, history, and the gods*. Berkeley, CA: University of California Press.

Deren, M. (1983). *Divine horsemen: The living gods of Haiti*. New York, NY: McPherson.

Desmangles, L. G. (1992). *The faces of the gods: Vodou and Roman Catholicism in Haiti*. Chapel Hill, NC: University of North Carolina Press.

Everett, A. (2009). *Digital diaspora: A race for cyberspace*. Albany, NY: State University of New York Press.

Giddens, A. (1991). *Modernity and self-identity: Self and society in the late modern age*. Stanford, CA: Stanford University Press.

Gitelman, L. (2006). *Always already new: Media history and the data of culture*. Cambridge, MA: MIT Press.

Hanegraaff, W J. Prospects for the globalization of new age: Spiritual imperialism versus cultural diversity. In M. Rothstein (Ed.), *New age religion and globalization* (pp. 15–30). Aarhus, DK: Aarhus University Press.

Herskovits, M. *Life in a Haitian valley*. New York, NY: Knopf, 1937.

Hurbon, L. (1995a). American fantasy and Haitian Vodou. In D. J. Constantino (Ed.), *The sacred arts of Haitian Vodou*. Exhibition catalog. Los

Angeles, CA: UCLA Fowler Museum of Cultural History.

Hurbon, L. (1995b). *Voodoo: Search for the spirit*. New York, NY: Harry N. Abrams.

Hurston, Z. N. (1990). *Tell my horse: Vodou and life in Haiti and Jamaica*. New York, NY: Harper Row.

Laguerre, M. S. (1984). *American odyssey: Haitians in New York City*. Ithaca, NY: Cornell University Press.

Laguerre, M. S. (1998). *Diasporic citizenship: Haitian Americans in transnational America*. New York, NY: St. Martin's Press.

Latour, B. (1993). *We have never been modern*. (H. Wheatsheaf, Trans.). Cambridge, MA: Harvard University Press.

McAlister, E. (2002). *Rara! Vodou, power, and performance in Haiti and its diaspora*. Berkeley, CA: University of California Press.

Metraux, A. *Voodoo in Haiti*. New York, NY: Schocken, 1972.

Miller, D., & Slater, D. (2000). *The Internet: An ethnographic approach*. New York, NY: Berg.

Nelson, A. (2002). Introduction: Future texts. *Social Text, 20*(2), 1–15.

Price-Mars, J. (1983). *So spoke the uncle / Ainsi Parla l'Oncle* (1928). Washington, DC: Three Continents Press.

Renda, M. A. (2001). *Taking Haiti: Military occupation and the culture of American imperialism, 1915–1940*. Chapel Hill, NC: University of North Carolina Press.

Richman, K. E. (2005a). *Migration and Vodou*. Gainesville, FL: University Press of Florida.

Richman, K. E. (2005b). The Protestant ethic and the dis-spirit of Vodou. In K. I. Leonard, A. Stepick, M. A. Vasquez, & J. Holdaway (Eds.), *Immigrant faiths: Transforming religious life in America* (pp. 165–188). Walnut Creek, CA: AltaMira Press.

Rigaud, M. (1969). *Secrets of voodoo*. (R. B. Cross, Trans.). New York, NY: Arco.

Romberg, R. (2003). *Witchcraft and welfare: Spiritual capital and the business of magic in modern Puerto Rico*. Austin, TX: University of Texas Press.

Roof, W. C. (1993). *A generation of seekers: The spiritual journeys of the baby boom generation*. New York, NY: HarperCollins.

Roof, W. C. (1999). *Spiritual marketplace: Baby boomers and the remaking of American religion*. Princeton, NJ: Princeton University Press.

Sheller, M. (2003). *Consuming the Caribbean: From Arawaks to zombies*. New York, NY: Routledge.

CHAPTER 10

Evangelical Media for Youth and Religious Authority in Brazil

Karina Kosicki Bellotti

The aim of this essay is to discuss questions of religious authority related to Evangelical youth in Brazil, especially in the twenty-first century, when this demographic has demonstrated a highly visible social action through music, public involvement, sports, and the arts in general. On one hand, there has been increasing investment by traditional and new churches in activities to attract young people to their pews, regardless of whether they were born in Evangelical[1] families. On the other hand, there has been increasing demand from at least some Brazilian youth to engage in religious activities, both formal and informal.

Therefore, the following questions constitute the main focus of this investigation: Is this two-way movement undermining religious authority of Evangelical churches, which may reflect a decline of religious institutional authority in Brazil as a whole, and a complementary rise of religious individual autonomy? Or is this creating new types of authority, to the extent that these activities for Evangelical youth expand the field of action of youth and adults, fomenting new relations of power and new negotiations of meaning within and outside the churches? Or do both situations coexist in different contexts? The limits and transformations of religious authority may display the challenges present in the Evangelical field in

Brazil, a country with a history of ambiguity and hybridity in relation to any type of authority.

I analyzed the following primary resources: media produced for youth by Evangelical churches and interdenominational organizations (Bibles, literature on counseling, music, blogs and websites), along with discourses produced by Evangelical youth about authority and individual religiosity and devotion, collected in websites, blogs, public virtual forums, and personal interviews with young people from different churches, engaged in a variety of activities. I also interviewed former church members who had attempted to initiate outreach to youth but felt excluded by the church leadership.

This chapter is divided into three sections: the first two, focusing on religious authority and youth in Brazil, and the strategies of churches to attract youth in the recent history, trace a conjectural overview of the factors that have transformed Evangelical culture in Brazil in the past twenty to thirty years, reshaping the roles and effects of institutional religious authority. The third part analyzes the trajectories of faith and action of three young people, one Adventist, one young woman from the small movement called Community Reach, and one former member of the Pentecostal denomination Assembly of God.

RELIGIOUS AUTHORITY AND YOUTH IN BRAZILIAN PROTESTANTISM

Authority in Protestant culture is attributed exclusively to the Bible, considered the only true command from God that human beings need obey on Earth. However, since the Reformation human authorities have emerged in Protestantism along with a fragmentation and differentiation of roles: pastors, preachers, evangelists, lay leadership, and so on. We can define religious authority as any institution or person that establishes a relation of power in relation to the lay membership. In the Western world, across the twentieth century, with the rise of individual religious autonomy the institutional authority of all churches and religious organizations decreased. In Brazil this occurred due to two main factors: the separation between the Catholic Church and the state with the proclamation of the republic in 1889, and the emergence of a competitive religious marketplace starting in the 1950s and 1960s.

Although Protestantism was introduced to Brazil in the early 1800s, when Catholicism was still the official creed of the empire, it was only with the Pentecostal growth since the 1960s that Evangelicals became a more visible social force in the country, competing with the Catholic Church for religious voluntary engagement. Religious autonomy increased to the extent that the generation of the 1960s and 1970s questioned the idea that to be Brazilian necessarily meant to be Catholic. On the other hand, those who were born in Evangelical families had the opportunity to experiment more frequently across Protestant churches, contributing to the growth of new Pentecostal churches.

Another factor should be taken into account regarding religious authority in Brazilian history. The religious monopoly enjoyed by the Catholic Church from colonization to the imperial period (1500–1889) was marked by the lack of evangelization of the masses, as they were obliged to attend the main rituals and festivities of the church. This exteriorized demonstration of devotion was not necessarily followed by a true commitment to Catholicism, a fact reinforced by the existence of the "new Christians," Jews of Portuguese origin who renounced Judaism in order to be accepted in Portuguese society in the modern age. Many of them immigrated to Portuguese America, bringing mixed attitudes toward institutionalized religion: irreligion, irreverence, suspicion, and strategic observance of the mandatory rituals. Furthermore, popular Catholicism used to mix its devotions with popular culture and African influences (Mello e Souza, 1998; Novinski, 1973).

The diverse forms of Protestantism should be equipped to adapt to this fluid religious reality, balancing between two possibilities: bringing a meaningful Christianity for "lost" Catholics while constructing a distinct religious identity. In the nineteenth century and the first half of the twentieth century, in common with the general Brazilian religious culture, Protestants established churches and creeds with the help of charismatic leaders who maintained strong authority with their flocks. Given the fact that these churches were a minority, and many of them were imbued with the American missionary spirit of Manifest Destiny, Protestantism in Brazil tended to create a closed culture in order to maintain its identity. Even the first wave of Pentecostalism in Brazil (1910–1950) was sectarian, which facilitated the concentrated institutional authority (Mendonça & Velasques, 1990).

Other factors that contributed to religious autonomy and the distancing of people from religious institutions were the general secularization of society and the expansion of modern means of communication by the 1940s and 1950s (radio) as well as the 1960s and 1970s (television). Although the media forms focused on entertainment, religious agents also used them to achieve cultural and social presence in the public sphere—the

Protestants were the first to use radio in Brazil (late 1930s), followed by the Catholic Church (1950s) and Pentecostals (1950s).

The focus on youth by Evangelical churches has increased in the past twenty years, visibly with the renovation of youth ministries in traditional churches (the Presbyterian Church, the various branches of the Assembly of God) and the creation of youth churches such as Snowball Church, among many others. Although the Evangelical marketplace does not offer as many products (books and gadgets) for youth as for children and adults, the exception is the recording industry, which is dominated by contemporary Christian music (called "gospel music" in Brazil), broadcast on gospel radio stations, in concerts, on DVDs, and at church services. Such artistic output is also one of the main attractions for youth, as many of them follow music groups maintained by churches and parachurch organizations (Cunha, 2007).

One may ask if this youth mobilization is reinforcing church authority, as it does bring youth to churches and parachurch organizations. One may wonder if the "world" is "invading" the church's boundaries when youth bring their language, dress, and lifestyle to holy spaces. It is notable that there is a two-way movement in which interdenominational initiatives are crucial: while many religious leaders make efforts to attract youth with rock and reggae concerts, skate and surf championships, and gospel nightclubs, young people from several churches, both new converts and not, engage on different fronts in order to evangelize, serve others in social assistance, play in gospel bands, preach, create blogs, and take an active part in the very music concerts, sports championships, and gospel raves sponsored by their churches. Thus my approach considers youth as a diverse demographic group, marked by gender, social class religious and cultural differences, and not always separated or differentiated from the adult world.

By the 1990s and 2000s, in terms of religious authority, the generation gap actually led to tension between youth and adults, especially between adolescents and adults, and this tension has reinforced the migration of dissatisfied teenagers and young people with new youth-oriented churches. This trend demonstrates the effects of the maintenance of institutional conservatism in some traditional churches, both Pentecostal and Protestant, which has left little space for youth. Other churches, concerned with the abandonment of their pews by youth, reinvented themselves in order to adapt to the new times. However, history and the received and remembered images of youth in Brazilian society may also be reinforcing the generational gap and the problematic communication between young and adults.

In the twentieth century the stereotype of youth in Western culture, mainly after the 1960s generation, was that they were rebellious, fond of novelty, defiant of authority, and broke down barriers, manifested in pop culture symbols and artists, feminism, and other social movements. Such generational influence was determinative of social and cultural changes in Western societies on different levels, despite the fact that not all young people of that time were directly involved. In Brazil, as in many Latin American countries living under dictatorships, some youth were engaged in urban and rural guerrilla activities along with other types of civil resistance. (The active role of Catholic Church in the public confrontation against dictatorship, as well as the Protestant ecumenical movement, inspired by the Social Gospel, should be noted here.) Since then, youth have been seen as a driving force of social change, which has led to tension with subsequent generations. Comparing these next generations with the received memory of their courageous and idealistic parents and grandparents, the new generations have been labeled apathetic, apolitical, accommodated, ignorant, insensitive to social problems, individualistic, and consumerist.

In religion, youth became a target of both Catholic and Protestant churches, both because youth is a delicate moment in the life course when many evade the institution in which they were raised, and because youth is considered an endangered phase of life threatened by drugs, casual sex, worldly activities, and lack of perspective. In both cases, some consider youth a special challenge for religious agents to "fix" and guide, while others, with the help of the same youth, aim to transform the problem into a blessing for church and society.[2]

STRATEGIES: SINGING, FIGHTING, AND SURFING FOR THE LORD

Moore (1994) demonstrated in his research on religious marketplaces the ability of some Protestant churches to adapt themselves to the social changes by using advertising techniques and entertainment to attract believers in the nineteenth-century United States. Brazilian Protestant churches were slow to follow this, especially because many of them were busy in maintaining their identity wholly separate from a Brazilian culture marked by Catholic and secular festivities and rites. Until the 1960s dance was strictly forbidden for many Evangelicals. The only type of music allowed for them was the official hymnody within the churches. No wonder many rushed to opportunities such as the National Crusade of Evangelization in São Paulo in the 1950s, where former Hollywood cowboy Harold Williams played his guitar and sang simple songs.

Music became one of the crucial elements of cultural change in many Protestant churches, especially since the 1970s, and more visibly by the 1990s. Besides the early musical ensembles, from ministries like Youth of the Truth, Winners for Christ, and Youth for Christ, there is gospel music, the term used to refer to music featuring Evangelical lyrics with popular rhythms, which became popular by the mid-1980s in the Evangelical circuit, due to the efforts of the Pentecostal (or Neo-Pentecostal, as many scholars call it; cf. Mariano, 1997) church Reborn in Christ, founded by bishop Sonia Hernandes and her husband, apostle Estevam Hernandes.[3] By the early 1990s not only did the church invest in gospel music, radio, and TV shows, but it also organized the March for Jesus, an Evangelical parade initiated in England in the 1980s.

The use of music has served many purposes for urban tribes. The Reborn in Christ Church has the Reborn Praise project, consisting of big concerts of gospel music, held in soccer stadiums and conducted by the Hernandeses and several singers, complemented by an immense choir and many dancers and musicians. Each church location has its own band that plays electric instruments in its services—called Ministry of Praise and Adoration—and the church has always invested massively in media, running a record company, a web portal, as well as TV and radio stations. Recently the church has targeted underground youth culture with the ministry Christian Metal Force, aimed at metal, goth, punk, and hardcore fans and former Satanists. The Golgoth Community, in the south of Brazil, also aims at the "excluded" from traditional churches—goths, headbangers, and former skinheads.

Another church that invests in music is the Snowball Church, founded in 1994 by the apostle Rina (who was at that time in his early thirties) in a borrowed space of the surf ware retail store Hawaiian Dreams. Rina took a surf long board as his pulpit, which became the trademark of the church, attracting surfers and other young people interested in extreme sports.[4] This church also maintains a contemporary band to play reggae and rock during services. This church is becoming known for attracting former Brazilian rock stars such as Rodolfo Abrantes e Catalau, who records for the church's own recently created record label, Bola Music. Musicians are regularly featured in festivities, sports championship matches, and camp meetings sponsored by the church.

A new, curious phenomenon that emerged in the 2000s was the "gospel nightclub" or "gospel rave." The Reborn in Christ Church promotes disco parties, and ministries such as Gospel Night and Balada Gospel promote parties with DJs, electronic gospel music, or other types of dance music (funk, hip hop, rap), where youth can dance, have fun, and meet new people in a wholesome environment—alcohol-free, drug-free, and with careful vigilance against any type of sexual activity.

Other types of festivities have also been adapted to Evangelical tastes: for instance, the Catholic festival of June (Festa Junina or "June Parties," celebrated on St. Paul's, St. Peter's, and St. John's Days) became Arraial Gospel, with all the games and the typical food of June Parties, amplified with gospel bands and a DJ pastor for the celebration. During Carnival time, while some churches promote camping activities to encourage reflective or contemplative time away from the hubbub, other churches and organizations promote street parties where believers can celebrate with their cohorts a time free from the drugs, sex, and violence sometimes associated with Carnival, enlivened by gospel music.

Such use of contemporary music and festivities is also seen in U.S. Protestantism, as described by Hendershot (2004). It is notable that the idea in Brazil is the same one that animated American Evangelical efforts— that is, to adapt "worldly" media, creating wholesome versions intended to attract new people and to create a subculture where youth can feel at ease with their faith without being considered "aliens" by their friends.

What is the relation between this use of music and religious authority? Cunha (2007) has demonstrated that the gospel music movement helps to diminish the authority of many traditional churches, as their members are empowered by the marketplace to bring new gospel music into their congregations. The circulation of gospel products undermines denominationalism by reinforcing a kind of interdenominational culture, especially among ministries of praise and adoration. At the same time, of course, the gospel market creates new types of authority through the leadership of gospel celebrities who not only praise but also preach and minister, competing with the ministries of local pastors in daily life. Celebrities are the main commodity of the Evangelical recording industry, where thousands of musicians vie for opportunities but few achieve stardom. Men and women of God follow a consistent pattern of presentation on the public shelves of the Evangelical marketplace: women are always dressed in ethereal and bright outfits (generally dresses to display their femininity), gazing at the sky with a clear background, as if they were walking in heaven; men generally wear short hair and somber colors, and also gaze at the sky or with eyes closed, in an attitude of reverence.

Despite the popularity of gospel music on the one hand and the existence of alternative Evangelical music, emulating rhythms of the "world" with sacred lyrics, on the other, there are young people who refuse to listen to either, or who only listen to the soft pop gospel artists. Such a trend can be discerned in the virtual forums of Orkut, a social-media website similar to MySpace and Facebook, popular among youth (and then among young adults and less among adults and middle-aged adults), which rose to popularity between 2004 and 2009 in Brazil and India.[5] There, within several virtual communities of interest, Evangelicals from different churches take part in interdenominational communities and in church communities. A good number of the young believers seek Orkut for counseling, debate, or confirmation of their creeds.

On Orkut I found communities related to several Brazilian churches—Snowball, Reborn in Christ, Universal Kingdom of God, Assembly of God, even the virtual community of the Christian Congregation of Brazil, which generally forbids their members to watch television or listen to radio. I also found interdenominational communities, such as Jesus and My 20 and Something Years, Believers That Think, and Evangelical Youth, among others, which gather critical opinions on practices of the Evangelical field. One of the topics that provokes fierce discussions is the following question: Should Christians listen to secular music and/or secular rhythms in gospel music? Or, in other words, what kind of entertainment is appropriate for Evangelicals?

In the forums, opinions are divided into two main and opposite ideas. One advocates that if the lyrics are truly devotional and the intention of the musician is to render praise to the Lord, the rhythm—worldly or not—is not a problem, especially if the music is capable of bringing new people to the Lord. The other opposes the use of rhythms such as forró, pagode, samba, rap, carioca funk, and heavy metal because of their worldly origin and the allegedly Satanist use of these genres—especially heavy metal and all its subgenres. Some users evoke studies (without further reference) that prove the malignant effect of such genres in the human body, which attests to the fact that Lucifer created attractive songs to deceive humans. Therefore, using such rhythms means bringing the world and Satan to the church.

In communities such as Jesus and My 20 Something Years, the issue of Christian entertainment was approached with irreverence and humor, showing the dissatisfaction of many young believers with the "gospel culture": "Christians have fun like other people . . . are they going to invent gospel entertainment now?" asked the young user Luiz on November 20, 2006. In fact most of the 185 responses to the prompt "How Christians have fun" alternated between sarcasm ("sex, drugs, rock . . . those things," wrote the user Zaratrusta) and sincere demonstrations of how "normal" they are ("Playing *Priston Tale*, chatting at the MSN, with topics like these, watching *Lost*, studying some musical instrument, reading books, mangas, watching animes, going to the mall . . . yes, there is life outside the church. What kind of paranoia is that [believers are not allowed to do all those things]?" wrote user Luciane).[6]

The idea that the gospel market has been creating other types of authority is suggested—and fiercely criticized—by users from this community and as well as the group Believers That Think. Many users demonstrate irritation with others who quoted several biblical verses in order to condemn worldly behavior and tastes. Therefore, religious individual autonomy is reinforced in the discourses and attitudes of such users.

On the other hand, it is the very idea of being part of an exclusive group that animates many young people to engage in their churches and watch their brothers and sisters in Christ, encouraging or admonishing them on Orkut, personal blogs, or websites. One subject deserves special mention here—the status of media for Evangelical youth, through the eyes of both adults and young people. In my research in the Evangelical marketplace, while I found a few publications for Evangelical youth, the main commodity was music. The debate over what Christians should hear and how they should enjoy their free time shows that not all youth consume gospel culture, even though the market offers these products and artists. The attitude that part of the Evangelical field maintains toward secular and Evangelical media suggests that religious authority becomes discredited when it turns its back on popular culture, showing prejudice and ignorance toward the things "of the world."

As Hoover (2006) points out, media should not be studied in isolation from the practices of everyday life and the life course of its consumers. Therefore, he suggests a broader definition of media, not only as texts or technological devices, but, more important, as practices of the everyday life of individuals. Therefore, the media in this study will be considered as a meaning-making tool for both producers and especially consumers, in order to understand its role in the transformations of religious authority in Brazilian Evangelical culture.

In Brazil, Evangelicals are a growing minority, who portray themselves sometimes as warriors against the devil's penetration into their daily lives and sometimes as a triumphant army raised by God to make the difference in a problematic country. Differently from their American counterparts, Brazilian Evangelicals do not identify with the subcultural sensibility that encourages some Evangelicals to be "in but not of the world" in terms of cultural consumption. On secular and gospel music, one Orkut user lamented that the gospel music does not have the same variety as the secular music; therefore, he chooses to listen to the secular groups and artists in order to learn more about music *and then* to compose his own gospel songs.

On the one hand, the discourse of many religious leaders demonizes "the media" in general, with the accusation that they bring moral corruption and degradation to society. Believers are strongly advised to stay away from these distractions and encouraged instead to serve the Kingdom. On the other hand, "the media"—that is, television and more recently the Internet—do not carry a good reputation among elites such as educators, and also in parts of public opinion, where they are accused of stimulating premature sexual initiation, violence, and consumerism.

The market for Evangelical goods has been growing, as evidenced by the Expo Christian Fair in São Paulo. But the articles for youth are few compared to the ones for children and adults. The only exception is gospel music. In a series of interviews with young Evangelicals and former Evangelicals, I asked them about the media they consume—secular and/or religious. My concern was to observe whether the counseling literature and the small number of other gadgets (games, outfit, fashionable Bibles) made for them were actually being consumed.

The former Evangelical Lais, a twenty-year-old undergraduate student of history at the Federal University of Paraná, disliked most of the counseling literature about sexuality produced by adults for the youth audience. When she was a devoted and active Evangelical, she preferred to read books of theology, wear Evangelical T-shirts, and listen to gospel radio, and she enjoyed all types of music. Today she occasionally listens to gospel music to remember the "good times" of her Evangelical life. At that time she refused to listen to secular music, but she never stopped watching television. The only thing that bothered her was the soap operas with Spiritist themes, which she watched with caution and a critical eye. For her, music was the main Evangelical entertainment. She also explored the Internet extensively, and by the time the interview with her was conducted in 2009 she took part in Evangelical virtual communities on Orkut.

AUTHORITY AND TRAJECTORIES OF FAITH

The dichotomy between "religion" (something created by people) and "the truth" (revealed in the Bible, not always followed by believers and churches) is as old as Protestantism. However, when I compared some opinions expressed on Orkut with the testimonies collected during my research, in light of the issue of authority, I concluded that young people find barriers within some churches. As a result, some churches create new spaces for youth in order to attract the dissatisfied, or to maintain the ones they have. Gender and age are crucial issues in determining who will be taken into account by the leadership. However, it is important to note that there is not an essence intrinsic to youth, such as a desire for innovation. Along with bold young people who tried to bring novelties to their church, there are others who took up positions of traditional leadership, as in the case of the Adventist pastor Douglas (discussed below).

One poignant characteristic of Brazilian youth traced in both the censuses of 2000 and 2010 was that the percentage of those young people who declared themselves to be "without religion" was higher than the percentage detected for the entire population—in 2000 it was 9 percent compared to almost 8 percent; in 2010 it was around 10 percent compared to 8 percent (9.4 percent for young people of fifteen to seventeen years; 10.3 percent for people of eighteen to nineteen years; 10.6 percent for people of twenty to twenty-four years; and 10.1 percent for people of twenty-five to twenty-nine years). Novaes (2006) observed that the religious circulation had intensified in the past thirty years, along with the spread of religious and spiritual references in media and popular culture, favoring a mixture of creeds and practices that attracted youth in particular. Youth have achieved a new status as consumers and citizens in the past thirty years in Brazil, being increasingly targeted by the industry, the media, and the tertiary sector of the nation's economy. Evangelicals are not immune to this, trend, as a portion of the young people try to understand religious creeds from their own experience within a transforming and globalizing society, where religion has to compete with many other practices.

Therefore, in this final section, I will analyze the activities of three young interviewees, between twenty and twenty-nine years old, from different parts of Brazil. One of them (Bertone) is a former Evangelical who still believes in God but has dropped out of church. One of them is Adventist (Douglas), and one is from the Community Reach movement (Thatiane). All of them converted or began to intensify their religious activities between the ages of twelve and fifteen, and each represents different relations with religious authority.

Douglas the Pastor

Douglas de Souza Reis is a twenty-nine-year-old Adventist pastor and writer with a degree in theology who lives in the city of Joinville, in the south of Brazil. From a Catholic-Spiritist background, he converted to Adventism at the age of fifteen. He had been involved in church activities (e.g., evangelism) since a young age, until he studied theology and became pastor. He has worked as a chaplain for Adventist schools: "Due to the function of chapel in Adventist schools, I had the opportunity to talk with young Evangelicals of different denominations. I realize that many of them are oriented by their own religious experiences, but they discard the Bible as a reference. I seek to follow the opposite way: to understand the Bible, and then look for the experience of proximity with God. Thus I seek to respect the creed of the other Christians, as at the same time I show them respectfully the aspects with which I disagree."[7]

When asked about his relationship (or lack thereof) with youth from other religions and/or churches, he endorsed the critiques of other Evangelicals about the gospel culture:

> The Seventh-Day Adventist Church, being a Protestant denomination, does not endorse evangelistic methods that contradict principles that it understands as biblical; while other denominations use gospel dance nights, the Adventists are opposed to the use of the nonreligious popular music in the liturgy. Particularly, I write a lot about this subject, concerned with the influence of the gospel on the denominational culture. . . . Along with most Adventists, I do not appreciate anything that suggests ecumenism. Events such as the March for Jesus are out of tune with what I believe. In fact, I see them just as a "Christianized" version of popular festivities. It is a mass, diluted Christianity, which does not seem compatible with the purity and the renunciation present in the Gospel.

In his interview he incorporated the discourse of authority—he is a religious leader, and little is known about the time he spent learning the faith, or the "Absolute Truth," as he calls it. Was it possible that he would have interpreted biblical lessons using this experience? Maybe, maybe not, but as he is a convert, it is possible that he would have gone through a process of seeking in the Bible to understand its truth in his daily life. His discourse shows that he has something to share with and to teach others, Christians and non-Christians alike. Therefore he should be an example of his faith. When asked how he defines himself as a Christian, or Evangelical, or Protestant, he refused to identify himself as "Evangelical," because it is a broad concept used to identify groups with few doctrinal affinities. He prefers to be known as Christian and Adventist: "I read the Bible every day, I try to share and teach what I learn with other people, in a spontaneous and conscious way. I kept myself virgin until marriage, I have followed for fourteen years a vegetarian diet, I observe Saturday as a sacred day, and I work for Jesus to come back as soon as possible to this Earth."

Thatiane and the "Big Soup"

Such activism can be found in the work of Thatiane, twenty-six years old, who lives in the city of Curitiba, in the south of Brazil.[8] She has an undergraduate degree in design and works as a designer for a secular company. Her family was not Evangelical, but she started to attend Evangelical churches in her hometown with her mother when she was a child. She attended different Evangelical churches due to their locale—it is common for Brazilian Evangelicals to change churches or denominations when they move from one town or neighborhood to another. She ended up at Community Reach when she moved to Curitiba to attend college. She stayed in the church because of friendships, and especially because of the pastor's preaching. For her, the issue of authority is based on the Bible—the true leader must serve others, like Jesus. Such a leader must also be firm in the Bible in his or her actions and words. Otherwise, Thatiane affirmed that she would not have any problem leaving the church or disobeying a leader who did not respect those principles. However, she had seen no such case in her life as a Christian.

Besides her resolute and contrary opinions on gospel culture, it is notable that she has run a social assistance project for the needy in Curitiba. With a small group of friends who had already done evangelism using theater and visiting asylums and hospitals, two years ago she started the free distribution of soup for the homeless and needy, with the help of donations. She and her friends did not consult the main pastor before doing these things, because they did not want to involve the name of the church or use it to publicize their work. They just wanted to serve and assist the disadvantaged. Only after months did the pastor came to know of the "big soup," as it is called in Portuguese, giving it his full blessing, as the congregation started to contribute to the work.

As a Christian, Thatiane defines herself as someone who likes to evangelize and to serve others. Currently she is leader of a cell group. Her concern with discipleship derives from her vision of evangelization. She enjoys the activity of counseling and Bible study, but her main focus is on the formation of disciples, of people who will make a difference in the world. When asked if she wanted to engage in an activity never tried before, she said that her heart "burned for work with abandoned children." She is also a religious authority, but in her interview the theme was more the process of becoming a Christian, of learning the biblical lessons—she said that now she is more mature as a person and a Christian, with a better and deeper comprehension of the biblical truths (e.g., she raised the issue of what the Bible teaches about adultery in the interview as an example of a biblical truth she had learned).

Bertone: Between Blind Faith and Reason

A former member of the Assembly of God, Bertone de Oliveira Souza, twenty-four years old, lives in the city of Imperatriz, in the state of Maranhão (in northeastern Brazil), one of the states with the highest rates of Catholic adherence. He is a Ph.D. candidate in history, with a research emphasis on the history of Protestantism in Brazil. He was born into an Evangelical family and was baptized at the age of nine in the (non-Pentecostal) Baptist Church of the National Convention. At that time, Pentecostalism enjoyed impressive growth in the south of Maranhão, and his family was attracted to the church because of its stories of God transforming into gold the teeth of his servants, and other supernatural manifestations. However, the distance of this church from his home made him change to the Assembly of God in 1997, where he stayed until 2002, when he was in his last year of high school.

During his adolescence, he had difficulty accepting all the practices of the Assembly of God—speaking in tongues, prophecies, miracles, screaming. He missed the traditional Baptist church, where the pastor "went to the door and greeted each person, he knew all in the family, called me by name, always friendly . . . we were religious but not fundamentalists."[9] This radically changed when he joined the Assembly, where there was constant preaching "on devils, hell, the dangers of television and cartoons (which I adored watching), dramatic preaching on the imminence of the Second Coming of Christ, the necessity for all to go on mission and be always sanctified, give testimonies everywhere. Those things made me, little by little, become an Evangelical with a strong sense of guilt, shyness, melancholy, alternating with moments of religious ardor, in search of experiences with the supernatural."

He was highly engaged in the activities of the church, read many books on theology, and dreamed of being a missionary. In the last months of high school the shy young man wanted to make friends and spread his wings. The influence of some of his teachers called his attention to history, geography, and philosophy. He read Marx and Nietzsche and started to question his religion, which made him drop the church. He went to college and majored in history. In the first two years he tried to go back to the church—first the Assembly, then the Baptist church, while his readings in the history course gave him another perspective on life. The recognition of different cultures and systems of belief as equally valid, and of the Bible as a human product, made him disbelieve in the infallibility of his religion:

> It does not mean only a personal conflict between faith and reason. I felt I did not want to take part in any religious institution, and I could not avoid doubting everything that is fundamental truth for Christianity. In the second semester of 2002 I left, definitely, the religion. For me it was very difficult to deal with the new situation in the first months, mainly after the conversion of my father. All in the family were Evangelicals, and I was the only one to abandon the faith; my lack of interest in practicing religion occurred in parallel to my increasing interest in studying it. For me, understanding religion, its ideas, its history, its psychology, substitutes for my desire to live it. Knowing became more important than believing.

Remembering the aforementioned discussions on Orkut, one sees the rejection of institutionalized religion and the endorsement of the social role of Christianity. Such topics echo the critiques of some behaviors allegedly fomented by the market—consumerism, social conformism, Christianity without Christ, and so forth. Are these critics right in being nonconformists, always unhappy with their imperfections, with the imperfections of the Christian culture, aiming at Christian perfection and sanctification? In the discussions observed on Orkut, the places where such things can be reached is the central issue.

Usually, those frustrated with religion tend to follow Bertone's steps—they drop religion and endorse a nonreligious group. Otherwise, they tend to change churches, which has become easier in the past twenty to thirty years. Sociologist Leonildo Campos (2008) listed a few reasons that can also explain the growth of Pentecostalism and the increase of religious transit within the Evangelical culture: the emergence of new poverty, resulting from unemployment, urbanization, precarious housing, the informal economy, and urban violence; along with the migration of Evangelicals from the South and Southeast to the North and Central-West regions of the country (which increased the percentage of Evangelicals, mainly Pentecostals, in those areas) (p. 35).

Lower-class youth are generally exposed to these social problems, with the important reality that the state does not provide good education, which aggravates the problem of lack of access to better jobs. Therefore, some churches, such as the Snowball Church, Reborn in Christ, and the Nazarene Church, and small communities like Community Reach, try to attract the youth that the more traditional churches have been losing due to the lack of communication between youth and leadership. Still, if such churches help to improve juvenile social action by giving youth a sense of citizenship, the gospel culture constructed in the past twenty years fomented a religiosity by consumption, which is criticized by many Evangelicals as illegitimate.

Such is the case with the youth leader and Nazarene pastor Ramon.[10] In an e-mail interview, he expressed his concern with the quality of devotion young Christians have been showing lately. The new senses of belonging using artifacts of the Evangelical marketplace are followed by suspicions of how profound this "postmodern Christianity," as he called it, actually is. He claimed that the problem for the next generation of Christians is the absence of a Christian identity, and the absence of Christ in the scriptures. For him, orthodoxy and the great theological themes have been neglected in the churches. Nowadays, Christ is depicted in gospel music as a "butler" who attends to everybody's needs, or as a powerful warrior who crushes enemies and gives victory to the believers. For the older generation there is no such thing as conversion because to them all youth look alike, or because these youth seem to care much more about big events like the March for Jesus than about being an everyday Christian. Furthermore, he complained that this generation does not read the Bible, or anything for that matter; they only listen to preaching online, on YouTube. He accuses the newer churches of neglecting the youth in terms of theological instruction, because these youth do not behave like New Testament Christians. But since the newer churches have the financial power to put out CDs and DVDs, the "real" Christians are not heard.

CONCLUSION

Critiques of the quality of Christian community share much in common with the serious problems of Brazilian society as a whole—the lack of quality formal education, which leads to poor instruction, illiteracy, and a low rate of reading. For the guardians of the "Religion of the Word," as Protestantism is known in Brazil, the accusation that youngsters do not read the

Bible is a crucial problem that threatens to compromise the core identity of Evangelical Protestants.

Beyond the well-known idea that the development of communication helped to diminish the authority of religious leaders, institutions, and orthodoxies, Evangelical music, commodities, and the broader uses of media by Evangelicals in Brazil can be shown to have helped to create new authorities—celebrities that boost an Evangelical culture to the sound of soft songs. These developments also help to fragment authority and empower young people who believe they can serve to the Lord merely by playing and enjoying a variety of musical genres.

At the same time, the use of media does not necessarily guarantee the formation of an individualized religion. As with the case of pastor Douglas, the media can be used by youth to propagate orthodoxy. But is this a matter of form versus content? That is, does the fact that modern methods of communication, such as the web, can be used to transmit conservative messages mean that those are not innovative ways to spread the word?

Another significant issue is the relationship of youth to the "authority who cares," as shown by Bertone—sometimes individuals (especially young people, who usually have an ambiguous relationship with any type of authority) do not want to be by themselves, while at the same time they seek self-affirmation. They can also look to such places for guidance in troublesome times. The central question of religious authority is who is drawing the lines between right and wrong and determining what is allowed and forbidden in a certain religious field. We can see that more and more people are involved in expanding the Evangelical field in Brazil using a number of means—media, marketing, rational choice, and face-to-face evangelism, among others. Each medium equips believers in the battle for God in Brazil, which means that more and more people take responsibility for the growth of the Kingdom of God. Each saint may feel that the Lord has given him or her the authority to go and preach—as can be seen in different ways among all the interviewees. However, not all saints feel called to evangelize. For them, Christianity can be just a lifestyle. Yet that does not mean they will not engage in evangelism at all. The qualitative analysis of life courses, or of a certain group of people, is a powerful tool for understanding the diverse paths through which individuals conduct their religious lives—sometimes differently from, sometimes exactly in the way that institutions prescribe.

Youth does not necessarily mean innovation, boldness, and adventurousness. These characteristics exist in some youth, and certainly they are important commodities in the marketplace of Evangelical lifestyles.

Churches and organizations that hold onto their conservative orthodoxy in practices, customs, and authority (like the Assembly of God in the case of Bertone), leaving little room for youth to act, have been losing people. There has also been a market segmentation of interests in recent Brazilian Evangelicalism—maybe as the result of the "invasion" of the market-oriented mentality in the religious sphere, maybe because of the increased role of youth in Brazilian society as citizens and consumers. Youth have been targeted as never before by many Evangelical organizations, using "their" language. With the national census of 2010 confirming the extent to which Brazil is an aging country, the near future of Brazilian Protestantism will carry the marks of such mobilization. But this is the subject for further research.

NOTES

1. I will use the term "Evangelical" in the commonplace usage in—and applied to—Brazil, where this word covers all Protestant groups. Therefore, the terms "Protestant" and "Evangelical" are synonyms in this text.

2. There are a few academic studies of religion and youth in Brazil. For studies on religion and youth in general, see Clark (2003) and Smith and Denton (2005), among many others.

3. In 2008 the couple was sentenced to eighteen months of prison in the United States for entering the country with money hidden in their Bibles. From their U.S. prison they transmitted church services to Brazil via the Internet.

4. These messages quoted, no longer available online, were drawn from http://www.orkut.com.br/.

5. Another church that created events for martial arts athletes was the Reborn in Christ Church, from which Snowball Church was created. Since the early 2000s the church has promoted "Fight Nights," in which young men attend a church service and/or a sermon, which is followed by competitions in mixed martial arts, boxing, karate, jujitsu, and so forth. One of its flyers reads, "Fight Night: The night in which the warriors gather to fight."

6. When this essay was concluded, in 2009, Orkut was the most popular online social network in Brazil; therefore, it was a rich source for research. Differently from Facebook, which became popular in Brazil only in the 2010s, Orkut had functionalities such as communities and forums that gathered heated discussions on infinite topics. In 2015, due to the popularity of Facebook and Google+, Orkut was shut down as it became obsolete after a heavy decrease in membership.

7. All statements were taken from an interview conducted over e-mail on July 5, 2010.

8. Personal interview, June 16, 2010.

9. E-mail interview, June 20, 2010.

10. E-mail interview, July 12, 2010.

REFERENCES

Campos, L. S. (2008). Os mapas, atores e números da diversidade religiosa cristã brasileira: Católicos e Evangélicos entre 1940 e 2007. *REVER:*

Revista de Estudos da Religião, 8, 9–47.

Clark, L. S. (2003). *From angels to aliens: Teenagers, the media, and the supernatural*. New York, NY: Oxford University Press.

Cunha, M. N. (2007). *A explosão gospel: Um olhar das ciências humanas sobre o cenário evangélico no Brasil*. Rio de Janeiro, BR: Instituto Mysterium & Mauad X.

Hendershot, H. (2004). *Shaking the world for Jesus: Media and conservative Evangelical culture*. Chicago: University of Chicago Press.

Hoover, S. M. (2006). *Religion in the media age*. New York, NY: Routledge.

IBGE (2010). *Censo demográfico, 2010: Características gerais da população, religião e pessoas com deficiência*. Rio de Janeiro, BR: IBGE.

Mariano, R. (1997). *Neopentecostais: Sociologia do novo pentecostalismo no Brasil*. São Paulo, BR: Loyola.

McDannell, C. (1995). *Material Christianity: Religion and popular culture in America*. New Haven, CT: Yale University Press.

Mello e Souza, L. D. (1998). *O diabo na Terra de Santa Cruz*. São Paulo, BR: Cia das Letras.

Mendonça, A. G., & Velasques F. (1990). *Introdução ao protestantismo*. São Paulo, BR: Edições Loyola.

Moore, R. L. (1994). *Selling God: American religion in the marketplace of culture*. New York, NY: Oxford University Press.

Novaes, R. (2006). Os jovens, os ventos secularizantes e o espírito do tempo. In F. Teixeira & R. Menezes (Eds.), *As religiões no Brasil: Continuidades e rupturas* (pp. 135–160). Petrópolis, BR: Vozes.

Novinski, A. (1973). *Os cristãos-novos na Bahia*. São Paulo, BR: Perspectiva.

Smith, C., & Denton, M. L. (2005). *Soul searching: The religious and spiritual lives of American teenagers*. New York, NY: Oxford University Press.

227

CHAPTER II

The Authority of the Image

*Sex, Religion, and the Text/Image Conflict
in Craig Thompson's* Blankets

Christine Hoff Kraemer

At a local bookstore I frequent, I struck up an acquaintance with the shop owner. Knowing my interest in religion and graphic novels, he had made a habit of pointing out relevant new releases, and as we chatted over the checkout counter one afternoon, he asked about my research. I replied that my current project was on religion and sexuality in literature. "Well, those don't go together," he grinned at me. "Don't you know that God hates sex?"

This perception is commonplace. It is inflected by a long history of American struggle over the proper relationship between religion and sexuality, but the visibility of the Christian Right in the United States over the past thirty years is its immediate context. Wilcox and Larson (2006, p. 6) describe the Christian Right as a movement seeking to organize Evangelical Protestants and other "orthodox" Christians into conservative political activism, usually on behalf of the Republican Party. The movement includes Mormons and Orthodox Jews and has reached out to Catholics, Muslims, and African American, Korean, and Hispanic Christians as part of its effort to prevent the legalization of same-sex marriage. Its primary constituency, however, consists of white Evangelicals (p. 7). The Christian Right considers itself a "pro-family" movement and is united over the idea that a return to Christian values is necessary for the health of the nation (pp. 6, 13). Christian Right groups include Focus on the Family, the Family Research Council, Concerned Women for America, and many local organizations that share, as Wilcox and Larson put it, "no single agenda but rather a collection of overlapping agendas": restricting abortion rights, banning same-sex marriage, reducing sexual material in television and movies, promoting prayer in public schools, and more (p. 9). Christian Right supporters portray the movement as protecting conservative Christians' religious liberties, which they believe are threatened by mainstream society. Critics charge that the heated rhetoric of the movement contributes to sexism, intolerance, and homophobia, and that the Christian Right does not merely wish to protect its constituents' liberties but also seeks to legislate enforcement of a single set of religious views (pp. 11, 18).

Many of the issues central to the Christian Right involve sexuality and gender. Seeing homosexuality as a sin that threatens to undermine civilization itself, Christian Right activists oppose laws that would protect lesbian, gay, bisexual, and transgender (LGBT) people from discrimination in employment or from being evicted from housing due to their sexual orientation (Wilcox & Larson, 2006, p. 148). Although many Evangelicals believe that homosexuals simply need to be "cured," some Christian Right activists support violence against homosexuals and believe that homosexual sex should be an imprisonable offense (p. 149). Although the Christian Right is particularly interested in limiting the freedoms of LGBT people, members of the movement are also active in antipornography and anti-"porn addiction" efforts and in restricting the circulation of explicitly sexual materials in general. Activists advocate a variety of agendas, ranging from the enforcement of age restrictions on the sale of such materials, to the criminalization of the sale or possession of all sexually explicit media (p. 153).

Journalists have touted the strength and influence of the Christian Right—and then, later, declared its defeat as a small, extremist group—many times over the past three decades. Wilcox and Larson (2006) estimate that, in actuality, public support for the Christian Right has been fairly consistent since the late 1970s, and that perhaps 10 to 15 percent of white Americans support its agenda (p. 5). Its effectiveness in mobilizing voters, however, has increased its influence. Although the Christian Right's power waxes and wanes—often in conjunction with the national election cycle—some of its tactics frighten other Americans. Wilcox and Larson write, "They see local organizations working to remove books from public libraries. . . . They see an elected official in Alabama fighting to ban all homosexual authors from school libraries. They hear some of the more extreme movement activists suggesting that known homosexuals be imprisoned, and they watch television accounts of the assassination of abortion providers by those on the fringe of the pro-life movement. To at least some observers, these extremists do echo Nazi persecution of gays and public book burnings" (pp. 14–15).

Iconic figures within the movement have provided clear articulations of its intentions. A 1995 fund raising letter from Pat Robertson proclaimed that the feminist agenda "is about a socialist, anti-family political movement that encourages women to leave their husbands, kill their children, practice witchcraft, destroy capitalism, and become lesbians" (Wilcox & Larson, 2006, p. 11), while Jerry Falwell's notorious September 12, 2001, statement accused "the pagans, and the abortionists, and the feminists, and the gays and the lesbians who are actively trying to make that an alternative lifestyle, the ACLU, [and] the People for the American Way" of having helped cause the terrorist attacks (p. 6).

That this is about both morality and politics has always been just below the surface. In her essay "Thinking Sex," anthropologist Gayle Rubin analyzes what she calls "sexual panics," describing how anxieties around deviant sexuality have been used both historically and in the present day to pass legislation enforcing dominant social, economic, and gender norms. Writing in 1984, Rubin predicted that the political right would use AIDS to encourage homophobia and combat the LGBT rights movement, an expectation that history has borne out.[1] These panics, she argues, affect the whole of society, not just the demonized minority: "There is systematic mistreatment of individuals and communities on the basis of erotic taste or behavior. . . . Specific populations bear the brunt of the current system of erotic power, but their persecution upholds a system that affects everyone" (Rubin, 1993, p. 35).

Today's controversy over same-sex marriage in the United States is not simply about extending legal rights to same-sex relationships: it touches on fundamental issues of religious authority and belief. The move to legally recognize same-sex unions, in the eyes of many observers, undermines the traditional heteronormative family. Further, to affirm expressions of eroticism that are explicitly forbidden by the Bible also condones the exercise of individual and group religious authority outside the structures of traditional religious institutions.

This debate is not taking place only in political terms, but in religious ones as well. On the political left, those outside the sexual mainstream have become increasingly willing to claim personal spiritual authority for the sacred practice of their sexuality, just as more conservative groups have claimed biblical or institutional authority for theirs. To declare eroticism to be not just sacred, but a primary source of spiritual experience raises human sexuality to the level of Tillich's "ultimate concern." From this point of view, sex becomes a rite of resistance for the liberation of all human beings. Given the intensity with which queer sexuality is debated in religious circles, this shift in rhetoric from secular to sacred human rights is not trivial.

"THIS WORLD IS NOT MY HOME": RELIGIOUS AND SEXUAL DIFFERENCE IN *BLANKETS*

"Queerness" is no longer simply a synonym for homosexuality (if it ever was). Instead, it has become a label for all kinds of sexual difference. Specifically because of the heterosexuality of the protagonist, Craig Thompson's graphic novel *Blankets* (2003) illustrates how conflicts over sexual difference and religious authority can affect those who are not members of any sexual identity group (not gay, lesbian, bisexual, transgender, etc.), making them also functionally "queer."[2] The autobiographical novel merges biblical imagery with a touching story of adolescent sexual awakening. Due to Craig's unusually intense childhood religiosity and artistic interests, he experiences himself as an outsider in his midwestern Evangelical community. Emotional abuse from both parents and teachers, in addition to sexual abuse by a babysitter, compounds Craig's sense of alienation. Attempts by others to stifle his urge to draw prove futile, and by adolescence Craig has resigned himself to a life of rejection. This resignation changes when Craig falls in love with Raina, a girl he meets at church camp. Craig makes an extended visit with Raina and her family and finds himself struggling with his faith in the face of his sexual awakening. At the climax of the book, Craig and Raina have an ecstatic sexual encounter. Craig's ethical confusion in the aftermath, however, is soothed by a religious vision in which he and his lovemaking with Raina are affirmed by an image of Christ. The experience, along with his own study of the Bible, leads Craig to abandon Evangelical Protestantism in favor of a biblically inflected personal spirituality.

Blankets was declared Best Comic of 2003 by *Time* magazine (Arnold, 2003) and received Harvey, Eisner, and Ignatz awards from the comics industry (Thompson, 2007). The work has not always been received positively, however. *Blankets* was removed from a Missouri public library in 2006 after complaints that the novel is pornographic (Sims, 2006). Clearly, the work treats a taboo topic: the sexual desires and experiences of adolescents. *Blankets* also portrays an adolescent girl as the initiator of sexual activity, challenging the cultural expectation that it is girls' duty to control sexual activity by repelling the advances of boys (Tolman, 2002, p. 15).

There has been a long history of attempts to censor comics in order to protect young people. Although comics are considered a legitimate storytelling medium for both children and adults elsewhere in the world, particularly in France and Japan, the U.S. comics industry has yet to solidly achieve this status. This is largely due to the industry's decision to submit to self-censorship in the mid-1950s following a public outcry against comics' alleged dangerous influence on youth.[3] In the decades that followed, the major comics publishing houses published exclusively with juvenile audiences in mind—a trend that did not reverse itself until the mid-1970s. Comics today have a lingering reputation both as children's literature and as youth-corrupting, sensationalistic pulp—both cheap, mass-produced, disposable products. To attempt a serious work of literature in comics still strikes many adults as doomed from the outset.[4]

The hybridity and ambiguity of the medium contributes to its transgressiveness.[5] In Blankets, Thompson is able to use and subvert biblical images and texts in a way that not only asserts the authority of his interpretations over tradition, but also allows images rather than words to convey the narrative's central messages. Such privileging of images is not universal to graphic novels—Art Spiegelman's acclaimed Holocaust narrative Maus sustains its primary narrative thread using text, for which images are supplements. In contrast, although text is also an important formal element of Blankets, the novel's practice in its climactic moments is either to use text as an element of visual design or to dispense with it entirely. Consequently, Blankets transgresses not just in its subject matter, but also in how it violates the traditional values of Western book culture by giving images precedence over words.

Blankets challenges the sexual mores of both Evangelical Christian and mainstream culture by presenting sexuality as a source of the sacred that is superior to the Bible and to church teachings. The book also champions individualism while showing how both Evangelical and mainstream culture perceive certain modes of nonconformity as synonymous with homosexuality. Craig struggles with his sensitive artistic temperament as one might with a minority sexual orientation, finally resigning himself to a closeted state that is breached only by Raina. Blankets illustrates how a sexual orientation that unites art, spirituality, and sexuality is perceived as threatening to Craig's community, where out-of-wedlock sex is believed to be dirty, sinful, and dehumanizing. Obscenity, as it is defined in Craig's community, has much to do with maintenance of the cultural and religious status quo.

Craig is conditioned early in his childhood to expect punishment for nonconformity. The book opens with an encounter with his abusive father, an enormous figure who looms over Craig and his brother (Thompson, 2003, p. 13). Misbehavior is punished by a night locked in the "cubbyhole," a tiny cupboard of which both boys are terrified. Thompson's illustration of the room turns the foldout cot into an enormous, toothed mouth, while demons lurk in the corners (p. 16). So intense is the experience of separation from his terrified younger brother that the incident later becomes Craig's personal vision of hell (pp. 62–63). At school he is beaten for his small size and dark hair, which to the larger, blond boys is a sign of being "Mexican" (p. 21); in class his teacher humiliates him publicly for writing a scatological poem about his abusers (pp. 28–29). At home Craig and his brother are molested by a male babysitter, an experience that leads the adolescent Craig to feel horror toward his own body (pp. 292–294).

Craig escapes into drawing and dreams of heaven, and so he reaches adolescence in a state of detachment. In response to other boys' catcalls of "Faggot!" and "You look like a fucking girl!" Craig reaches for the greater reality of the spiritual over the physical, thinking, "This world is not my home; I'm only passing through" (Thompson, 2003, p. 53). Yet, while Craig experiences school merely as the world's rejection, his isolation at church camp strikes him as a rejection from God (p. 79). There, he is taunted by the other boys for his religiosity while simultaneously mourning his lack of athletic and social talents (pp. 79–80).

Craig also feels alienated by his male peers' performance of their gender and sexuality. For Craig, as a preadolescent, his church camp experiences include exposure to the other boys' aggressive sexuality and objectification of girls. When Craig attends church camp as an adolescent, he finds this tendency exaggerated even further. In the boys' bathroom, two jocks converse while one urinates, saying, "You know, Jake. Church camp is the best place to score pussy.... I was feeling up that one blonde girl last night; what's her ... Cindy. Yeah, and I'm talking 34 Double-D, I swear it!" (Thompson, 2003, p. 117). To the speaker, his sex partner's bra size is far more memorable than her name.

Craig's gentle approach to Raina—holding her hand or tentatively stroking her hair (Thompson, 2003, p. 128)—stands in contrast to this attitude, suggesting that the other boys' perceptions of Craig are partially accurate: he *is* different. When held up next to the macho behavior that is expected among his peers, there is something deviant about Craig's approach to sexuality, a difference that is emphasized further by his later experiences of spiritual sex. While for the jock, Cindy is merely her breasts and genitals, Craig's attraction to Raina frames her as a muse and an angel. Nor are adolescent boys the only people to associate Craig's personality traits with a deviant sexual orientation. Late in the book, Thompson includes a satirical exchange between Craig and a member of his church. The well-meaning parishioner warns Craig not to attend art school and asserts that drawing nudes will lead inevitably to pornography addiction and homosexuality. In the minds of Craig's fellow church members, an artistic temperament like Craig's puts him at risk for what they see as perversion.

Craig's family also teaches him about the baseness of sexual desire. When Craig is a child, his parents chastise him for his drawing of a naked woman. "The body is beautiful, Craig, but not like that," his mother tells him. "God created us, but sin has made us impure. . . . God gave you a talent and we don't want you to use it for the Devil" (Thompson, 2003, pp. 206–207). The mother's statements imply that representing a naked human body is an act of impurity, and that a desire to see a naked body is evil. As the child Craig cries, he looks at the picture on the wall, a print of Warner Sallman's *Head of Christ* (1940). The figure, initially seen in profile, begins to shed tears over the boy's sin. As Craig reaches pleadingly toward the image, Christ turns away in disappointment (p. 208). The shame of this incident is carried into the present when, in Craig's imagination, his memory of the childhood drawing blurs with the reality of Raina. In a series of four steps, the cartoon image of the woman acquires Raina's head and body, a transformation that suggests Craig's sexual desire for her is objectifying and sinful (p. 209).

Craig's artistic urges in general are also discouraged, both by adults in his life and by the system of religious values he has begun to internalize. In Sunday school, when Craig suggests he might draw in heaven, his teacher laughs and replies, "How can you praise God with drawings?" (Thompson, 2003, p. 137). When Craig replies that he wants to "draw His creation," the teacher again dissuades him by saying that God has "already drawn it for us" (p. 138). As an adolescent, Craig's reading of Ecclesiastes triggers a fit of self-disgust over the escapist aspects of his art. "A profusion of dreams and a profusion of words are futile. Therefore fear God," one panel quotes (Eccles. 5:7; Thompson, 2003, p. 56). Suddenly seeing his drawings as a meaningless distraction from the higher truth of his faith, Craig burns them in the same barrel where his family burns garbage. The act is portrayed as an exorcism: Craig's head whips from side to side, then is thrown back as his drawings burst from his mouth (see figure 11.1; Thompson, 2003, p. 60). The eerie image of an empty-eyed Craig, kneeling with his palms turned up in supplication, is emphasized by Thompson's use of a splash page, a single panel that occupies the entire space.

FIG. 11.1 From *Blankets* by Craig Thompson, p. 60. Used by permission. Photo: Top Shelf.

The Authority of the Image

Despite Craig's attempt to cleanse himself of his urge to draw, more often his art frames the holiest moments of his life. Craig's childhood collaborations with his brother Phil give him a sense of precious connection that he otherwise lacks: "These were the only wakeful moments of my childhood that I can recall feeling life was sacred or worthwhile" (Thompson, 2003, p. 44). Later, after the meeting at church camp, Raina sends Craig a letter. Craig frames his artistic and emotional renewal in religious terms: "Her letter renewed my faith in the notion of making marks on paper" (p. 142). His doubt and desire to sacrifice his talent for his religion are swept away by Raina's affirmation of their connection, and he immediately draws a picture of himself and Raina sitting together in a tree. This positions Raina as Craig's muse, as a goddess-like figure of artistic inspiration (pp. 143, 337). Just a few pages later, however, Thompson repeats the word "faith" in a different context: a series of panels shows Craig writhing in ecstasy as he masturbates to one of Raina's letters, while the caption reads, "You probably wouldn't believe me—if I told you this was the one and only time I masturbated my senior year—but such are the will powers provided by faith" (p. 147). Here, "faith" refers to the religious beliefs that require Craig to reject his sexuality as impure, views that conflict with Craig's newly resurrected faith in art as a means of connection. The marks that Craig makes on paper this time—smears of semen—make him deeply ashamed, and he crumples the paper and throws it away, collapsing to the floor in a posture of despair (p. 148).

Craig's faith in his connection with Raina—and by extension, the efficacy of his art—is confirmed by Raina's phone call, telling Craig that her parents are getting a divorce. This affirmation gives Craig something his Christian faith does not—not only "hope," but also "proof" of their connection (Thompson, 2003, p. 165). Craig convinces his parents to allow him to visit Raina, and soon he is off to spend two weeks with her and her family.

Craig's sexual awakening during his visit with Raina is framed by art and religion, beginning with the handmade quilt that Raina gives him upon his arrival—a gift that Craig calls "sacred" (Thompson, 2003, p. 184). When Craig insists he give her something in return, Raina proposes an exchange of his art for hers: a painting on her wall (p. 187). Later, Craig lies on Raina's bed reading, and then hurriedly gets up, feeling that he is disrespecting a sacred object with his casual sprawling: "Instead, I should be removing my sandals (socks?) and averting my eyes" (p. 201). That Craig perceives both the bed and the quilt as holy ground anticipates his affirmation of sacred eroticism when he and Raina sleep there together. Later in the novel, images of the holy begin to include the natural world, particularly the blanket of new snow that Craig sees as "clean and pure" (p. 244). He and Raina share their first kiss in a snow-covered forest (p. 256). Thompson chooses this imagery for the cover of the book: the couple standing together, framed by dimly seen trees and snowy whiteness. As the book develops, the winter landscape becomes a reflection of the purity of the characters' youthful romance.

CHRIST SMILED: SPIRITUAL AUTHORITY THROUGH EROTIC ENCOUNTER

Thompson portrays Craig's sexual awakening as a healing of his relationship with his body and with the material world. His sense of displacement from his body dates back to his childhood and is specifically associated with the experience of being molested (Thompson, 2003, pp. 291–292). When Raina asks Craig to sleep in her bed with her, Craig agrees, but his mind floods with Bible verses condemning fornication, lust, the flesh, and the world (p. 304). This fog of worry lifts when he sees Raina in her nightgown, however; instead, he remembers a line from the Song of Solomon as he visualizes Raina with a halo and angel wings: "All beautiful you are, my darling; there is no flaw in you" (see figure 11.2; Song of Sol. 4:7; Thompson, 2003, p. 306). The two curl up under the blanket Raina made for Craig, but Craig stays awake far into the night, whispering "a prayer of gratitude to God" as he admires Raina's sleeping form. For the first time in the novel, Craig unapologetically declares the sacredness of the body, and the book's images grow more and more erotic as Raina tosses and turns in her sleep, culminating in a splash panel that shows Raina surrounded by trumpets and sensually curling spirals: "She is yours / She is perfect / a temple / with hair spilling over her temples" (p. 311). Against the body-condemning faith of his parents and church, Craig instead uses the New Testament image of the human body as a temple to affirm Raina's sacredness (see John 2:21 and 1 Cor. 3:16–17, 6:19, for examples). Rejecting the thought that he should feel guilty for his desire, Craig instead asserts, "I feel as clean and pure as the snow" (p. 313). Craig's mental landscape has become identified with his experience of the natural one, with the effect that both are affirmed as holy.

As the visit continues, Craig observes that the intimacy he and Raina share at night is not matched during the day, when she interacts with friends, takes care of her parents and two mentally disabled siblings, and escapes into poetry or drug use. Craig's declaration of love is later met by Raina's melancholy remark that everything ends, and that she doubts the

FIG. 11.2 From *Blankets* by Craig Thompson, p. 306. Used by permission. Photo: Top Shelf.

value of getting started. Yet the narrative also repeatedly affirms the worth of imperfection. Craig declares that the first mark he makes on Raina's wall—a mere dot—is a mistake, and Raina responds, "Even a mistake is better than nothing."[6] Later, Craig kisses Raina's pimples, exclaiming, "They prove that the rest of this perfection isn't merely a dream! Without the zits, I'd have no proof of you as reality" (Thompson, 2003, p. 399).

On their last night together, Craig and Raina share an intensely erotic encounter, which Thompson illustrates in a series of soft, organic images, uninterrupted by sharp panel borders (Thompson, 2003, pp. 418–424). The omission of borders recalls an earlier scene in the novel, where Craig and Raina hide beneath a curtained platform in order to avoid a chapel service at church camp. In an intimate moment, Raina naps on Craig's jacket while he strokes her hair; the lack of hard lines and the overlapping of images suggest that normal social restrictions have been temporarily removed (pp. 125–126, 128–129). In bed with Raina, Craig remembers the words of his church's communion ritual and applies them to their lovemaking: "For as often as you drink this cup' . . . it is never enough." The "milky," "salty," and "sweet" tastes of Raina's flesh are substituted for the symbolic body of Christ. Instead of recalling a sacrifice and death, Raina's flesh represents unending desire to Craig. But this is not a despairing thought. The words "it is never enough" caption a splash page of Craig and Raina gazing into each other's eyes and smiling (p. 424). Rather than contrasting their encounter with the sacredness of the communion ritual, the words of the liturgy instead confirm the sacredness of their sex.

After Raina falls asleep, Craig covers her with the quilt, "aware that she'd been crafted by a divine artist" (Thompson, 2003, p. 429). For the first time, Craig unconditionally acknowledges art as holy by identifying it with the creative power of God and, by extension, asserts the worthiness of his own talent. The chapter closes with a sequence showing nothing but the shapes of snow and trees, captioned with a poem that both describes the scene and reflects on Craig and Raina's lovemaking: "Sky and earth became one, / Trees outstretched their naked limbs, / Snow drifts shifted shapes— / Washing away to reveal tufts of briar" (pp. 446–447). The panels tastefully suggest entangled limbs, white skin, and pubic hair; a ridge captures the curve of a hip. These images of creation portray the divine as artist, both of the natural landscape and of the human body. Further, both nature and the human body are erotically charged. The phrase "Sky and earth became one" suggests mystical union; in the accompanying panel, the whiteness of the sky and the snow on the ground has erased the horizon. This image functions as a metaphor for the union experienced in sex, as sky and earth also represent human flesh. These affirmations demonstrate the degree to which Craig has broken with his community's Evangelical religion during his two-week visit with Raina. Craig has begun to see his artistic talent, his bodily desires, and the natural world as sacred. He is asserting his own spiritual authority by privileging his personal experiences above the authority of his parents and adults in his church.

Craig continues to dialogue with the Bible, but he has embraced the right to interpret the text for himself by representing and affirming sexuality with biblical imagery. Although the events of his childhood seemed to conspire to crush his individuality, his experiences of being an outsider have strengthened his ability to stand apart. Now catalyzed by transformative sex, Craig's individualism has recentered itself on a positive source of value: the sacredness found in the body and in nature. Whereas previously Craig interpreted his difference as a sign of God's disfavor, his experience of sexual love leaves him feeling uniquely blessed. In the aftermath of his lovemaking with Raina, he gazes up at the wall at Raina's print of *Head of Christ*—the same portrait the child Craig once imagined turning away from his sin. This time, however, Christ turns from a profile view to face forward and smiles radiantly at the viewer: both Craig within the frame and the reader taking in the page. As Craig gazes at the portrait, the candles in the room suddenly snuff out, leaving the room dim. Smoke drifts from the wicks, suggesting the departure of a spiritual presence (see figure 11.3; Thompson, 2003, p. 431).

As historian of religion Stephen Prothero (2003) notes, over five hundred million copies of Warner Sallman's *Head of Christ* have been produced, making it the most common religious image in the world (p. 116). The image's appearance in courtrooms and government buildings throughout the mid-twentieth century made it an icon of an American Christianity, linked with patriotism and nationalism (Morgan, 2005, pp. 250–251). During the 1990s, visual culture scholar David Morgan surveyed Americans on *Head of Christ*. He discovered that Evangelicals especially were likely to see the painting not as an artist's rendition of Christ, but as a portrait of Jesus himself, an "exact likeness."[7] Some respondents credited miracles to the image or asserted that their visions of Jesus had verified the painting's accuracy. Historical research further revealed a small number of personal accounts of the painting turning to look at and address believers (Morgan, 1996, p. 189). Although Sallman had intended the portrait as a corrective to overly effeminate portraits of Jesus, eventually the portrait was attacked for its femininity and, ironically, its queerness. According to Morgan (1998), in the 1950s one Lutheran seminary professor criticized

FIG. 11.3   From *Blankets* by Craig Thompson, p. 431. Used by permission. Photo: Top Shelf.

Head of Christ as "a pretty picture of a woman with a curling beard who has just come from a beauty parlor with a Halo shampoo!" (p. 120; quoting Roth, 1958, p. 9). This distaste for gender ambiguity became explicitly homophobic when Morgan (1996) solicited letters and interviews regarding the reception of the portrait in 1993; he quotes one United Church of Christ minister as saying that some of his colleagues "couldn't have Sallman's portrait of Christ in their churches because the finely spun hair of Christ as portrayed in the painting was too much of a come-on for the homos in the parish and the community" (p. 201).

The graphic novel form enables Thompson to both use and subvert *Head of Christ*. In Craig's childhood, his mother uses the image in the chastisement she gives Craig for his drawing of a naked woman. Directing the boy's attention to the painting, she asks Craig how Jesus feels when he sins, and he sees the figure's face wet with tears before it turns away (Thompson, 2003, p. 208). The boy reaches toward the painting in supplication, asking for forgiveness, but meets with no response. As a sinner, Craig is worthy only of God's pity, not his love. The sequence is an effective representation of the image's use in Craig's Evangelical family: as a focus for prayer and devotion, as well as an all-seeing eye that weeps over human beings' sins. As an adolescent, while sitting in Raina's bedroom for the first time, Craig perceives *Head of Christ* as "keeping watch over the bed" (p. 201) and providing a deterrent against sin. Under the painting's gaze, Craig remembers Christ turning away from him in his child's imagination and refrains from touching Raina (p. 221).

Yet, when Thompson represents *Head of Christ* turning toward Craig to affirm his sexual love for Raina, he undermines the meaning of the image in Craig's family and church community. No longer does the image serve as a representation of proscriptive religious authority. Craig's internal experience of his sexuality is that it is sacred, something that makes him feel "as clean and pure as the snow" (Thompson, 2003, p. 313). This experience is reflected externally by the painting, much like the natural landscape that shelters and visually mirrors the young couple's love. Additionally, by using an image that for many Evangelicals bears the spirit of Jesus himself, Thompson affirms not just Craig's sexuality, but also his own spiritual authority in drawing the book. The image's approval confirms the primacy of Craig's experience over the traditions of his community (or, perhaps, positively usurps the countertradition that the *Head of Christ* Jesus is queer). Further, the fact that we as readers are included in the figure's gaze as it beams from the page affirms the sexuality and spiritual authority of individuals in general. That so many layers of meaning can be contained in a short sequence of images demonstrates the formal potential of the graphic novel. Without writing a word, Thompson couches his challenge to Evangelical beliefs about sexuality and religious authority as a criticism that comes directly from the Savior himself.

As an art form, the graphic novel is especially equipped to challenge traditional religious words and imagery. Its history as a medium is tied up with children's literature, as well as with pulp fiction, and these connotations paradoxically make comics an ideal form for a religiously and sexually transgressive story like *Blankets*. Aside from its exploration of adolescent desire and its challenge to Evangelical culture, *Blankets* also repeatedly returns to the nihilistic message that Craig encounters in the earliest textual layer of the book of Ecclesiastes, a text that continues to fascinate him well after leaving the Protestant Church. In the "Footnotes" chapter, Thompson illustrates the difference between the pessimistic voice of the oldest Ecclesiastes sections and the reassuring voice of a later writer's interpolations. "What does a man get for all the toil and anxious striving with which he labors under the sun? All his days his work is pain and grief; even at night his mind does not rest. This too is meaningless," reads a text box, under which shivers a naked man surrounded by bones (Eccles. 2:22–23). The following verse (Eccles. 2:24) is illustrated by a pair of pigs clinking beer glasses next to a newly built house: "A man can do nothing better than to eat and drink and find satisfaction in his work" (Thompson, 2003, p. 547). Simultaneously, Thompson demonstrates the conflicting tones of this biblical text and establishes an aesthetic through which passages of *Blankets* may be interpreted.

Raina's frequent struggles with the seeming meaninglessness of her life resonate with Craig's traumatic childhood and hopeless adolescence. After Craig's return home from the visit, Raina withdraws from the intensity and perceived responsibility of their long-distance relationship, and Craig is again pictured reading Ecclesiastes as he observes the melting of the snow. "Nothing fits together anymore," he comments aloud to the landscape (Thompson, 2003, pp. 506–507). He and Raina attempt to remain friends, but Craig eventually finds their reduced intimacy too painful. He breaks off the contact and burns every memento of Raina except the blanket she made for him. The chapter closes with an image of a hand rolling white paint over the mural that Craig once put on Raina's wall, an image of the couple sitting together in a tree. Notably, it is not just the image itself that disappears under the paint, but also the panel borders, suggesting that is not just the relationship that is disappearing, but also Craig and Raina's memories of it. Ecclesiastes's message about the ephemerality of all things is reflected in the empty space that remains; that the painting ever existed is represented only by a smudge at the bottom of the page (p. 543). Similarly, although the warmth of Craig's family and his affirmation of doubt in the "Footnotes" epilogue provide a hopeful note to the book's close, the novel's final panel bears a significant resemblance to the earlier image of the dark forest of Ecclesiastes. Though the final splash page is not nearly so dire as Thompson's illustrations of the suffering man—Craig stands in a snowy landscape under a dark sky, surrounded by trees that neither shelter nor ominously reach for him—the book's final word is "temporary," as Craig notes the simultaneous satisfaction of making art and its inherent transience (p. 582). Here, the white space representing the snow resonates with all the complex meanings it has been given in the book—the purity of Craig's sexual and spiritual independence, the infinite potential of a blank page, and the emptiness after the erasure of his relationship with Raina. That relationship has been reduced to a blanket and the occasional vivid dream, suggesting that life, too, is characterized primarily by ephemerality; however, as with art, the ability to create moments of beauty and joy is sustaining. Despite the sweetness and light of much of the narrative involving Raina, *Blankets* ends on a bittersweet note that celebrates transformation and ecstasy within a wider context of struggle, loss, and pain.

HYBRIDITY AS BLASPHEMY AND OBSCENITY: THE UNSETTLING FORM OF *BLANKETS*

To present sophisticated adult material in a supposed children's medium is disturbing; so also is presenting a story about divine embrace in a medium associated with sensationalistic pulps. Readers who were exposed to biblical Sunday school comics, such as *Picture Stories from the Bible* (first published by Educational Comics between 1942 and 1946) or Jack Chick's conservative Protestant evangelism tracts,[8] may experience an additional level of dissonance at encountering sexuality and meditations on life's impermanence in a medium they associate with easy-to-digest moral lessons. *Blankets* pays homage to the Bible story genre of comics in sequences where Craig reads his Bible: biblical verses appear in a font that resembles printing, with illustrative images beneath (Thompson, 2003, pp. 198–200, 217, 546–547). Unlike in the novel's climactic moments, here the images are subordinate to the text and merely provide a pictorial version of the events described—an aesthetic that reflects traditional Protestant values.

As art historian Joseph Leo Koerner (2004) explains, Protestant ani-
conism did not end Protestant art, but rather reworked it to better embody
the Protestant embrace of the Word. He writes of Lutheran engravings:

> Tablets, book, preaching and sacraments visualize what fills and 245
> makes the true church: God's words. To Protestants, the triumph
> of the verbal over the visual is a proper reformation of the image.
>   *Sola scriptura* was a rallying cry in a territorial war between
> rival communicative media. On the one side stood the word, that
> which (to its partisans) was apostolic and is now, once more, "spe-
> cial dispensation" of truth. On the other side stood the image,
> instrument and emblem of the Roman Church's deceit. (p. 46)

Early Protestant artists, rather than abandoning visual representation,
chose instead to ensure that their religious images focused on the textual
and spoken elements of the religion, not the sensuality of the purely visual, which was associated with Catholicism. Thompson retains some of
this sensibility when he inscribes scripture on the page. At times biblical
verses are presented in a font like that of a printing press, emphasizing
their orderly authority over Craig's scrawled thoughts (Thompson, 2003,
pp. 56, 219); at others, verses penned in wild, slashed letters harass Craig
like a flock of attacking birds (p. 305). When applied to Raina, however,
verses appear in a lush, swirling script that emphasizes the beauty and joy
of Craig's experience of her (pp. 422–423). Words themselves become images in these instances.[9] Yet in the silent splash pages that mark the novel's
most significant moments—Craig's sacrifice of his art, his vision of Christ,
the mandala-like icon of the young couple embracing—*Blankets* sets words
aside as firmly as the college-aged Craig shuts away his Bible (Thompson,
2003, pp. 551, 563). The book's formal structure dramatizes the rejection of
the primacy of Logos in favor of the visual and tactile sensuality of divine
Eros.

This Protestant aesthetic has had a profound influence on American
culture. For many Americans, the perceived conflict between words and
images—and the superiority of words—is deeply ingrained, such that the
rise of primarily visual media has sometimes been associated with the decline of civilization. As new media theorist Anne Frances Wysocki (2003)
observes, any medium that gives more weight to visual elements than it
does to textual ones is commonly seen as either not worth taking seriously or properly used only for children (p. 38). This perception leads to the
familiar claim that film and television viewing is producing generations of

relative illiterates. Comics theorists, however, argue that the comics form is a particularly engaging, interactive, and demanding form of media. Drawing on reader-response criticism, critics such as literary scholar Charles Hatfield (2005) emphasize that the form's hybridity is unusually adept at creating the sense of incompleteness that invites the reader's act of interpretation (2005, p. xiii; referring to Iser, 1978, pp. 166–170). Hatfield notes that American criticism on comics reading tends to fall into two camps: that comics are a "stepping-stone" toward literacy because they are "easy," or that they discourage the development of complete literacy because they are "easy" (p. 36). Yet the ability to read a comic deeply requires a complex grasp of the many ways comics represent time, interrelate word and text, and use borders and layout to indicate narrative sequence. The tension between formal elements (word and text) that he sees as central to the medium insists on a "different order of literacy," one that is visual as well as textual (p. 67).[10]

Following sociologist Bruno Latour, Mary E. Hocks and Michelle R. Kendrick (2003) argue that media that combine words and images confront the rigid binaries of modernist thinking and enable audiences to recognize the hybridity of culture. Such an awareness, however, can arouse fears about disintegrating social order and "induce widespread cultural anxieties over borders, purity, chaos, miscegenation, and contamination" (p. 3). Like the controversial horror comics of the 1950s, *Blankets* sparks all of these anxieties: The book has pictures; is it meant for children? But some of the pictures are explicitly sexual; does that mean it is pornographic? Yet the work also tells a tale of sexual abuse, artistic awakening, and deeply felt, spiritually inflected love; does that mean the book is not pornography but "art"? And if we consider it art, who is its appropriate audience?

In *The Female Nude: Art, Obscenity, and Sexuality*, Lynda Nead (1992) articulates a number of theories about how and why people draw the line between art and pornography. She writes, "The obscene body is the body without borders or containment and obscenity is representation that moves and arouses the viewer rather than bringing about stillness and wholeness" (p. 2). Nead continues, "Put very simply . . . obscenity is that which, at any given moment, a particular dominant group does not wish to see in the hands of another, less dominant group" (p. 92). Both of these suggestions have the potential to shed light on why Thompson's work has been considered pornography. At the same time, however, the claim calls attention to some of the novel's most important aspects. If Nead is correct that the artistic body is one that is safely contained, while the obscene body implicates the sexuality of the reader, then *Blankets* clearly has "obscene" potential. Would *Blankets* so effectively challenge Evangelical beliefs if it did not seek to arouse the reader with erotic devotional images? In the final chapter of *Blankets*, Thompson includes a full-page image of a half-nude Craig and Raina embracing while falling toward the snapping mouths of demons. As their mouths meet, angels appear to lift them out of danger, as if the kiss itself had summoned holy forces to assist (see figure 11.4; Thompson, 2003, p. 570). The erotic appeal of this image is necessary for it to have an impact on the reader: we are invited, like Craig, to associate desire with an experience of sacred union.

Susan Sontag's (1966) observations on the similarities between pornography and religious literature also resonate here: they are both genres that seek to spur readers to action. Of pornography, she writes, "Its celebrated intention of sexually stimulating readers is really a species of proselytizing. Pornography that is serious literature aims to 'excite' in the same way that books which render an extreme form of religious experience aim to 'convert'" (p. 47). Similarly, art historian David Freedberg (1989) draws parallels between the censorship of art found to be pornographic and the destruction of images believed to be idolatrous. Freedberg surveys human beings' responses to images over thousands of years of history, observing that people have consistently reacted to images as if they have life and "could effectively be used to shame or punish those represented on them, or actually to harm them, or to serve as a means of seduction." He explains further:

> Since so much of the evidence for live images involves a tacit or explicit sexual relationship, a bridge is provided from religion to sexuality. In the material on arousal by images, one can begin to understand the problem of fear. If the image is, in some sense, sufficiently alive to arouse desire (or, if not alive, then sufficiently provocative to do just that), then it is more than it seems, and its powers are not what we are willing to allow dead representation; and so these powers have to be curbed, or what causes them eliminated. Hence the need to censor. (p. xxiv)

These observations are particularly relevant given the association between image-focused media and children. Inappropriate images are understood as especially powerful and dangerous to children, as well as to improperly prepared adults.

Earlier obscenity cases have also focused on the accessibility of libraries in assessing a book's danger to a community. Nead (1992), for instance,

FIG. 11.4 From *Blankets* by Craig Thompson, p. 570. Used by permission. Photo: Top Shelf.

Case Studies

describes the 1961 British trial of D. H. Lawrence's *Lady Chatterley's Lover.* In the course of the trial, Judge Mervyn Griffith-Jones pointed out that the book (which Penguin was planning to release as a paperback) would then be available in public libraries. Nead quotes Griffith-Jones: "Would you approve of your young sons, young daughters—because girls can read as well as boys—reading this book? . . . Is it a book you would even wish your wife or your servants to read?" (p. 91). This trial excerpt highlights the classism and sexism of social attitudes toward erotic material. Pornography may be safe and acceptable for a dominant group, but it is dangerous to subordinate groups (working-class people, women, adolescents) because it may cause them to flout sexual norms. Definitions of pornography, then, serve the goal of controlling sexual expressions of those in less powerful groups.

Blankets portrays specifically adolescent desire and has mainly been challenged in school libraries. The book mirrors and therefore legitimates the desires and experiences of adolescents, and these features may make *Blankets* problematic for adults who prefer to uncritically categorize any person under the age of eighteen as a child. Perhaps we as adults deprive adolescents of knowledge that should be rightfully theirs when we keep such books out of their hands—the knowledge that adolescent desire is simultaneously normal, dangerous, and potentially holy.

CONCLUSION: CONVERSION TO THE SACRED EROTIC

Blankets is a sophisticated book whose combinations of words and images demand active involvement from the reader. The novel ultimately privileges images over text, a decision that transgresses against Western culture's historical logocentrism. More disturbing, however, is the way the form may involve, excite, and then invite readers—especially adolescents—to adopt the author's point of view. Accordingly, those who charge the book with being pornographic may be reacting to a genuine threat to their religious structures' ability to characterize and control sexuality. As Freedberg says, some images have a power that renders them more than dead representation; readers may experience *Blankets* as tempting them to convert.

Craig's simultaneous sexual, artistic, and spiritual awakening drives him to art school against the advice of his community—a decision that leads him to intellectual and social freedom. In *Blankets* the experience of the divine immanent in the body and nature provides not just a place to resist oppressive social structures and religious dogma, but also an alternative source of religious authority: bodily experience. Ironically, this path is given structure by the biblical imagery with which Craig is raised, despite the fact that his family and community see the impurity of sex as a fundamental lesson of the Bible. Thompson offers up a solution to both sexual repression and spiritual alienation that does not require a like-minded group. Since sexuality is both a potent force and a part of all individuals, to approach it through a model of divine connection gives every person the opportunity to tangibly experience God: the only thing, according to Ecclesiastes, that gives meaning to an inherently transient world.

Claiming religious authority on the basis of individual experience is nothing new in American culture; one need look no further than Emerson and the Transcendentalists to find a rich vein of this tradition. But to locate the source of that authority so squarely in the body, and specifically in sexuality, is historically a more subversive perspective, and one that has become increasingly significant as issues of sexuality, gender, and the body have become politically polarized. Theologian Marvin M. Ellison (1996) argues that political and social oppression inevitably involves violations of the body, whether through stripping individuals of the right to refuse sexual contact, criminalizing particular sexual behaviors, or socially sanctioning violence against those who deviate from sexual norms (p. 15). In this analysis, advocating for the sacredness of the body and for the right of the individual to have pleasure is a political act, one that *"empowers the moral agency of the sexually abused and violated"* and lays the groundwork for collective action (p. 29). While it is possible to read *Blankets* simply as a sweet personal account of a sexual and artistic awakening, when framed by this political context it prefigures the possibility of greater religious and sexual pluralism. The ability of artists like Thompson to harness both traditional and alternative religious language in celebration of the erotic, therefore, marks a significant strategy in the struggle to end social and political inequality based on sexual difference.

NOTES

1. See Rubin's note to the 1992 revision (1993, p. 27).
2. Jungkeit (2010) independently uses the label "queer" to describe the character of Craig (p. 337). See this article also for further examination of how *Blankets* privileges images in the context of Christian and post-Christian erotic theology.
3. For a typical account of psychologist Fredric Wertham's successful assault on the comics industry as a corrupting influence on American youth, told from the point of view of the comics

industry, see Daniels (1971). For a more nuanced, book-length examination of Wertham as a liberal who did not promote censorship of comics, but rather age requirements, see Beaty (2005).

4. For an overview of the history of comics reception in the United States, see Bongco (2000, pp. 1–18); see also pp. 19–44 for a discussion of how comics' status as a "popular" medium has obscured its potential complexity for many readers.

5. See Bongco (2000, pp. 45–83) for an introduction to the language of comics that emphasizes text-image conflict.

6. After this exchange, Craig internally wonders, "And what if I ended up as a mistake to her?" (Thompson, 2003, p. 340). Raina later withdraws from the intensity of the relationship, leading the heartbroken Craig to break off the friendship entirely. Later, we see a hand cover Craig's painting of the couple sitting in a tree with white paint. In the second printing of the book, a smudge of the painting remains on the otherwise white page that closes the chapter—a representation, perhaps, of the mistake that was better than nothing (p. 543). In later printings, however, this smudge is omitted, suggesting that the relationship has left no trace at all, not even in memory. Credit goes to my Fall 2006 Writing Seminar at Boston University for noticing this subtle detail, which radically changes the meaning of the chapter.

7. Sallman himself at times claimed to have received the image in a vision (Morgan, 1996, p. 185).

8. See the official site for Jack Chick (2007) as well as the following archive site containing material from both fans and detractors: *Jack T. Chick Museum of Fine Art* (MonsterWax, 2007).

9. For examples, see McCloud (1993, pp. 138–161). Gene Kannenberg Jr. (2001), describes the comics artist Chris Ware's more advanced version of this technique, where text not only reads as an image, but is also used as a design element in order to present "simultaneous narrative strands" (p. 175).

10. The definitive descriptive work on how to read comics is McCloud (1993), which itself uses a comics form to approach its material and also emphasizes a reader-response model of interpretation.

251

REFERENCES

Arnold, A. (2003, December 18). Best comics of 2003. *Time.* Retrieved from http://content.time.com /time/specials/packagesarticle /0,28804,2001842_2001833 _2002066,00.html.

Beaty, B. (2005). *Fredric Wertham and the critique of mass culture.* Jackson, MI: University Press of Mississippi.

Bongco, M. (2000). *Reading comics: Language, culture, and the concept of the superhero.* New York, NY: Garland.

Chick, J. (2007). *Chick publications.* Retrieved from http://www.chick .com/.

Daniels, L. (1971). *Comix: A history of comic books in America.* New York, NY: Bonanza.

Ellison, M. M. (1996). *Erotic justice: A liberating ethic of sexuality.* Louisville, KY: Westminster John Knox Press.

Freedberg, D. (1989). *The power of images: Studies in the history and theory of response.* Chicago, IL: University of Chicago Press.

Hatfield, C. (2005). *Alternative comics: An emerging literature.* Jackson, MI: University Press of Mississippi.

Hocks, M. E., & Kendrick, M. R. (Eds.). (2003). *Eloquent images: Word*

and image in the age of new media.
Cambridge, MA: MIT Press.

Iser, W. (1978). *The act of reading: A theory
of aesthetic response*. Baltimore,
MD: Johns Hopkins University
Press.

Jungkeit, S. (2010). Tell-tale visions: The
erotic theology of Craig Thompson's
Blankets. In A. D. Lewis and C. H.
Kraemer (Eds.), *Graven images:
Religion in comic books and graphic
novels* (pp. 333–354). New York, NY:
Continuum.

Kannenberg, G., Jr. (2001). The comics
of Chris Ware: Text, image, and
visual narrative strategies. In R.
Varnum and C. T. Gibbons (Eds.),
*The language of comics: Word and
image* (pp. 174–197). Jackson, MI:
University Press of Mississippi.

Koerner, J. L. (2004). *The reformation of
the image*. Chicago, IL: University of
Chicago Press.

McCloud, S. (1993). *Understanding comics:
The invisible art*. Northampton, MA:
Kitchen Sink Press.

MonsterWax. (2007, April 29). Jack T.
Chick museum of fine arts. *MonsterWax*. Retrieved from http://
www.monsterwax.com/chick.html.

Morgan, D. (1996). "Would Jesus have
sat for a portrait?": The likeness of
Christ in the popular reception of
Sallman's art. In D. Morgan (Ed.),
*Icons of American Protestantism:
The art of Warner Sallman* (pp.
181–203). New Haven, CT: Yale
University Press.

Morgan, D. (1998). *Visual piety: A history
and theory of popular religious
images*. Berkeley, CA: University of
California Press.

Morgan, D. (2005). *The sacred gaze:
Religious visual culture in theory and
practice*. Berkeley, CA: University of
California Press.

Nead, L. (1992). *The female nude: Art,
obscenity, and sexuality*. New York,
NY: Routledge.

Prothero, S. (2003). *American Jesus: How
the Son of God became a national
icon*. New York, NY: Farrar, Straus
& Giroux.

Roth, R. P. (1958, March 2). Christ and the
muses. *Christianity Today, 2*, 8–11.

Rubin, G. (1993). Thinking sex: Notes
for a radical theory of the politics
of sexuality. In H. Abelove, M. A.
Barale, & D. M. Halperin (Eds.),
The gay and lesbian studies reader
(pp. 3–44). New York, NY: Routledge. (Reprinted from *Pleasure and
danger: Exploring female sexuality*,
pp. 143–178, C. S. Vance, Ed., 1984,
Boston, MA: Routledge & Kegan
Paul.)

Sims, Z. (2006, October 5). Library board
hears complaints about books:
Decision scheduled for Oct. 11
meeting. *Marshall-Democrat News*.
Retrieved from http://www.mar
shallnews.com/story/1171432.html.

Sontag, S. (1966). *Styles of radical will*.
New York, NY: Farrar, Straus &
Giroux.

Thompson, C. (2003). *Blankets: A graphic
novel*. Marietta, GA: Top Shelf.

Thompson, C. (2007, April 29). Books >
*Blankets. Craig Thompson: The Blog
of Craig Thompson*. Retrieved from
http://www.dootdootgarden.com/.

Tolman, D. L. (2002). *Dilemmas of desire:
Teenage girls talk about sexuality*.
Cambridge, MA: Harvard Univer-
sity Press.

Wilcox, C., and Larson, C. (2006). *Onward
Christian soldiers? The religious
right in American politics* (3rd ed.).
Boulder, CO: Westview.

Wysocki, A. F. (2003). Seriously visible.
In M. E. Hocks and M. R. Kendrick
(Eds.), *Eloquent images: Word and
image in the age of new media* (pp.
37–60). Cambridge, MA: MIT
Press.

Afterword

The Media and Religious Authority

Lynn Schofield Clark

In the context of today's rapidly changing media systems, it seems that there are more opportunities than ever before for individuals to challenge authority. And yet, as Stewart Hoover notes in the introductory chapter to this volume, even in this emergent digital environment, key questions endure, such as "Where does [authority] come from? How is it established? Who is involved? Who or what might be challenging or changing it?" This essay seeks to point out common themes that emerged as this volume's contributors grappled with these questions in relation to the realm of religion, considering common and divergent theoretical frameworks. This final essay also raises some questions that have largely remained unexamined in the current text but that, with the preceding works as a foundation, are ripe for further development. We begin with some discussion of the context for questions of authority as they're emerging in relation to today's media systems, and then also discuss why the study of religion, media, and authority is particularly relevant today.

Within media studies, and in particular among scholars interested in communication and political theory, a great deal of scholarly attention has focused on struggles over authority that are playing out in the contemporary challenges to political arrangements of power, as witnessed in the Arab Spring, Occupy Wall Street, Spanish *indignados*, and the Greek *Aganaktismenoi* movements, as well as in the student protests in Hong Kong and the United States arising in the aftermath of lethal interactions between law enforcement officials and persons of color. To a significant extent, these social movements have been facilitated within digital and mobile media platforms, raising new questions about how media might facilitate challenges to authority. And as these new movements unfold, a central question has become: Are these activities truly bringing us closer to democratic decision making and thereby undermining traditional sources of authority that were rooted in enduring systems of power? Or, in contrast, is it naïve to hope that those engaging in protest activities would somehow manage to overcome the many ways in which existing power structures are already embedded in the systematic workings of new media?

Central to these questions is a Weberian understanding of the linkage between power, authority, and legitimacy that also guides the work in this volume. Authority, as Peter Horsfield noted in his contribution to this volume, has two dimensions: there are questions of power and dominance, and there are questions of legitimation. As people protest current regimes of power, they call into question the legitimacy of those regimes. Two central and interrelated questions emerge, then, that link issues of authority and social change: how do some people or groups go about claiming authority, and how do those same people or groups come to have authority ascribed to them by others?

The media are widely recognized as playing a key role both in how would-be movement leaders come to lay claim to authority and in how others come to see those would-be leaders and movements as legitimately authoritative. Furthermore, the media are industries with complex social, legal, and political histories that have shaped how and in which economic and political contexts these processes of claiming and ascribing authority may occur. It is not surprising, then, that many in media studies today are calling for more research that explores the specific mediated contexts through and in which challenges to authority are taking place.

As the essays in this volume have revealed and as will be discussed below, religion has been involved in political change in various ways, sometimes providing justification for change and at other times providing legitimation as things remain the same. At the same time, religious organizations and practices are also constantly undergoing change themselves, raising the question of how mediated resources have been marshaled in the claiming or challenging of authority. As Hoover notes in his chapter, "The marketing of religious charisma might actually legitimate sources as authoritative." But this volume's contributors do not uniformly agree with the assertion that "the market" has the power to "relativize" authority. The contributors have instead found various ways in which media and the marketplace present challenges or affirmations or become sites for new forms of religious expression (see also Clark, 2007). Exploring instances of *how* and *where* and *when* authority is claimed or ascribed is thus central to this book's contributions.

MEDIA, RELIGION, AND AUTHORITY IN HISTORY

Religion is an interesting case in relation to questions of media and challenges to or affirmations of authority, because we know that historically the Christian religion, state power, and the manuscript culture of the *scriptorium* were structurally linked during the medieval era of European monarchies and monasteries, and similar traditions of leadership-sanctioned copying and preserving of the Qur'an existed in the Muslim world with both calligraphers and, more controversially, woodblock printing. Although there were relatively few specific moments in history when the interests of church and throne were completely aligned, there is little doubt about the linkages between the two in terms of power and authority during the Middle Ages of Europe and the Middle East. By the eleventh century, most clergy were drawn from the nobility and were considered a separate class from the parish priests, who were drawn from the peasant class; European Jews and Muslims were forbidden from owning land and were actively pressured to convert to Christianity, while Christians and Jews in the East voluntarily converted to Islam to avoid lower-class status. European kings consolidated their power and worked in concert with popes to challenge the Seljuk Turks during the Crusades of the eleventh through the thirteenth centuries, often conducting pogroms against the local Jewish population as another part of the effort to suppress religious and cultural difference and retain cultural and political authority. But, as we now know, the links between religious, state, and manuscript authority were not to last. Historians have argued that a large shift began to occur in the aftermath of the Black Death, which saw the demise of some thirty-five million people in the fourteenth century, and which resulted in a widespread redistribution of land and resources among survivors. This spurred a decline of serfdom in western Europe and a weakening of state power just as controversies and heresies dominated in the church hierarchy and as emergent city republics and widened trade routes were fomenting a commercial revolution. Elizabeth Eisenstein (1979) has noted that the printing press, invented around 1440, functioned to aid in processes of change that were already occurring, as manuscript culture gave way to printed materials that were widely and commercially available at a far lower cost than ever before. Importantly, Eisenstein argues that it was not the communication technology itself, but rather its functions, that enabled the dissemination, standardization, and preservation of thought that aided in the developments of the Protestant Reformation, the Renaissance, and the scientific revolutions of early modernity.

Eisenstein's model of exploring not only media change but other contributing and preexisting factors is an approach echoed in Horsfield's examination of the emergence of what he terms the "Catholic brand" of Christianity in the third century. He argues that this "brand" became the dominant strand of what we now recognize as the Christian tradition through an interlocking series of events that included the development of a particular hierarchical structure, a worldview amenable with several traditions of the time, and the prodigious writing and distribution of letters that standardized practices and theology in a way that differentiated the Catholic approach from its Jewish Christian, Gnostic, Marcionite, and Montanist Christian competitor traditions of the day. Horsfield thus provides a social constructionist approach to religious and media history that deepens our understanding of how media and religious authority collaborated in the third century and sets the tone for the essays that follow, as each of the contributors has sought to challenge a simple story of technological determinism in the ways we think about the relationships between media, religion, and authority.

RELIGION, MEDIA, AND INDIVIDUAL AUTONOMY

Within studies of religion, scholars have long debated the extent to which modernity ushered in a new era of secularization. As Mark Chaves (1994) argues and as Peter Horsfield points out in his essay in this volume, secularization is perhaps best understood not as a decline of religion per se, but as a recognition of the declining scope of religious authority, particularly as that authority has been vested with the institutions of religion. This shift in religious authority has led to significant interest in the rise in individual autonomy, or the ways in which people believe themselves to be capable of authoritative decision making when it comes to how, where, and when they will or will not engage in practices of religion.

Not surprisingly, then, the theme of individual autonomy runs throughout the chapters in this volume. Alf Linderman's essay, for instance, suggests that individual autonomy is central to the way that what Grace Davie terms "vicarious religion" plays out in the Swedish context. Linderman points out that more than half of Sweden's citizens support the public broadcasting of religious services, even if they do not choose to watch the programs themselves. In a society like Sweden that values the individual's right to claim authority over one's religious observances, Linderman notes that it is important that such religious practices be available when needed. Furthermore, as it's critical that such practices be consistent with the recognized expertise in traditional institutions, a secondary level of religious authority is also evident and is linked with the primary level of individual autonomy. In other words, for the individual to be able to exercise religious authority over her own practices, she needs to be assured that leaders in such practices will be available and can be trusted to maintain religious traditions even in her absence. In this case, then, media provide legitimation for traditional authority as it is vested in the institutions that sanction and credential individuals for religious leadership.

Pauline Cheong is similarly interested in the ways that religious practitioners, through their ascribing of authority to the new celebrity leaders of American evangelicalism, seem to provide an affirmation for traditional religious authority even as such authority operates in new locations of social media. Like Horsfield's work on the early development of a particular "brand" of Christianity, Cheong explores how a subset of privileged evangelical leaders employ social media to enhance their social capital and thereby affirm their authority among their constituents. Like Linderman's, Cheong's chapter points to some of the continuities in religious authority that persist even in an environment of individual autonomy.

Karina Kosicki Bellotti also raises questions of individual autonomy in her chapter on evangelicalism and the rise of the gospel music movement in Brazil. Yet, unlike Cheong's and Linderman's explorations of continuities in Christian ascriptions of authority, Bellotti argues that this new evangelical movement in Brazil has diminished the traditional authority of churches. This has happened, she argues, as such emergent movement leaders and their practices reinforce interdenominationalism and affirm new celebrity authorities within the evangelical community. She wonders how to characterize this new movement, particularly in relation to questions of individual autonomy and new relationships of power both within and outside churches. Claims to traditional authority are evident as traditional religious bodies name such new phenomena a "watered-down" version of evangelical Christianity. Similar claims are also heard among some Christian clergy who object to religious broadcasting and the celebrification of white male evangelical social media superstars. Such cases as these point to the continuing struggles over media and authority that characterize the evangelical traditions in North and South America.

Christine Hoff Kraemer's essay also speaks to questions of individual autonomy, particularly as she highlights the work of an author who takes it upon himself to claim the authority to construct his own personal identity as distanced from traditional evangelical religion in the work of his autobiographic graphic novel *Blankets*. Kraemer is interested in author Craig Thompson's melding of sexuality, art, and spirituality in the novel, as his creation affords him a way to privilege his personal experiences over the authority of his family and their church. Thompson's work exemplifies the ways that artists and others located outside of institutions are able to lay claim to the authority both to critique those institutions and to construct their own identity apart from them, a theme that also emerges in Missouri's study of afroreligiosity in third cinema film, as discussed below.

MEDIA, INDIVIDUAL RELIGIOUS EXPRESSION, AND AUTHORITY OUTSIDE THE WEST

Whereas Linderman, Cheong, Kosicki Bellotti, and Hoff Kraemer focus on individual autonomy as understood in relation to Western traditions, chapters by Maroon, Zeamer, Lee, Boutros, and Missouri consider questions of individual religious expression and authority that, due to the differing contexts for these practices, may not be viewed as direct challenges either to religious leadership or to religious authority. This set of essays thus advances questions of the relationship between media, authority, and religion by foregrounding cultural context and religion, the state and the media arrangements of power that differ markedly from those in the West.

In her essay on television viewing in both domestic settings and in cybercafés of Muslim Morocco, Bahíyyah Maroon explores how Muslim practitioners are called on to self-regulate in accordance with their own understanding of Muslim morality. She notes that as individuals negotiate television viewing in the home and in public spaces, they weigh the potential for harm associated with television with the desire for choice. She argues that exercising this authority is an expression of practical morality that operates in situations that are circumscribed, but that are also constantly changing in relation to expectations of what is deemed permissible in Muslim society. This essay thus offers an interesting contrast to the decision making on the part of Westerners, as decision making in public and even in home settings may seem more consequential and less likely to accede to the commercial in the context of a more collectivist and less consumerist society.

Like Kosicki Bellotti and Hoff Kraemer, Joonseong Lee also looks at the rise of individual practices that seem to challenge traditional religions. Rather than exploring threatened religious organizations and leadership, however, Lee is interested in how individuals take it upon themselves to engage in practices of memorializing that were once associated with shamanism. As a deep part of the spirituality of Korea, shamanism is something that has taken new forms in the online context, and Lee notes that many shamanic leaders now promote themselves online. What's of even more interest to Lee, however, is that through online memorial sites dedicated to the memory of those who have died, individuals can now engage in rituals once reserved solely for shamanic leadership, and through these rituals they soothe their *han* (their feelings of grief, resentment, regret, or spite). Lee notes two particularly interesting facets of this emergent phenomenon: first, women, long denied the opportunity to participate in shamanic rituals, are able to soothe *han* in relation to memorial culture through these sites. And second, because these sites operate at some distance from state authority, it's also possible for memorial sites and rituals to become places where individuals can express their resentment about unjust deaths that have resulted in relation to power imbalances in society. Thus, whereas participation in online shamanic practices challenges traditional religious authority, it also contains within it the possibility for challenges to traditional state authority as well.

Emily Zeamer explores the ways that individual autonomy and modernity are worked out in the context of Thai Buddhism. Rather than finding evidence for political challenge like Lee, however, she explores how it is that these practices both reflect aspects of modernization and seem to offer support for rather than a challenge to state authority. Zeamer observes that the modernist development of looking for evidence has become an important and taken-for-granted aspect of all storytelling, including in relation to the stories of "ghosts" or of karma. In Buddhism, the most important knowledge is that which is gained firsthand. But, as she notes, it has become common for people to look for *phisut*, or evidence, that supports a story of karmic balance or imbalance. Because people believe that they must seek their own understanding and yet have frequently done so within a political context that is fraught with corruption, Zeamer argues that even as people in Thai public culture remain deeply committed to the search for truth, they also see political debate and critique as risky. Thus folkloric tradition tends to function in a way that preserves a traditional ethos of seeing one's experiences in the world as the inevitable and rather unchangeable result of karma.

Alexandra Boutros is also interested in individual practitioners of religion and the ways that these practices and relationships between practitioners are mediated in the digital realm. In her study of what she terms techno-Vodou, or Vodou as it is present on the web, Boutros considers the ways that traditional Vodou practitioners have migrated to online spaces and have become spiritual entrepreneurs in the process. She notes that the link between religious practice and business acumen is not new to Vodou, but the digital allows such relationships to become disembedded across time and space, thus extending both the reach and the responsibilities that are a part of the relationships between Vodou practitioners and Vodou followers. In her work, Boutros notes that the religious practices of Vodou were never as centrally organized as those available elsewhere, and thus the Internet is a logical extension of the intersubjective relationships that have long been central to the ways that practitioners engage in rituals and exchange payment in various forms with one another.

Like Christine Hoff Kraemer, with her interest in artistic expression as a form of challenge to authority, Montré Aza Missouri is also interested in the art form and its relationship to religious understandings, as noted earlier. Yet, whereas Hoff Kraemer explores an individual's attempt to challenge the perceptions of religious authority he associated with his family and his conservative evangelical tradition, Missouri is interested in filmmakers who seek to create narratives that affirm a tradition of black nationalism and, in Missouri's view, fail to be as emancipatory as they could be. Missouri explores the ways that the Obeah religion of the Americas and the Akan system of Africa embedded in Jamaican tradition become woven into the afroreligiosity of third cinema, a form of filmmaking that intends to move people toward black nationalistic pride and action. But these films are deeply patriarchal in their message, Missouri argues. She thus offers an important critical/cultural studies critique that suggests that even as certain authority systems are challenged in cinema and art, others may be reaffirmed.

Like Hoff Kraemer, Missouri is interested in authority as it relates to and is embedded within an ideological system rather than in authority as it relates to the intentions of leaders or institutions of religion. Both Hoff Kraemer's chapter on religious expression in the graphic novel *Blankets* and Missouri's exploration of afroreligiosity in third cinema offer opportunities to explore the extent to which an artistic effort succeeds, or not, in challenging certain notions of state and religion. This approach represents a continuation of work that has been done in the area of religion and film and religion and literature, and in this context highlights the value of analyzing media texts for insights into the workings of and challenges to religious authority (see, e.g., Asamoah-Gyadu, 2007; Pype, 2014).

Aside from these two essays on media texts and Cheong and Horsfield's studies of religious leaders who have succeeded in utilizing media to achieve some form of cultural dominance, the remaining essays in this volume are interested either in how practitioners ascribe authority to differing practices or people, or in the extent to which an artistic effort succeeds in challenging certain notions of state and religion. Overall, the volume reflects a poststructuralist sensibility that foregrounds not what leaders of religion intend, but what people actually do in their everyday lives, and how such collective practices become encoded into ideological systems that are then challenged or affirmed within the symbolic workings of mass- mediated storytelling. As is evident in most of this volume's contributions, the interest is in how, where, and when religion is "produced," as Hoover mentions in his introductory essay, rather than in questions of the intent of religious leaders.

Campbell (2007, 2010) has referred to this as an interest in the *religious structures* or practices of traditional religious authority. This is one of four realms of traditional authority, she notes. First, there is *religious hierarchy*, which refers to the roles of those who lead religious organizations, as seen here in Horsfield's essay, on those who emerged as religious authorities in the early Christian church, and in Cheong's study of evangelical leaders who use Twitter to garner authority. A second form of authority rests with *religious texts*, or the gathering of recognized or official teachings of a community. This focus emerges to some extent in Horsfield's chapter on how some teachings became authoritative in early Christian history in relation to the practices of letter writing. A third form of authority relates to *religious ideology*, or the set of commonly held beliefs or worldviews common to a religious community. This is apparent in Linderman's chapter on the Swedish desire for religion's availability, Missouri's study of the ideologies encoded in the afrospirituality of third cinema, and Zeamer's exploration of Thai Buddhist views about evidence and karma. Finally, as noted, it is *religious structures*, or the patterns of practice that guide religious activities, that seem to be of particular interest in this volume. An interest in the authority of religious practices is at the forefront in Kosicki Bellotti's chapter on those who plan and participate in gospel music events, Maroon's exploration of practices related to television viewing in domestic and public spaces in Morocco, Lee's chapter on how people engage in religious practices in memorial sites online, Hoff Kraemer's chapter on constructing a new body-affirming sensibility in contrast to evangelicalism, and Boutros's study of how Vodou practitioners engage in relationships with one another online. An emphasis on particular practices is also evident in Zeamer's discussion of how people incorporate understandings of karma and "ghost stories" into everyday explanations, and in Horsfield's discussion on how certain practices—including the arrangement of power and authority—came to be viewed as authoritative. But do these interests in religious practices represent a movement toward more democratically organized forms of religious expression, or is it that varied forms of expression have long existed and it is the *scholarly interest* in these practices that is relatively new? As is the case within media and religious studies generally, the challenge today is in parsing out the new from the continuous, which is always difficult given the constantly changing mediated landscape. In an increasingly plural world, both religiously and culturally, many of the essays in this volume assist in thinking through this task.

Prior to this volume, numerous scholars had considered how forms of media were used to legitimate or rework traditional and charismatic religious authority (Campbell, 2011; Echchaibi, 2011; Mandaville, 2007; Rosenthal, 2013; Sounaye, 2014). Traditions of authority differ in both Judaism and in Islam, as Turner (2007) has observed. In Jewish and in Muslim traditions, authority is derived as teachers come to be respected and recognized for their ability to offer insights into matters of spiritual import. Authority also remains somewhat open in these traditions, as teachers continually engage in disputation. Turner argues that this democratizing tradition of disputation has extended onto the Internet, so that anyone who is capable of providing learned responses to spiritual questions can claim religious authority. Some of the essays here, notably those by Hoover, Cheong, Maroon, Kosicki Bellotti, and Linderman, are a continuation of this work as they explore the extent to which traditional religious leaders, institutions, practices, or texts maintain authority. Other essays, such as those by Zeamer, Boutros, and Lee, as noted above, call into question the relationship between media and religious authority, as do other recent works (see Dorman, 2012). In particular, these chapters and similar works help scholars to reflect on the cultural assumptions that too often direct our 263 attention to traditional arrangements of authority as embedded in Western society and in monotheistic religions, and thus they offer an important counterpoint for further development.

WHAT IS MISSING?

What is somewhat striking is that there is as of yet little attention either in these essays or in other works to the ways in which emergent commercial media entities—notably, Facebook, Google, Amazon, and Apple—are participating in the struggle for commercial dominance that, by default, has large implications for the organization of power and authority within society. To my mind, this is the frontier for future studies in religion, media, and authority, as I have argued elsewhere (Clark, 2011a, 2001b; see also Hjarvard, 2014). Scholars such as Alex Galloway (2006, 2012), Tarleton Gillespie (2014), and Lev Manovitch (2002, 2013) suggest exploring authority as vested not in individuals or in institutions, but in code, protocol, and algorithm. Each of these scholars contests the idea that the Internet or, more widely, the media provide spaces for individual freedom and democratic action. They instead point to the ways that the computer has become a kind of "meta-medium" that borrows techniques from other media even while giving birth to new forms of media, noting that we know relatively little about the ways that algorithms organize what we see online. I'd argue that whereas most of the contributions in this volume and in previous work on religion and authority have focused on religion and its relationship to either traditional or charismatic leadership, the field would benefit from greater attention to the rational/legal authority that Weber and Weberian scholars have equated with the rise of bureaucracy and with these less-visible forms of control. Some interesting work is taking the notion of protocol or media logic into a glance backward, tracing relationships between religious imagination and earlier communication forms such as the telegraph and the clock tower that served to organize and control our relationships with and through time and space (Durham Peters, 2012; Stolow, 2012). But much work in this area and in relation to more contemporary questions is needed.

Critical media scholar Christian Fuchs (2013) has argued that institutions tend to benefit when individuals believe that they hold voluntary control, pointing out that such a view supports the idea that collective power is the random outcome of individual choices. A "googlized" view of the world would then see Google not as exercising a form of power in its creation of algorithms but is simply responding to consumer choice (Vaidhyanathan, 2011). But are we truly becoming more democratic and more free to choose, or are we instead moving toward a world in which social control and surveillance are taken for granted as an inescapable part of what it means to be human? And if the latter is the case, then what new questions emerge in the relationship between religion and authority?

To me, one of the most important questions relates to issues of both power and human dignity. It could be that in the Internet age, with its emphasis on "choice," it's unlikely that we will see an outright censorship of religion. Attempts to close down discussions have become much more sophisticated in the era of big data that Andrejevic (2012) terms the time of "post-comprehension knowledge," in which we are invited to think that data "speaks for itself." In this context, information management has become a key aspect of power and authority. It has become more difficult to blatantly ignore certain minority religions, for instance, even as it has become easier to see a version of reality that screens out certain perspectives because an algorithm has already determined that you are unlikely to agree with or appreciate that view. And it's also still true that certain racialized, gendered, and abled bodies are more likely to be subject to surveillance than are others. Thus, even in the emergent digital context, questions remain regarding the extent to which religions continue to interact with the social and political organization of power. In the context of Western societies, religion has never been completely separate from the organization of power, of course, and this volume's contributions affirm that perspective. But if we assume that systems of power always work in the interests of the commercial and the powerful, then what do those in religious communities need to do to guarantee the human rights of the less powerful in today's highly mediated and interconnected societies? What does "religion" or "religious community" or even "religious practice" mean in relation to issues of Internet neutrality, digital divides, big data, and lack of corporate accountability, such as in the recent cases of women's rights violations at Uber and in Facebook CEO Mark Zuckerberg's attempts to woo Chinese leadership by agreeing to the very state censorship guidelines it purportedly rejects? There are many human rights issues at stake, from the silencing of certain religions to the lack of accountability of leadership, that could warrant attention in relation to many religious traditions.

It seems clear that we as scholars need a better understanding of the connections between religion and human rights to guide our discussions of religion, media, and authority, just as we also need to continue to update our ideas of media and authority in relation to evolving concerns in the realm of technologies and politics. The preceding essays provide an important series of case studies through which to begin to consider such questions. And yet, going forward, I believe we need to understand much more about the intertwined relations of algorithmic and commercial authority with other societal forms of authority. Otherwise, it is possible that all religious authority will be rendered either useful and usable by, or largely irrelevant to, larger systems of governance and power.

As I have argued elsewhere (2014), researchers today are being called on not only to analyze what is, but to think about what, collectively, we might become. Today's digital, satellite, and mobile media make it impossible to imagine a world that is not deeply interconnected. We need to develop ways to think about these interconnections and about how various media have both served and continue to serve in the processes of claiming and ascribing authority. But, as scholars in media, religion, and authority, we are also well positioned to consider both how today's interconnections came to be and what these interconnections look like as they evolve and reshape our societal institutions, including those of religion.

Scholars cannot be expected to do the work of activists, yet we can partner with people who are working to envision what might happen if we as a society do or do not act in certain ways in response to the pressing challenges that face us. We might wish to embrace a vision of scholarship as not only a critical evaluation of current and past arrangements of power and authority, but also an important voice that offers a means to critique and envision a different future. There is, in other words, an important heuristic value related to the study of religion, media, and authority. Even as studies such as those contained in this volume call into question the arrangements of power and authority as they are, they may also provide glimpses of what might be different, better, and possible.

REFERENCES

Andrejevic, M. (2013). *Infoglut: How too much information is changing the way we think and know.* New York, NY: Routledge.

Asamoah-Gyadu, K. (2007). Blowing the cover: Imagining religious functionaries in Ghanaian/Nigerian films. In L. S. Clark (Ed.), *Religion, media, and the marketplace* (pp. 224–246). New Brunswick, NJ: Rutgers University Press.

Campbell, H. (2007). Who's got the power? Religious authority and the Internet. *Journal of Computer-Mediated Communication, 12,* 1043–1067.

Campbell, H. (2010). Religious authority and the blogosphere. *Journal of Computer-Mediated Communication, 15,* 251–276.

Chaves, M. (1994). Secularization as declining religious authority. *Social Forces, 72*(3), 749–774.

Clark, L. S. (Ed.) (2007). *Religion, media, and the marketplace.* New Brunswick, NJ: Rutgers University Press.

Clark, L. S. (2011a). Considering religion and mediatisation through a case study of J + K's big day (The J K wedding entrance dance): A response to Stig Hjarvard. *Culture and Religion, 12*(2), 167–184.

Clark, L. S. (2011b). Religion and authority in a remix culture: How a late night TV host became an authority on religion. In G. Lynch, J. Mitchell, & A. Strhan (Eds.), *Religion, media, and culture: A reader* (pp. 111–121). London, UK: Taylor & Francis.

Clark, L. S. (2014). Mediatization: Concluding thoughts and challenges for the future. In A. Hepp & F. Krotz (Eds.), *Mediatized worlds* (pp. 307–323). New York, NY: Palgrave Macmillan.

Dorman, B. (2012). *Celebrity gods: New religions, media, and authority in occupied Japan.* Honolulu: University of Hawai'i Press.

Durham Peters, J. (2012). Calendar, clock, tower. In J. Stolow (Ed.), *Deus in machina: Religion, technology, and the things in between* (pp. 25–42). New York, NY: Fordham University Press.

Echchaibi, N. (2011). From audio tapes to video blogs: The delocalization of authority in Islam. *Nations and Nationalism, 17*(1), 25–44.

Eisenstein, E. (1979). *The printing press as an agent of change.* Cambridge, UK: Cambridge University Press.

Fuchs, C. (2013). *Social media: A critical introduction.* London, UK: Sage.

Galloway, A. (2006). *Protocol: How control exists after decentralization.* Cambridge, MA: MIT Press.

Galloway, A. (2012). *The interface effect.* New York, NY: Polity.

Gillespie, T. (2014). The relevance of algorithms. In T. Gillespie, P. Boczkowski, & K. Foot (Eds.), *Media technologies: Essays on communication, materiality, and society.* Cambridge, MA: MIT Press.

Hjarvard, S. (2014). Mediatization and the changing authority of religion. Paper presented to the preconference of the International Communication Association, Seattle, WA.

Mandaville, P. (2007). Globalization and the politics of religious knowledge: Pluralizing authority in the Muslim world. *Theory, Culture and Society, 24*(2), 101–115.

Manovitch, L. (2002). *The language of new media.* Cambridge, MA: MIT Press.

Manovitch, L. (2013). *Software takes command.* London, UK: Bloomsbury.

Meyer, B., & Moors, A. (Eds.) (2006). *Religion, media, and the public sphere.* Bloomington, IN: Indiana University Press.

Pype, K. (2014). Religion, migration et esthétique des medias: Notes concernant la circulation et la réception des films provenant du Nigéria a Kinshasa. *Social Compass, 61*(1), 30–38.

Rosenthal, M. (2013). Infertility, blessings, and head coverings: Mediated practices of Jewish repentance. In M. Lovheim (Ed.), *Media, religion and gender: Key issues and new challenges* (pp. 111–124). London, UK: Routledge.

Sounaye, A. (2014). Mobile Sunna: Islam, small media and community in Niger. *Social Compass, 61*(1), 21–29.

Stolow, J. (Ed.) (2012). *Deus in machina: Religion, technology, and the things in between*. New York, NY: Fordham University Press.

Turner, B. (2007). Religious authority and the new media. *Theory, Culture and Society, 24*(2), 117–134.

Vaidhyanathan, S. (2011). *The googlization of everything (and why we should worry)*. Berkeley, CA: University of California Press.

CONTRIBUTORS

KARINA KOSICKI BELLOTTI is Professor of Contemporary History at the Federal University of Paraná (Curitiba, Brazil) and holds a Ph.D. in cultural history (State University of Campinas, Unicamp, Brazil, 2007). She has published two books (*A Mídia Presbiteriana no Brasil*, 2005; and *Delas é o Reino dos Céus*, 2010), in addition to articles and chapters on media, culture, youth, and Brazilian Protestantism. In 2005 she was Visiting Researcher at the University of Texas at Austin, and from 2006 to 2008 she was researcher for the project Faces of God in Latin America, coordinated by Dr. Virginia Garrad-Burnett (UT–Austin), funded by the Templeton Foundation.

ALEXANDRA BOUTROS is Associate Professor of Communication and Cultural Studies at Wilfrid Laurier University, Waterloo, Ontario. She holds a Ph.D. in art history and communication from McGill University, Montreal. Her research focuses on the mediation of religion in popular and consumer culture, including contemporary mediations of Afro-Caribbean religions. She is the author of numerous articles and chapters and co-editor of two volumes. In addition, she has received research and scholarly awards from a variety of foundations and other sources in both the United States and Canada.

PAULINE HOPE CHEONG is Associate Professor of Communication at the Hugh Downs School of Human Communication at Arizona State University. She is also a graduate faculty member of the School of Justice and Social Inquiry, and Women and Gender Studies, and an affiliate faculty member with the Department of Film and Media Studies and the Center for the Study of Religion and Conflict. She is currently co-leading a multidisciplinary project on extremist narratives and is co-author of *Explosive Narratives: Islamist Extremism and the Role of Rumors in Strategic Influence* (2012). She is also the co-editor of *Digital Religion, Social Media, and Culture: Perspectives, Practices, Futures* (2012) and *New Media and Intercultural Communication: Identity, Community, and Politics* (2012). She has presented more than fifty papers at international conferences and has published in leading journals on communication technologies, including *New Media and Society, Information Society, Information, Communication and Society, Bulletin of Science and Society, M/C Journal: A Journal of Media and Culture, Journal of Computer-Mediated Communication, Journal of International and Intercultural Communication, American Behavioral Scientist,* and *Journal of Communication.*

LYNN SCHOFIELD CLARK is Professor and Chair of the Department of Media, Film, and Journalism Studies and Director of the Estlow International Center for Journalism and New Media at the University of Denver. She is the author/editor of five books and more than sixty articles and book chapters. She is also an Affiliate Professor with the University of Copenhagen and a Fellow with the Digital Ethnography Research Center (RMIT) and served as President of the International Society on Media, Religion, and Culture for 2014–16. In addition to scholarship on media and world religions, her participatory action and public scholarship research centers on the ways in which youth politics and publics are being transformed in relation to today's technological and demographic shifts. Her most recent book, *The Parent App: Understanding Families in a Digital Age* (2013), explores how socioeconomic difference has shaped how U.S. youth and their families integrate digital and mobile media into their lives together. She was the University of Denver's 2012 Service Learning Faculty Member of the Year.

STEWART M. HOOVER is Professor of Media Studies and Religious Studies at the University of Colorado at Boulder, where he directs the Center for Media, Religion, and Culture. His field of scholarship is media audience research, media history, and the social and political impact of the media. He is an internationally recognized expert on media and religion, and the University of Colorado's Center is one of only four in the world devoted to this important and emerging field of study. Professor Hoover has studied and written about a diverse array of topics in this field, including televangelism, religion journalism, religion in secular and entertainment media, and religion in the Internet and digital media. He and his colleagues have studied the ways audiences today find religious and spiritual meaning in the media: from books, television, and film to Facebook and the other social media. Through these studies and the center's outreach efforts, they hope to build public understanding of the ways that religion is being changed by the media age, and the forms through which religion persists in the twenty-first century both nationally and globally. Their work on Islam has looked at the ways it is understood through the media and the ways it is being formed and shaped by the media practices of different groups across the world. Their work on Christianity has most recently focused on popular forms, including neo-Pentecostalism. Professor Hoover's efforts have been supported by grants from the Ford Foundation, the Lilly Endowment, the Social Science Research Council, and the Porticus Foundation. Professor Hoover holds a Ph.D. from the University of Pennsylvania and a master's in ethics from the Graduate Theological Union, Berkeley. He is author or editor of ten books, including *Media, Home, and Family* and *Religion in the Media Age*.

PETER HORSFIELD is Professor of Media Studies and Director of Graduate Studies and Research at the Royal Melbourne Institute of Technology. He has been an active scholar and writer on media and religion for two decades, having conducted the first research on the phenomenon of American televangelism. He has published extensively in the media studies, theology, and religious history literatures, in both print and digital formats. He directs the Porticus Global Doctoral Fellowship Program, which has supported the graduate work of over twenty students from the Global South. Through his extensive international experience and profile, he has become one of the central figures in the field of religion and the media.

CHRISTINE HOFF KRAEMER is Assistant Professor of Religious History at Cherry Hill Seminary. She holds a Ph.D. in religion and literature from Boston University. Her work focuses on religion and sexuality in contemporary literature and popular culture, and has already received wide attention in academic circles, including an important profile at the American Academy of Religion. She is author of numerous articles and chapters on sexuality, body imagery, and paganism, all in relation to their expression and understanding in and through popular culture.

JOONSEONG LEE is Associate Professor of Communication at California State University, San Marcos. He is an active scholar of media and religion, having written on religion in contemporary entertainment television in the United States and Korea, on religious meaning-making in online media, and religion in game culture. His dissertation focused on the phenomenon of officially sanctioned cyber memorial zones in Korea. He has received a number of research and other grant awards.

ALF LINDERMAN is Director of the Sigtuna Foundation and Professor of Sociology of Religion at the University of Uppsala, Sweden. He is one of the founders of the field of media and religion studies, having directed the first conference in Uppsala in 1994. He has researched and written on religion and meaning in media cultures, both in Western nations and in the global south. Among his early works were important contributions on the international implications of American religious broadcasting. The foundation he directs is the leading Swedish institution bridging academic and popular discourses about religion in contemporary arts and media. Its publications, conferences, seminars, and fora regularly attract scholars from across Europe, Scandinavia, North America, Asia, and the Middle East.

BAHÍYYAH MAROON, Ph.D., researches culturally informed patterns of eudaimonia, morality, and free will in establishing and transforming social structures and organizational structures. A dedicated public scholar, she is an international speaker whose work highlights a global conversation on compassion and well-being. When she is not teaching her course "Happiness and Culture," speaking, or researching, she can be found sharing bursts of ideation in Twitter land (@BDMaroon).

MONTRÉ AZA MISSOURI is Associate Professor in the School of Communications at Howard University. Previously she was a lecturer at London Metropolitan University. She holds a Ph.D. from the School of Oriental and African Studies in London, where she conducted research on the mediation of race and gender through contemporary African and African American filmmaking. In addition to her published work, she is also a producer, writer, and editor of film, video, and digital-video documentaries.

EMILY ZEAMER is a social anthropologist whose research interests include the social production of knowledge, the construction of social difference, and cultures of technology and practice. A lecturer at the University of Southern California, she teaches courses on time, social subjectivities, ethnographic (qualitative) research methods, and cultures of modernity.

INDEX

Douglas the pastor case study, 219–21, 225

dreams, karmic, 135

E

ecclesiastical discipline, 58

Economy and Society (Weber), 19–21

ecumenical churches, on media in United States, 24

education, privilege-disadvantage of clergy by, 100

empires, importance of writing in construction of, 60

empowerment

of black women, 189

of disaffected and disenfranchised people, 182

disempowerment, 179

of individuals, 126

by the marketplace, 215

by media age, 32–33

of sexually abused people, 250

of slaves, 178, 181

by social media, 85

through shamanism, 168–69

of the womanist gaze, 172

of young people, 225

enlightenment, 130, 171, 173

entertainment media

importance of, 3–4

readings of doctrine in, 3

religion in secular, 2

See also radio programs and hosts; television

epistemic authority, 94

eroticism

in *Blankets*, 236, 237–44 (See also *Blankets* [graphic novel])

in films, 187

in images, 187

as sacred and spiritual, 231

the sacred erotic, 250

social attitudes toward, 249

See also pornography

erotic power, 230

Estonia ferry, 70, 71

ethics

of authenticity, 77

ethical frameworks, 48

human reality conditioned by, 140

shared ethical orientation, 147 n. 11

ethnicity, 18, 20, 189 n. 2, 198

Europe

arthouse cinema in, 180

fundamentalist groups in, 78

hybridity of African ancestry in, 187

immoral programs of, 106

influence of print media on early modern, 53–54

media-cultural dynamics of, 65

media influence on religion in, 73

medieval, 255–56

monarchies of, 255

religious development in, 69–70, 72

European colonial influence, 129–30, 186

Evangelical Christianity, 197, 207 n 1

alternative music in, 215–16

in Brazil, 213–14, 217–18, 257–58

festivities adapted to, 215

ministries in, 214

National Crusade of Evangelization (Brazil), 213–14

restrictions on dance/music in, 213

revival in United States of, 2

targeting of youth by, 226

views of homosexuality in, 229

evangelism, 19, 33, 225

exclusion/inclusion factors, 55

F

Facebook, 86, 216, 226 n. 6, 263, 264, 271

faith

archaic, 105

in *Blankets*, 236

blind, 222–24

common ideas of, 42

conflict between reason and, 223

contexts of, 236

cultural expressions of, 122

legitimization of power through, 41

practices of, 111

qualities of, 18

teaching of, 44

traditional doctrines/domains of, 81, 83

trajectories of, 218–24

in youth subculture, 215

faith brands, 89

faith memes, 97

279

competing, 81–82
music, 216
in relationship between religion and
media, 19
tension between youth and adults, 212
Twitter, 6, 81
analysis of tweets, 100 n. 1
appropriate uses for, 99
clergy branding on, 89
clergy who use, 100, 261
cross-marketing purposes of, 92
examples of tweets, 92–97
publications on use of, 87, 88
strategic promotions using, 91
tweeting prayers, 95–96
tweetups, 94
usernames examples, 90–97
uses of, 83
See also microblogging

U
understanding, attaining deeper, 126
United Church of Christ, 242
United States
evangelism in, 33
Haitian-American relations, 193
religious attitudes of, 69
religious landscape in, 19
revival of Evangelical Christians in, 2
South Korea Status of Forces
Agreement (SOFA), 164–65,
168
unity, in Christianity, 62
universal authority structure, 58
universality, 59, 60
universal unity of bishops, 62
usernames (handles), 90–97

V
value, definitions of, 26
value-rational authority, 41
Vatican, 3, 29
vicarious religion, 78–80, 168, 257
ability to measure, 76
definition and description of, 68–73
dismissal of concept of, 70–71
examples of, 69
invisibility of, 74
principles of, 72

rituals in, 69–74
taking part in, 72–73
videos, music, 3, 111–12
violence
toward black women, 175
toward homosexuals, 229
virtual worlds, 196
vision, unifying, 51
visual imagery, 51
visual memories, 45
Vodou
ceremonies of, 198, 199
client-specialist relationship in, 194
concept of cyberspace in, 196
Houngan Boniface, 201–6, 205
houngans, 193, 201–6
Internet influence on, 197–206
long-distance practices, 203–4
malevolent spiritual practices, 207 n. 2
mambos, 193, 197–201, 204–6
Mambo Sandrine, 197–201, 204–6,
205, 206
meaning of "house" in, 203
online marketing of, 196, 198–99
rituals practices of, 202, 203–8, 260
territorialization and
deterritorialization online,
196–97
traditions and practices of, 193–97
See also Haiti

W
Ware, Chris, 251 n. 9
Weber, Max
on authority, 5–10, 27, 30
categories of authority, 7–10, 39
on charismatic authority, 29
on consent, 30
criticisms of typology of, 41, 42
Economy and Society (Weber), 19–21
on legitimization, 39, 41–42
pure types of authority, 40
on religious authority, 32
theories of authority, 21
on traditional authority, 43
on web of culture, 52
Weberian scholarship, 263
web/Internet. *See* Internet
web of culture, 52–53, 55

www.ingramcontent.com/pod-product-compliance
Lightning Source LLC
Chambersburg PA
CBHW032117020426
42334CB00016B/980